PENGUIN BOOKS

THE PRIVATE LIFE OF THE BRAIN

Susan A. Greenfield is a leading neuroscientist based at the Department of Pharmacology, Oxford. She is the Director of the Royal Institution of Great Britain and is the author of *Mindwaves, Journey to the Centres of the Mind* and *The Human Brain: A Guided Tour*. She presented a six-part television series on the brain, called *Brainstory*, for BBC2, and is author of the accompanying book of the same name. She is an Honorary Fellow of the Royal College of Physicians. In 2000 she was awarded a CBE and a Life Peerage in 2001.

THE PRIVATE LIFE
OF THE BRAIN

Susan Greenfield

PENGUIN BOOKS

PENGUIN BOOKS

Published by the Penguin Group
Penguin Books Ltd, 80 Strand, London WC2R 0RL, England
Penguin Putnam Inc., 375 Hudson Street, New York, New York 10014, USA
Penguin Books Australia Ltd, 250 Camberwell Road, Camberwell, Victoria 3124, Australia
Penguin Books Canada Ltd, 10 Alcorn Avenue, Toronto, Ontario, Canada M4V 3B2
Penguin Books India (P) Ltd, 11 Community Centre, Panchsheel Park, New Delhi – 110 017, India
Penguin Books (NZ) Ltd, Cnr Rosedale and Airborne Roads, Albany, Auckland, New Zealand
Penguin Books (South Africa) (Pty) Ltd, 24 Sturdee Avenue, Rosebank 2196, South Africa

Penguin Books Ltd, Registered Offices: 80 Strand, London WC2R 0RL, England

www.penguin.com

First published simultaneously in the USA and Canada
by John Wiley & Sons, Inc. 2000
First published in Great Britain by Allen Lane The Penguin Press 2000
Published in Penguin Books 2001
Reissued 2002

3

For
David Brynmor Thomas

CONTENTS

Preface

This book initially started life as a neuroscientist's exploration of pleasure. I was fascinated by what motivated so many of my colleagues and friends to work hard, to accrue money, and to invest long hours in a library or office, when instead they could simply have been sitting in the sun or enjoying a good claret. Obviously, they needed to survive and feed and clothe their children, but many of us in Western society can achieve those goals without working the long hours that many do. And the price paid seemed crazy. You have only to look at children splashing in a paddling pool, and in general living for the moment, to feel that one has, perhaps, lost the plot. What has actually happened in the brain?

The human condition seems to entail an uneasy vying between times of abandonment when we "let ourselves go" and other times—most of the time, in fact—when we are "developing" or "broadening" our minds, where above all, we have a strong sense of ourselves and some partial control, at least, over what is happening around us. The more I tried to translate into brain terms this dichotomy between the sensual, momentary existence and the self-conscious adult human mind-set, the more I realized that it did not apply to pleasure alone, but to a far wider range of basic emotions. Hence the quest for a neurophysiology of pleasure widened into a consideration of all the emotions, both how the brain can accommodate their diversity, as well as whether there might be a common basic factor that distinguishes an emotion, in general, as such. My "solution," as you will see, is that emotions and the mind are not stark polar opposites, but rather the ends of a continuum.

In order to match up what we feel to greater or lesser extents at any time with what is going on in the brain, I was thankful for my earlier training in neuropharmacology; it seemed to me that drugs offered the perfect Rosetta Stone, a bridge, for relating two sets of phenomena, one objective (physical events in the brain), the other subjective (what you are feeling), that normally are hard to link up with each other. Nonetheless, by looking at various conditions resulting from the use of both prescribed and proscribed drugs, it seems possible to work out a more general scheme for the human condition and how it unfolds from one moment to the next in the brain. Yet such a journey inevitably leads us to the most challenging question of all: How does the brain generate the firsthand experience of feeling, of consciousness?

I do not presume to have come up with The Answer here, but in the final chapter, I do offer some thoughts that I hope will make a contribution to the debate. Having suggested a theory in my earlier book *Journey to the Centers of the Mind*, I have now been able to develop the basic idea that consciousness varies in degrees that are correlated with highly evanescent assemblies of neurons. The final chapter outlines the different factors that govern formation of these assemblies, and describes how in turn their configuration and size in the physical brain indicate different states of mind. Finally, we turn to the important issue, often overlooked by neuroscientists, that brain functioning must always be seen as an integral part of the whole body: I suggest a means whereby the brain and body function in concert and argue that it is the iteration between body and brain that *is* consciousness. For those with a taste for the technical, the Appendix offers a more detailed, physiological account of the scheme.

The basic message of this book is that emotions such as pleasure necessitate a temporary abrogation of the self, the individual carefully developed throughout a lifetime. Perhaps this is an idea that has long lurked in our folklore, captured in expressions such as "blowing the mind," but which is now rooted here in the physical brain. As such, I hope this book may provide some more insight into why and how we do what we do for pleasure or otherwise.

Many people have helped bring the manuscript to fruition. First are my editors, Emily Loose at Wiley and Stefan McGrath at Penguin, who have seen the text through various incarnations and who have given invaluable advice. In addition, my agents, John Brockman and Katinka Matson, should be thanked for their unstinting support and help. I am also very grateful to the following colleagues for helping with endless queries: Henry Marsh, Nick Rawlins, Ole Paulsen, Kim Jobst. But above all, I wish to acknowledge my husband, Peter, for providing continued support, advice, and encouragement, and without whom I would never have been able to have even started this project.

This book is dedicated to David Brynmor Thomas. I first met David in 1996, when he was supposed to have retired but was acting head of the technology transfer unit of Oxford University. My colleague David Vaux and I were filing a patent and were interested in starting a biotech company as a consequence. Without David Thomas's flair, humor, imagination, and courage, we would never have gotten past first base. Just as the company, Synaptica—where he ended up as Secretary—was starting to flourish, David tragically developed a fast-growing cancer and died within a few months, in May 1999. Both David Vaux and I feel his loss keenly, not only as a valued mentor professionally, but also as someone who came to be a very close friend. This book is not about companies nor technology transfer, but I hope David would have liked it.

Susan Greenfield
Oxford
October 1999

I

THE IDEA

If someone told you that tomorrow you would lose your consciousness forever, how would you feel? Perhaps that you might as well be dead. And yet if your fate were commuted instead to losing your mind, then your prospects, though not very palatable, would seem less gloomy. Your consciousness and your mind, therefore, cannot be the same thing. This book is all about what these two distinct entities actually are and how they might relate to each other.

For as long as I can remember, I have been fascinated by how such sophisticated and elusive concepts fit in with what we know about our sludgy, physical brains. After all, your unique, highly personal view of the world—your mind—hardly lies in the mechanical workings of your liver, heart, or lungs. As medical technology marches forward, these vital yet impersonal organs will be transplanted with increasing ease and frequency. Working as I do every day on the chemistry of the brain, I have to admit to some bias. Even so, it is the brain, after all, when assaulted by drugs, psychiatric and neurological disorders, and head injuries, that is primarily at the root of any changes in character, emotions, or consciousness. There, among the tangle of invisible cells, electrical impulses, and molecules ranging from the awesome intricacy of proteins to the spooky simplicity of gases, down there where time counts to less than a thousandth of a second, somehow a unique, subjective experience is generated in each one of us—an experience of consciousness.

One thing for sure is that consciousness always entails some sort of feelings. Until relatively recently, philosophers have had a monopoly on exploring this subjective aspect of the mind: the mystery and apparent miracle of how things actually *feel* to an individual. Such flimsy, subjective phenomena are traditionally an anathema to us newcomers in the study of the brain, the scientists. Brought up as we are on the basic rule of being objective, we prefer to tinker around with the physical brain. But by disregarding the obvious yet frustrating fact that consciousness is a highly private event, scientists are throwing out the baby with the bathwater: The philosopher John Searle has remarked that studying the brain without an interest in consciousness is like studying the stomach without an interest in digestion. As I see it, we need to be bilingual, by which I mean that we must investigate both the neuroscience—the physical workings of the brain—and the subjective phenomena of feeling. We must develop a familiarity with the issues involved in the study of both the physical and the epiphenomenal events in the brain if we are ever truly to understand either.

In 1799, a stone was found near the town of Rosetta, thirty-five miles northeast of Alexandria in Egypt. Dating back to 200 B.C., this tablet was bilingual: it bore inscriptions describing the benefactions of the then Pharaoh, Ptolemy V, in two languages, Greek and Egyptian. For the first time, there was a key to extrapolating the meaning of the previously mysterious hieroglyphics of the Egyptian language. What we need now, over two hundred years later, is a neuroscience Rosetta Stone—a system of matching up our sense of consciousness and what we feel with what happens physically in the brain. Only by so doing will we ever have a chance of understanding how a physical brain can be responsible for creating consciousness and the powerful phenomenon of emotions. But there are no obvious clues as to what this neuroscience Rosetta Stone might be.

Perhaps one of the most straightforward ideas is that each different region of the physical brain has its own mental function. This model of the brain suggests that we ought to be able to find physical centers for the production of emotions and consciousness. The notion of physical centers for functions is inspired by the fact that brains—of all animals— are divided into easily identified, discrete parts. All brains are symmetrical around a middle axis and have a surface that resembles a walnut and a cauliflower-shaped appendage (a region known as the *cerebellum*) at the back. There is nothing else like this in the world nor, as far as we know, in the universe.

Of course the shape of brains does vary from species to species. Look in any continental butcher's window, and you will see that mammalian brains, say that of a rabbit compared to that of a sheep, will look somewhat different. Each species has a brain with a distinctive appearance, the makeup of which is the product of evolution. Over the years different parts of the brains of different animals have expanded and prospered in importance, while others have remained relatively unchanged, all in accordance with the demands of the lifestyle of the species.

But despite variations in size from one species to the next, and in the exact configuration and relative size of different brain regions, the basic structure of the brain is the same. The most fundamental component, common to all vertebrates, is the swollen extension of the spinal cord, which contains all the neuronal wherewithal to breathe, generate biorhythms, and control the hormones that are pivotal in the regulation of food, fluid, temperature, and sex. This primitive *brain stem* is the pivotal core, enfolded around which are the more complex and sophisticated parts of the brain: it deviates relatively little in a vast range of species, from reptiles to humans.

A good half century ago, psychologist Paul MacLean[1] advanced a revolutionary theory that accounted for the similarity of the brain stem from one species to the next. The bottom line was that the brain stem was the source of the driving power, the energy that underscored everything we did. In this sense MacLean's view of the function of the brain stem was akin to Sigmund Freud's *Id* — the provenance of blind, brute urges to copulate and attack, to create and destroy.[2] These most basic building blocks of human behavior, argued MacLean, could be unmasked, independent of the niceties of an obvious or appropriate context. If someone murdered your spouse, you might hate him or her, with good reason. But the blind and unquestioning devotion stirred up by the Nazis in the Nuremberg rallies of the 1930s had far less rationale — it was an emotion ignited by the heat of the moment. In fact, MacLean cited behavior at the Nuremberg rallies[3] as an example of the human brain stripped down to its reptilian essentials, whereby the brain stem operations are unleashed and allowed to run free. He proposed that emotions were, therefore, most of the time, suppressed in some way by logic and reason.

The great pioneer Sigmund Freud had first presented a version of this idea of unfettered mental forces a good fifty years earlier, with the concept of the *Pleasure Principle*.[4] According to this principle, the drives of the Id served to reduce tensions, to uncoil a cerebral spring being wound up tighter and tighter by the *Ego*, the organized, rational aspect of brain function. The Ego normally held the Id in check: this supervisory Ego had no precise anatomical location, but was a kind of umbrella term for the cohesive set of memories and values, the individual view of the world, that characterizes the adult human mind. The Ego itself was suppressed still further by standards of critical morality—the *Superego*—a sort of conscience.

But Freud had abandoned neurology for psychiatry: he was interested not in the intricacies of the brain itself, but in why people thought and behaved as they did. Given the still sparse knowledge of neurophysiology at the time and the even cruder research techniques, it is not surprising that Freud was not attempting to discover how such sophisticated processes could be realized from the mire of the physical brain. Instead, it was MacLean, benefiting from the progress of several decades of brain research, who identified a particular part of the brain as crucial in the suppression of the basic urges. The *limbic system* describes a variety of brain regions that cluster around the hub, or the brain stem, and thereby cushion and channel its atavistic demands.

To a certain extent, the idea of this conglomerate of regions as the regulator of emotion has been borne out. In many cases, damage to the limbic system results in inappropriate emotion. For example, *Klüver–Bucy*[5] *syndrome* occurs when a certain part of the limbic system, the *amygdala*,[6] is damaged. Patients exhibit a high sexual drive, directed not so much toward a prospective partner as toward anything around them, even inanimate objects. Along similar lines, removal of another region, the *cingulate cortex*,[7] in experimental animals results in "sham" rage—a pattern of behavior that contains all the outward features of a genuine, infuriated state but that occurs for no obvious reason.

Blanketing the limbic system is yet another layer of brain, the *cortex*, Latin for *bark*.[8] This structure is so named because it wraps around the rest of the brain, forming an outer layer as its arboreal namesake does around a tree trunk. The cortex is spectacularly exaggerated in our own species, double the size in places that it would be for a primate of our size. Because its surface area is so much larger in primates in general, and because damage often leads to relatively sophisticated impairments of thought, the cortex has quite reasonably been assumed to be involved with logic and the ability to rationalize.

MacLean had the novel insight that not only was the brain stem held in check by the limbic system, but that the limbic system in turn was suppressed by the cortex. This idea was inspired by the fact that the cortex is, even to the naked eye, clearly a distinct structure from the limbic system below it. In dissection the two areas prize apart cleanly and easily, like the skin from the flesh of a tangerine. Although it was Freud who drew a distinction between what we want to do and our final censored actions, it was MacLean who pointed specifically to distinct physical brain regions, respectively attributing them with emotions or thought processes. Because this idea of a brain hierarchy seems intuitively attractive, and because the brain anatomy seems to correspond to a neat and rigid escalation in abilities, scientists and nonscientists alike have accepted for decades the paradigm that emotion and logical thinking—so-called *cognitive processes*—can be segregated.

Some might even have been tempted to associate a certain brain region—the *prefrontal cortex*—with the generation of personality. One of the earliest and most famous cases that drew attention to the prefrontal cortex as a candidate "center for" personality took place in Vermont, in 1848: Phineas Gage, a railway foreman, was tamping down dynamite with an iron bar when the explosive detonated prematurely. The four-foot-long tamping bar, thick as several fingers, was shot through the front part of his brain. As the story goes, incredibly, none of Phineas's faculties seemed impaired. His movements and speech were normal, and all his senses were intact. There was just one problem: over the next few months, Phineas's whole demeanor changed from that of an easygoing team player to a quick-tempered and uncooperative egocentric.

Almost a century later, a Portuguese neurosurgeon, Egaz Moniz (1875–1955), heard of a procedure whereby destruction to—a *lesion of*—the front part of the brain suppressed "neurotic" behavior in a monkey. As a consequence, in an era when the mentally ill were simply put in straitjackets, locked into padded cells, or injected into insulin comas, Moniz developed a seemingly most humane, surgical treatment for violent patients that was soon extended to a variety of mental disorders: *leukotomy*—literally, "cutting the white matter."[9] *White matter* is the general term used for the fiber connections between groups of brain cells, in this case the connections between the frontal lobes and the rest of the brain. The aim of the leukotomy procedure was to isolate the prefrontal cortex so that it no longer could play any part in the functioning of the patient's brain, and hence of his or her life. At a time when drugs for psychiatric conditions were hardly heard of, leukotomy came to be used as a treatment of choice to calm down agitated and aggressive patients right up until the 1960s. Those who had undergone surgery became so calm that they were often listless and completely unmotivated.

Now, if changes in the physical brain underlie changes in character, it seems reasonable to search for a physical provenance of our "selves." But as it turns out, the brain cannot be so easily compartmentalized. We now know, thanks both to clinical observation and to neuroscientific research, that there is no simple one-to-one matching between a function and a particular part of the brain. For example, in the generation of movement, at least three different extensive systems in the brain are involved, each with a different aspect of motor control.[10] Instead of a brain region being an autonomous center for this or that, it seems more likely that areas of the brain, especially zones within the cortex, work in a way that is more reminiscent of the interactive harmony produced by instruments in an orchestra. On the one hand, many instruments converge to contribute to a single moment of sound in a symphony; yet any one of those instruments will make very different sounds when playing a work by Stravinsky versus one by Wagner. A comparable convergence and divergence are at work in the brain: any one function depends on the contributions of many brain areas, yet any one brain area will participate in any number of diverse functions. For example, the visual system uses at least thirty different areas of the brain, while any single region, such as the prefrontal cortex, which lies behind the forehead, has been associated with functions as diverse as depression, memory, and as we have seen, personality itself.

Also arguing against a simple structural provenance of our selves in the brain is the fact that one human brain looks so much like another. If your and my prefrontal cortices were laid side by side on a slab, they would look more or less identical. So, it is still far from obvious to see where the individuality of each human being might creep in: we will have to search for some further clue, buried somehow, somewhere in the actual fabric of the brain, within each region.

This fabric of brain tissue, from which each brain region is made, can be broken down into complex, overlapping interstices of circuits formed in turn from vast numbers of brain cells, *neurons.* The 100 billion neurons in the adult human brain have been likened previously to the number of trees currently in the Amazon rain forest. Yet I now think that a bustling metropolis, like New York City, would be a better analogy. New York City can be divided up on a gross scale into different boroughs, then into different districts and neighborhoods, and finally into blocks. But within each block there is an incessant activity both restricted to local spheres of influence as well as interaction with the "higher" levels of neighborhood—district, borough, and so on. Any one room in a building on a block could, perhaps, be fancifully likened to a neuron. The constant activity within any building, with people darting, lingering, resting, and rushing between rooms and out into the wider world of the street and the city itself, would be similar to the chemicals, or *transmitters,* that are used as messengers from one brain cell to the next. Transmitters are used to bridge the gap, the *synapse,* between neurons. First, one neuron generates an electrical signal lasting a thousandth of a second, and of an amplitude ranging anywhere from some sixty thousandths to ninety thousandths of a volt: this is the *action potential,*[11] an electrical blip that hurtles down to the end of the neuron at speeds of up to 250 miles per hour.[12] Once it reaches the end of the neuron, the electrical impulse acts as a trigger for the transmitter to be released.[13] The transmitter then diffuses rapidly across the narrow synapse between the two cells, and joins in a molecular handshake with an appropriate custom-made chemical (*receptor*) embedded on the outside of the target neuron.[14] This molecular handshake, perhaps more akin to a hand fitting in a glove, initiates the final step, the generation of a new action potential in the target cell. This process, *synaptic transmission,* is the best-known mechanism by which brain cells communicate with one another; it is regarded as the basic building block of virtually all brain operations.[15]

Let's stretch the New York City analogy to the breaking point. We can now reduce brain operations to a level even smaller than the neuron itself, to that of the synapse—the behavior of a person constrained by the dimensions and layout of a room that perfectly fits their needs to eat, sit down, or stretch out. And even at the synapse the units can be broken down further, analogous to the person opening a certain cupboard and reaching for a certain glass. There are, for example, *channels*[16] in the wall of the cell that allow ions such as sodium and potassium to traffic between the interior and exterior of the neuron, and so change its voltage (the imbalance in charge between the inside and the outside of the cell). This interplay of ions results in the all-important, highly transient electrical signal. There are *pumps*[17] in the cell wall, too, a little like molecular revolving doors, that allow the ions to return to their original sites once the electrical signal has been generated.

Given this complexity of structures in the brain, a next reasonable question might be what creates each of these structures and controls their functions. One part of the answer is clear: genes. Each of the hard-working complexes of molecules in the brain—ion channels, ion pumps, transmitters, and receptors—will have, as do the myriad other components of the neuron, different genes responsible for their expression within different circuits within the brain. So, if one of these genes is defective, clearly the transmitter, receptor, or ion pump will malfunction, and the whole system will become perturbed. Due to the apparent ease and agility with which molecular biologists now manipulate lifeforms by manipulating their genetic makeup, the importance placed on genes has understandably swelled. There has even been talk of the "gene for" criminality, for homosexuality, or more recently, for good parenting skills.

So impressive is the power of genes that some scientists, such as the geneticist Richard Dawkins[18] or the psychologist Steven Pinker,[19] argue that the traditional focus on the Self as the most important unit of life is misplaced. The Self is largely unimportant in evolutionary terms, and to Dawkins or Pinker the course of evolution is the subject of primary interest. The most basic unit of life can be boiled down to the immortal gene as it is passed on from one generation to the next and serves as the ultimate controller of how each brain is made.

In this "reductionist" spirit, one of the Nobel laureates who discovered the structure of DNA, Jim Watson, claimed that ultimately all science was "reducible" from biology to biochemistry to chemistry to physics, and hence that everything other than physics was "just social work." This stark type of view has been robustly opposed by the biologist Steven Rose,[20] who instead hypothesizes that every organism has its own "lifeline," its own trajectory in space and time that gives it a unique narrative. Rose has pointed out the fairly incontestable fact that genes on their own are, after all, merely a few strands of the nucleic acid DNA. The critical issue is how one component relates to another, how they are organized—be it one brain cell forming a synapse with another, a synapse forming with another into a circuit, many circuits forming brain regions, or brain regions forming into a brain.

My father used to enjoy telling me when I was a child that all we humans were was "ten shillings' worth of chemicals" (I am old enough now to have been young in the days prior to the decimalization of British currency). But what I never thought through in my ignorance and innocence was that there is of course far more to a body than a mere cauldron of chemicals: it is how these chemicals are actually organized within the cells of each organ, how in turn those cells are configured to make up each organ, and eventually how the organs relate to one another, that is critical. As soon as a system, be it a symphony or a curry or a whole human body or a brain, is reduced to its tiniest components, something special is lost.

Undeterred, the reductionist genetic train of thought fuels the currently highly fashionable concept of a gene for this or that. Yet even a clear pattern of heritability can be misleading. Consider the most famous experiment demonstrating the inheritance of traits, conducted by Gregor Mendel in 1865. Mendel demonstrated a systematic and predictable appearance of traits in peas for, for example, one of two different colors, yellow or green. But we cannot infer from this observation that a percentage of the pea population in question had a "gene for yellowness." Instead, what Mendel had really identified were peas with a gene for an additional enzyme that destroyed the green pigment chlorophyll, which in turn played a part in the complex process of its metabolism. The net effect of yellowness was thus not due to a direct one-to-one matching with a single, autonomous gene responsible for a different color of pea.

Not only might many genes be for some such unsung, covert phenomenon as opposed to the observable end product, but the genes themselves are hardly independent little units of destiny. As a crude analogy, take a simple component of the internal combustion engine, such as the spark plug. It is an essential component of the car, but there is no automatic, autocratic ability to motor along conspicuously locked into its design. Placed on a coffee table, a spark plug goes nowhere and does nothing. Only when placed in the correct, complex context of the engine, with the engine placed in a car, is the spark plug's potential realized. Only then can the car operate properly—so long as a host of factors additional to the spark plug are also operational.

I am not arguing here that we are born as blank slates, but rather I am attempting to place the admittedly vital role of genes, literally, in context. We have seen that it is misleading to expect there to be a whole, macro brain region for a committed, single function. Following a similar argument, surely it is even more absurd to dissect the composition of the brain into even smaller parts and expect a sophisticated function to be preserved, locked into a few strands of DNA.

Now think again about the gene that contributes to the expression of a protein that will make up a channel in the wall of a cell so that ions can pass in and out. Or consider a protein that contributes to a molecular target, a receptor—any one of many types of tiny chemical sites opening out from the wall of a neuron that enables a transmitter to exert an effect on the target cell. How crazy to expect a one-to-one relationship between such a disembodied protein, the product of a purportedly autocratic gene taken out of all context, and the final outcome of the human brain—some sophisticated behavior or other.

Quite recently, some studies have tried to combine the ideas of "genes for" and "brain regions for" to understand the physical bases of the vagaries of human character, emotional disposition, and thought processes. Imagine an experiment where, by the wonders of molecular biology, you were able to shuffle genes around with such dexterity that you could engineer a mouse containing extra rations of either its mother's or father's genes, instead of the usual fifty-fifty arrangement. Eric Keverne and Azim Surani in Cambridge have actually succeeded in skewing the allocation of genes from one parent or the other.[21] Of course, the resultant embryos, some of which survived the three weeks to full term, were hardly the murine counterparts of Marilyn Monroe and Errol Flynn—ultrafeminine or ultramasculine. But the brains of the genetically manipulated mice had higher concentrations of either paternal or maternal genes in certain brain areas. Paternal brain cells tended to aggregate in the limbic system—the area that MacLean and others after him have identified with emotions—while the maternal cells were found in the cortex, the area purportedly responsible for more cognitive processes such as abstract thinking.

Such observations do not prove, however, that intelligence is a feminine attribute and emotion a masculine one. All that we might be able to say is that the propensity for different types of mental processes would be genetically traceable to your father, others to your mother. Just because a trait is inherited from your father does not mean that it is a masculine one, any more than hemophilia, say, is feminine, simply because, as in the notorious example of Queen Victoria's family and her great-grandson, the doomed son of the last czar of Russia, it is passed through the female line.

A further worry with this type of interpretation is that it still rests on the assumption hearkening back to MacLean, that emotions and reason are separate and mutually exclusive phenomena: the idea of emotions and instincts from father, and a mutually exclusive intelligence from mother, is predicated on the old paradigm that each process operates exclusively within one area or the other, either the limbic system or the cortex.

There is, however, a possible alternative interpretation to account for the predominance of maternal-derived cells in the "higher" centers, paternal ones in the "basic" areas. The issue could simply be one of certain genes favoring a fast rate of brain growth. Wherever such genes were operating, the brain region might grow faster and end up larger. My reason for suggesting this more humdrum scenario is that, as well as the cortex, another structure lying deeper within the brain and more associated with thoughtless generation of movements—the *striatum*[22]—turns out too to be rich in maternal-only cells. Both these areas, cortex and striatum, are actually quite bulky: in contrast, the more superficial limbic system structures, the septum and amygdala—which are conspicuous for being chiefly composed of paternal cells—are relatively modest in volume. It is possible then, since the maternal genes in this study appear to favor growth of the brain in general, that it is beneficial for these genes to go to work in whatever brain regions happen to be larger—where more cells will be needed anyway. This is just an idea, but one that illustrates that there is at least one alternative for which the maternal or paternal genes, in this case, might truly be "for."

Of course, that does not mean that gross modifications in function will not result from loading the genetic dice in one brain region or another. The severe disorders of movement and mental ability seen in

Angelmann Syndrome,[23] or disorders in sex and eating drives that characterize Prader-Willi Syndrome,[24] for example, are undoubtedly genetically related impairments. But we do not know what the direct product of the gene actually does, what the gene is, after all, "for."

There is no doubt that our genes play vital roles in shaping our personalities and regular behavior, just as a spark plug does for a car. But our mental functions, whatever they are, are in no way reducible to the products of our genes. In fact, the degree to which overall brain operations are genetically preprogrammed varies from one species to the next, and with that variance the potential for individualization also varies. In the case of goldfish, say, the genetic blueprint for a generic goldfish brain is pretty much unencumbered by interference from what happens to the individual goldfish, swimming out his or her fishy existence in the uneventful environment of a glass bowl. If a pet goldfish happened to expire overnight, a substitute rushed in early the next morning would circumvent the need to break the otherwise upsetting news to one's offspring. The behavior of the substitute would be indistinguishable from its deceased counterpart. As the brain becomes more sophisticated, however, it is increasingly hard to regard individual animals as interchangeable. The swift trip to the pet shop would be less likely to work even for a hamster that had been used to handling, and of course would not even be countenanced over the death of a pet cat or dog.

To illustrate the point that genes alone cannot simply control or create our personalities and behavior, the neurologist Richard Cytowic[25] has made the following, illuminating calculation. The number of human genes has been estimated to be at most about 1,000,000. The number of synapses in the adult human brain, however, is far more, some 1,000,000,000,000,000 — which is 1,000,000,000 times in excess of the basic genetic elements. These connections between brain cells are, to return to the New York City analogy, a little like the rushing of people in and out of a building, as well as within it: connections constitute an intermediate level in brain organization between genes and macro brain regions.

So if we now turn to the vital role of the connections between brain cells, we are led to consider the role of the chemicals in the brain that operate through a network of synapses. What happens when the processes of chemical transmission across synapses are stirred into a maelstrom by drugs? Certainly, the effects of alcohol on character are all too familiar in turning a pleasant and considerate human being into, for example, a belligerent or sullen bore. Similarly, the dreamlike stupor of the heroin addict and the literally "mindless" state sought by those who take Ecstasy all suggest that changing levels of brain chemicals play a vital role in changing states of consciousness. So are brain chemicals the key to the generation of our subjective feelings?

Just because changes in the chemical composition of the brain can change personality does not mean that we can simply attribute a change in personality or behavior to the chemicals themselves. Recently, on a science program on national TV, I have heard speak of one transmitter, *serotonin*, as the "chemical brake" on behavior, while another, *dopamine*, was described as the "molecule for pleasure."

To think this way is to revisit precisely the same fallacy as the "gene for" or the "brain region for" some type of behavior or cognitive function. It is yet again the same old idea that we should be able to express a sophisticated, outward function in terms of one brain feature alone—if not a gene or a brain region, then this time, a chemical transmitter. Rather, the real challenge is to incorporate brain chemistry into a new way of looking at overall brain operations that can also apply to subjective feelings: the neuroscience Rosetta Stone.

One exciting area of research in neuroscience with some promise in this endeavor is the study of brain *plasticity*, where physical changes can be seen in the degree and extent of connections between neurons in certain brain regions, as a result of injury, or more commonly, simple everyday experience. As the brain becomes more sophisticated, it appears to exploit instinct less and less and instead uses increasingly the results of individual experience, of learning. Hence individuality, I would argue, becomes more evident: the balance starts to tip correspondingly away from nature toward nurture—the effects of the environment. It is in this personalization of the brain, crafted over the long years of childhood and continuing to evolve throughout life, that a unique pattern of connections between brain cells creates what might be best called a "mind." I shall be trying to show that the mind should not be regarded as an airy-fairy alternative to the physical brain but that, at the same time, it is something more than a generic lump of gray matter. My particular definition of *mind* will be that it is the seething morass of cell circuitry that has been configured by personal experiences and is constantly being updated as we live out each moment.

So, important factors in making you, a human being, the person you are, are the personal experiences that you alone have had—what amounts to your memories. If you buy into my suggestion that the mind might well be the personalization of the physical brain, and if the personalization of the physical brain is driven not so much by genes as by individual experiences, then the concepts of *memories, mind,* and *Self* will be very closely related.

On the other hand, there is still something more to my state of mind at this very moment other than a mere inventory of all the things that have happened to me in my life. I like to think of myself, as I'm sure you do too, as a holistic and essentially feeling entity.

For example, one Christmas vacation, on a long flight my husband and I were taking from London to the Caribbean, a woman was caught persistently smoking in the rest room: unlikely as it might sound, she actually ended up being physically restrained in a straitjacket and handcuffs, two rows behind us, screaming. I felt a strange combination of what in retrospect I can label as alarm and anger: my heart automatically thumped through my chest and my throat went dry. I felt as though I was being taken over by reactions that I had not consciously initiated, and which I could not control. Yet it was an experience within my own private interior. No one else could climb into my body, to experience the particular sensations I was accessing firsthand.

No doubt my fellow passengers were experiencing some state that was indisputably just as private but comparable—even similar—to my own. After all, emotions are far more predictable than thought: most of us would feel extreme sadness at the death of a parent, or anger at someone caught stealing one's car, or love as we stood by our new spouse at a wedding. The outward responses, too, are so similar that they can be described in the same single word and documented, as they were by Charles Darwin over a century ago, as common coinage between all humans,[26] for instance, *joy, high spirits, surprise, fear,* and *horror.* Everyone who is happy expresses that emotion with the same facial expression—the universal smile. Similarly, it is hard to mistake anger in another human being, wherever one is in the world. If emotions are less individualistic, perhaps they are a very basic part of brain function, both in the animal kingdom as well as in each human brain.

Already we have seen how MacLean, and Freud before him, saw raw emotion as something unleashed from the bounds of calm reason. Yet the intuitively appealing idea of emotions as something different from our normal, logical state was far from new, even in the last century. The dire consequences of a clash between emotion and reason can be found in a play written almost two and a half thousand years ago by the Athenian author Euripides. Euripides wrote of two basic opposing forces within the human mind. His play[27] tells of the Bacchae—women who were becoming uncontrollable due to their abandoned, ecstatic worship of Bacchus, the god of wine. The king, Pentheus, wishes to impose order and stop their orgiastic revels altogether. However, he is warned by the blind seer Teiresias that things will turn out very badly if he does. There are two forces in man, Euripides has Teiresias explain, the "wine" force and the "bread," or rational, force—as I would have it, a mind employing reason based on experience: both are needed in a dynamic equilibrium if one is to remain mentally healthy.

Now notice that a common factor in the Euripides/Freud/MacLean schemes of things is the basic assumption that when you are thinking, being reasonable, and indulging your individual memories, there is no emotion present at all. But surely the idea of no emotion at all is alien to our ideas of being human. Any friend or colleague who acts in a way seemingly devoid of emotions is soon disparaged as "cold-blooded," a mere lower form of automated life, or worst still perhaps derided as a "robot," some kind of oblivious entity with no consciousness within at all.

In a classic paper written in 1959, Bruno Bettelheim documented the moving account of "Joey, the mechanical boy."[28] Joey's problem was that he saw himself as a machine: for example, in order to eat he needed to attach tubes to himself. He had to be programmed, and all his responses were carefully thought out first. After an extensive and largely successful period of treatment, Joey took part in a procession, holding a banner that read, FEELINGS ARE THE MOST IMPORTANT THING UNDER THE SUN. "With this statement," concludes Bettelheim, "Joey entered the human condition."

Since it is generally abnormal to behave like a robot, then surely the corollary is that feelings are actually with us to greater or lesser extents all the time. Although, as adults, we might not be oscillating between sobs, ecstasy, and terror, that does not mean that we have no feelings at all. On the rare occasions when there are no immediate problems in my lab, I am aware still of an underlying anxiety, a mental radar beam panning around and around, on the alert for trouble, strife, or stress. Similarly, everyone knows those fortunate souls who have a sunny disposition as they work their way through the day. People whistle and sing in the corridors of my institution, giggle and groan as they wait for the elevator. True, they are not being emotional in the usual sense of the word, but they could hardly be described as robots, bereft of all apparent feeling.

Emotions must somehow be incorporated into any neuroscience Rosetta Stone. My own view of brain operations departs early on from the simple Euripides/Freud/MacLean division of emotion versus reason, in that I am suggesting that some sort of basic emotional state is present *whenever you are conscious*. And if emotion is a phenomenon that is inextricable from consciousness itself, then it should be a high priority for neuroscientists. Yet surprisingly, emotions have to date received relatively scant attention. In basic physiology courses, for example, nothing is said of laughter, not even regarding its mechanical bases— those unbidden familiar contortions of muscle, breathing, and vocalization. It is almost as though laughing, and the emotion of happiness that engenders it, was too frivolous for the heavy machinery of scientific investigation. I remember vividly how in one student lab in which I demonstrated, the medical students were told by the senior member of the faculty that one of the side effects of morphine, along with constipation and constricted, pinpoint pupils, was euphoria—as though one of the most overwhelming experiences imaginable was something as banal as an intestinal contraction.

One notable exception to the coyness seen among many scientists regarding the study of emotion was a series of experiments carried out over forty years ago; this work was to initiate a particular approach that promised a glimmer of insight into the generation of emotions in the brain. Two psychologists, Olds and Milner, showed that a rat would repeatedly press a bar to stimulate its own brain in preference to any other activity in the rodent repertoire.[29] The electrode via which the current was delivered had to be implanted in certain key regions, but then the animal would carry on pressing the bar until it was exhausted. The most obvious interpretation was that the rats were experiencing some sort of rodent pleasure. And if rats can feel some sort of pleasure, it is no great conceptual leap to point to the tail-wagging dog, the purring cat, and indeed the gurgling, grinning baby who can smile and laugh way before he or she will be able to speak or reason.

There is no way of knowing, of course, what the actual sensation is like for the rat, just as it is impossible to know what it feels like generally to go through life covered in fur, sporting a long scaly tail, and being able to jump from a standing start at least several times higher than your body height. As the philosopher Thomas Nagel famously pointed out with regard to bats,[30] we cannot enter the skull of another person, let alone another species, to experience directly the emotions that rats or bats actually feel. All we have access to is the mechanical, external behavior that may or may not accompany a certain type of emotion. In the case of the bar-pressing rats, all we know for certain is that they are working for a reward: hence the brain sites eliciting self-stimulation would be more accurately described as "reward centers" than the arguably more tempting "pleasure centers."

Yet such studies do hint at a crude portfolio of different rodent emotions. There are also behaviors comparable, yet antithetical, to those of the frenzied bar-pressing of a rat presumably experiencing pleasure: over the intervening years, psychologists have made much use of the idea of *aversion* and *aversive stimuli*.[31] In the behavioral sciences, it is possible, just as with self-stimulation experiments, to contrive scenarios where an animal, usually a rat, will make a demonstrable effort not to experience a certain outcome: a mild electric shock to the feet, or indeed stimulation to certain other parts of the brain that are anatomically distinct from the misleadingly dubbed pleasure centers—the areas of the brain that the rat will work to stimulate. An alternative scenario is to work to prevent stimulation: *active avoidance*. In this case, the strategic behavior on behalf of the rat can be distinguished from *passive avoidance,* since this time the rat will actually not take action—it will refrain from a behavior, in order to avoid a certain outcome.[32] Just as the experimenter infers from the incessant bar-pressing of self-stimulation that the animal must feel some sort of pleasure, so they will also assume, when observing avoidance behavior, that the animal feels something unpleasant, such as fear.

But an emotion, a feeling such as fear, is not identical to a behavior such as avoidance. After all, as you lay sweating and terrorized in the lonely house in the middle of the night, you are undertaking no overt avoidance behavior, but you are still very frightened. Avoidance behavior, then, is a good reason to suspect that animals feel fear rather than concrete and exclusive evidence that they do. This distinction between what rats—or indeed people—do and what they feel is important to remember when tying to understand emotion.

Within the last few years, emotional behavior versus the subjective feel of an emotion has been dissected out, into different brain circuits. The neurophysiologist Joseph LeDoux[33] has described an elegant segregation between two different anatomical systems in the brain, which correspond to two distinct processes involved in fear. The system that LeDoux uses is one comparable to that of the famous Russian psychologist Pavlov, who is of course celebrated for training dogs to salivate at the sound of a bell that they had been conditioned to associate with food. Similarly, in LeDoux's studies, an erstwhile neutral stimulus becomes associated with pain; in the future this previously innocuous stimulus will elicit a conditioned reaction of fear just as the familiar buzzer in Pavlov's experiments evoked involuntary salivation.

LeDoux has shown that conditioning a fear reaction in this way to an otherwise neutral trigger takes place using two simultaneous yet distinct systems in the brain. One circuit is via the cortex: the processing here is relatively lengthy but will eventually mean that one has a conscious experience of fear. By contrast, the second circuit bypasses the cortex: LeDoux proposes that this system has evolved not because some region below the cortex is, as MacLean would have argued, the emotional center of the brain, but instead because in evolutionary terms, processing of information via this route would result in quicker avoidance action, compared with a conscious response necessitating the scenic detour through the cortex. The particular brain region that lies below the cortex and that is the lynchpin to this "quick and dirty" circuit is the amygdala.

LeDoux's keenness to incorporate the amygdala is not particularly surprising, since that structure has long been implicated in emotion. As far back as 1939, lesions of the amygdala were used to suppress violent behavior, and indeed could lead to bizarre syndromes, such as the Klüver-Bucy syndrome we met earlier. Conversely, consider that electrical stimulation of this area in cats, for example, can lead to sham rage—a phenomenon where there is no obvious cause of the behavioral pattern of responses of flattened ears, erect fur, and spitting. So is the amygdala the "center for" emotion?

When I was small, one of my favorite comic strips was "The Numskulls." The Numskulls, living up to their name, spent their existence inside a man's head and got him up to no end of mischief. They looked a little like a three-year-old's drawing of a person, consisting entirely of a large oval head from which protruded, as an afterthought, four single lines as vestigial limbs. I was delighted recently when I was able to procure a slide from the original of some forty years ago: the benighted, balding hero is shown in cartoon profile, with his brain divided up into rigid compartments. Each Numskull is engaged in a particular job: there's the chip-eating zone behind the mouth, with each morsel being carefully passed along from one matchstick pair of arms to the next, while another is busily operating a telescope behind the eye. Yet a third department shows a Numskull sweeping the inside of the nose with a broom, while arguably the best job of all, in the highest compartment, involves a slightly irate Numskull screeching down a telephone, instructing general operations: the center for consciousness, no less. Much as one might smile at such a scenario, it is easy to slip into thinking that this is how the brain really does work, as though each distinct region were a mini-brain in its own right—almost a little person, with a separate brain of its own.

If we focus in on the amygdala with regard to emotion, then we run into the Numskull problem of regarding it as an autonomous brain within a brain, a "feeling" center. Just imagine the miniaturized brain of the Numskull himself: does it too have mini-Numskulls at work? Similarly, we might ask what happens inside the amygdala that is so special. If you were to look at the amygdala under a microscope, you would see a confluence of neuronal circuitry, like any other brain region. Of course the particular arrangement of certain groups of neurons would be special to the amygdala, but in itself this configuration would not bestow any unique, qualitatively distinguishable properties. The amygdala is an aggregation of many networks of neurons: not only has it no inner observer, but there is not even an inner proactive, driving force deciding what actions to instigate.

On the other hand, the amygdala is indeed in a key anatomical position, effectively an intermediary between the *hippocampus*,[34] a region contributing to memory consolidation, and the *hypothalamus*,[35] an area intimately involved in the regulation of hormones and thus with basic drives such as hunger, thirst, and sex. The amygdala, therefore, is a neuronal crossroads, perfectly positioned for the meeting of previously unassociated inputs converging from different brain regions. Herein lies its appeal to models of the brain, such as LeDoux's, where a behavior is learned as a Pavlovian reflex—a stimulus-response conditioning not requiring thought. But a confluence of anatomical pathways does not in itself offer an explanation of what an emotion, the actual feeling as opposed to the reflex behavior, actually is.

Emotional behavior, albeit unconscious, robotlike reflexes, is important as a key player in evolutionary terms—in survival value. After all, if a snake slithers across your path, it is important to take avoiding action as quickly as possible. LeDoux has argued that each emotion has evolved separately according to our evolutionary needs. Yet we still have no idea, if we follow his scheme, of the role of the amygdala, say, in differentiating rage from fear, or of explaining how the amygdala plays a role in positive emotions, such as pleasure.

A more basic problem still is that in LeDoux's scheme, a behavior is studied at the expense of the actual feel of an emotion. Emotion as a subjective sensation has been replaced by an emotional behavior—an objective, observable event. The important question here, of course, is what we think is the most important feature of an emotion. LeDoux sees the behavioral response with or without consciousness as the "wider" view: but I would disagree and argue that the whole crux of emotion is not so much the response but the conscious, subjective feeling itself of fear, or indeed, of pleasure. The concept of an unconscious emotion is, at least for me, a paradox.

In support of my particular disregard for mere behavior over actual feelings, other recent work suggests that what you feel, as opposed to what you do, can actually be differentiated inside the brain. Ned Kalin[36] has shown, for example, that young rhesus monkeys will behave in the same way for two very different situations. These monkeys will coo either to express a desire for the mother's embrace or, on different occasions, will coo as a threat-induced plea for immediate help, because they are frightened. To us nonsimians this difference might seem like nitpicking—surely the two acts amount to pretty much the same type of emotional state. However, Kalin has demonstrated that according to the context in which the response is being generated, different chemical messenger systems will come into play. Surely then consciousness, one's prevailing inner emotion, cannot be equated with a stereotyped, outward behavioral response. My own conclusion is that emotion itself is independent of outward behavior, but is completely impossible without consciousness, and vice versa.

Unlike MacLean, Freud, and indeed Euripides, who treated emotion as an occasional outburst of a different type of brain state, and unlike LeDoux, who bypasses the feel of an emotion altogether, I am arguing for a different paradigm in which emotions are with us all the time, albeit at a spectrum of intensity. I am going to try and convince you that at one end of the spectrum pure emotion—the type of sensation experienced during road rage, a crime of passion, an orgasm, or at a rave—can best be viewed as the core of our mental states when, as when we are infants, feeling is not greatly tempered with individual memories, with cultural or private meaning, or, most important of all, with the self. Feelings just are.

When people lose their minds, blow their minds, or are out of their minds with fear or ecstasy, they are no longer accessing that highly personalized set of values, history, and unique view of life. They are no longer making full use of their personalized configurations of brain connections, which I have defined as the mind. Instead, they are traveling back to the time when they were very young, before such internal connections existed, when the external world therefore had no personal meaning, and indeed when they were swamped with emotions. Emotions, I am going to try to convince you, are the building block of consciousness. Emotions are with us all the time, to a greater or lesser degree, depending on how much you are using, or losing, your mind at any one moment. I shall be arguing that you cannot understand consciousness without understanding emotion, and that consciousness is not purely rational or cognitive as some, particularly those working in artificial, computational systems, have implied. Above all, not until we establish what emotions actually are and how and when they are generated—when we lose our minds or blow our minds—only then will we truly appreciate the mind itself. The idea that has prompted this book is that the more we are feeling emotional, the less we are accessing our individual minds, the less we are being ourselves; ultimately, we have let ourselves go!

Of course, this is just the outline—I would never imagine that you would buy into the idea just yet: you will be, I'm sure, wanting to see robust arguments and scientific evidence. But if true, then the idea would have profound implications, not just for how you understand the mind and brain, but more importantly, how you view yourself and your life. Why is it that we all seek to have more fun, but that anyone who spends his or her life as an out-and-out hedonist is usually the target of pity or scorn, rather than envy? Why do the activities we pay so much money to pursue, be it sports, partying, or travel, only sometimes bring the anticipated pleasure? Why do people take drugs? Is there any way in which we might better understand the scourges of modern life, such as schizophrenia and depression, and if so, will such understanding pave the way to better treatment? These are hardheaded, practical concerns that will be tackled in the journey toward the loftier goal of understanding how a brain weighing only some three pounds and with the consistency of a soft-boiled egg can generate the private world that only you know, and which makes normal living in any way different from virtual death—existence in a coma or simple sleep.

The conceptual corners I hope we shall turn are that: (1) emotion is the most basic form of consciousness; (2) minds develop as brains do, both as a species and as an individual starts to escape genetic programming in favor of personal, experience-based learning; (3) the more you have of (1) at any particular moment, then the less you have of (2), and vice versa.

The question of how the ebb and flow of a highly developed mind can be catered to by a physical brain, and the related question of how the one impacts on the other, are the hardest-ever challenges to human ingenuity and imagination. Yet we are living in a time that is unprecedented in its enthusiasm for probing the workings of the brain. At the most recent meeting of the American Society for Neuroscience, there were some 30,000 delegates who, collectively, could claim to have a very good idea of how our most personal body part is put together, how it develops in the womb, what it is made of, and what kind of processes and phenomena occur within it. Moreover they, or rather we, have access to meticulous reports of how the electrochemical intricacies that underpin brain function can be perturbed by injury or disease, as well as by drugs, both prescribed and proscribed. It is scarcely surprising, then, that an ever wider scientific constituency of biologists, mathematicians, physicists, and clinicians finally are gaining the confidence to break the monopoly of philosophers on the biggest and most tantalizing questions that we can ask about who and what we are.

Let's see first what progress has been made so far by both philosophers and the wider scientific community. We will then be able to go on and explore the extent to which the path outlined here is validated by empirical evidence, what the practical implications might be, and whether any new theoretical advance emerges as a result.

2

THE STORY SO FAR

"Let me show you what I mean," jabbers the generic scientist, snatching at an envelope, restaurant napkin, or even the knives and forks. A curious Martian or an ordinary mortal seated at the next table might be amused to observe an excited dialogue unfold over an ever-louder and more jargon-laden exposition of a sequence of hypothetical events, as a succession of silverware is laid end to end at each step; or the observer might be baffled by the intense concentration elicited by an unassuming paper napkin, now contaminated with a spreading stain of spidery, cabalistic symbols. The creation of models is a mainstay of the scientific mind-set. The idea is to capture the critical feature or essence of an otherwise slippery or complex phenomenon. Unlike the leggy paragons of the catwalk, a scientific model can take any form, depending on the expertise and proclivities of its proponent. When it comes to the nervous system, a model might be anything from a series of statements couched in mathematical formulae to a psychologist's doodling of spaghetti junction boxes and arrows to represent brain regions and connections. The idea is to capture the overall picture of a system, in our case the brain, without getting bogged down in the details of algaelike neurons, minute electrical signals, marinades and jets of different chemicals, and the mystifying conglomeration of interlocking brain regions. Before hacking our way into the neurophysiological jungle, we first need to see if the expedition proposed in the previous chapter is even necessary.

Let's start by looking at the success, or otherwise, of current models of the brain that boil thought processes, and indeed consciousness itself, down to the starkest possible explanation—one seemingly lean and abstract enough to be devoid of neuronal frills.

One way of circumventing the messy and still largely mysterious workings of neurons is to liken the brain to something else, to come up with a good metaphor that is as different as possible from the brain itself, save for the very aspect being described. For example, the psychologist Bernard Baars has developed the metaphorical model of the theater.[1] A theater of the mind/brain is not new. In the sixteenth century, the Milanese philosopher Giulio Camillo introduced the idea of memory as a theater: in his scheme, the critical feature was the bounded enclosure of reality within a framework—a theater building or a brain—based on a combination of a fixed number of components, such as drapery and footlights, or in the biological cast, macro brain regions.[2]

I would certainly go along with the idea that the image of the theater provides an appealing framework for describing brain function. The stage, for example, is small and limited, just like a moment of conscious experience. We can press the comparison further: behind the stage, the conscious experience, is a vast area of offstage activities, both past and present, that sets the context that will give the momentary experience a particular quality. A center stage scene, an idea, could be described as an idiosyncratic mixture, a confluence of disparate, earlier images spawned by personal experience. The attention needed at any one moment can be likened to a spotlight, reminiscent of a similar metaphor of a searchlight already celebrated by biologist Francis Crick in his description of consciousness.[3]

However, Baars sees attention not so much as consciousness itself but rather as the means for searching out what type of consciousness to have. And once under way, this consciousness, the momentary performance, will inspire the audience, the unconscious brain processes, to allow themselves to be pressed into service. True, a conscious thought to leave a room sets in train a cascade of complex unconscious to-ing and fro-ing at a host of junctions between the nerves and muscles that orchestrate the myriad shifts in weight, body position, and locomotion needed. But the Baars metaphor is counterintuitive: How can an audience be unconscious!

Even more problematic is the inevitable question of who is directing the show, namely, what is the nature of the Self. Using the theater metaphor, it is impossible to draw clear distinctions between self-consciousness and the consciousness of, say, a rabbit. According to Baars's model, the Self is the actual compilation of the multiple contexts, the painstakingly assembled props and draping that decorate the stage within each individual edifice. Although such an analogy is fair enough, it is not particularly helpful. If the Self is flavored and colored by previous experience, a suggestion that is hard to refute, then the big challenge is surely to ask how such a process happens in the real brain.

But it is not just scientists who have attempted to capture the essentials of our cerebral functioning in an arresting image uncluttered by chemical or anatomical details. Philosophers, too, often model complex events or ideas by using thought experiments, literally fantastic, highly improbable scenarios that by their very absurdity accentuate the essence of the argument. One such thought experiment that illustrates the problem of coming to grips with the physical basis of the Self is that of the "teletransporter," a hypothetical device conjured up by the philosopher Derek Parfit.[4]

Parfit invites you to imagine that a replica of yourself could be built from transported data downloaded from your brain. However, a sad consequence of doing so would be that the original cells would be killed; on the bright side, they would be reconstructed again in exact replication. Your replica would be effectively you, because he or she would have inherited your brain, along with all its memories. The replica would think that it had been you all the time, when really it may only have been so for a trice. So this particular model emphasizes that there is, after all, really no such thing as an enduring Self. All there is is a brain in a body, which at any moment gives a snapshot of awareness, an illusion of perpetuity. But as with any collection of snapshots, there is not necessarily any continuity.

Imagine a photo of a village landscape. There may well be the *illusion* that a tree has been growing forever, that a church was built long ago, and that all will endure into the future, but the snapshot is actually only one frozen moment of time. Within a pack of snapshots, of course, each photograph may feature the same subject—or maybe not. It would be just as easy for an erstwhile tourist to take a snapshot of a village church and tree, and then one of rocks piled up at one end of a beach. Each shot would be self-contained and consistent within itself, with an illusion of a history and a future, but there need not be a connection or any consistency at all between the scenarios of the village church and the beach. So it might be with brains. Any waking moment has an illusion of a past and hopes of a future, but a continuity of a single individual is merely a trick of the neurons, a particular property of the state of consciousness—the snapshot taken at that particular time.

This radical and somewhat brutal denial of an enduring Self, captured in the thought experiment of the teletransporter or the analogy of the snapshot, has also been vividly illustrated by another philosopher, Dan Dennett, this time with a metaphor of "multiple drafts."[5] Dennett argues that at any one moment there is a salient brain state, amounting to a complex consciousness, that is highly transient, just one of many different drafts of one's take on the world. As with the snapshot, in that frozen moment, each draft gives the illusion of permanence. According to Dennett, then, the Self would be equivalent to the inexorably aging, generic brain caught in a sequence of snapshots;[6] the individual, as an enduring entity, could never exist as such.

Parfit's thought experiment and Dennett's metaphor offer a sophisticated last resort to the solution of the mind-brain problem, how the illusion of a Self with an individual mind can, in reality, be generated by a generic, physical brain. But the issue of the transitory nature of the Self so strongly emphasized by Dennett and Parfit is in a sense missing the point. Even if we have only borrowed for the present moment the brains we happen to be using right now, what is the basis of the apparent individuality? It is not enough to overlook the obvious similarity between brains and imagine instead that these inert, wrinkled, and indistinguishable lumps can in some unspecified way be special to each of us. Baars's suggestion that the Self is a compilation of personal memories seems reasonable, as suggested already in Chapter 1. But if this idea is to have any value, then surely the actual process by which a brain becomes personalized into a mind is critical.

An additional difficulty, not catered to by Parfit's or Dennett's scenarios, is how consciousness comes into the picture. After all, when we fall asleep and lose consciousness, we do not expect to lose our minds as well. Our brains, personalized by whatever means, are there when we sleep, waiting to be accessed next morning. So, in addition to the conglomeration of memories, however they are realized in the brain, some special, additional process or airy entity is at work amid the bump and grind of our otherwise automated gray matter.

Baars suggests that consciousness takes place within working memory, a kind of mental shortlist from which the final moment of consciousness transiently transpires. For neuroscientists, *working memory*[7] refers to certain ongoing rules and assumptions kept in mind while performing some task. For quite some time, working memory has been one of the diverse functions attributed to the prefrontal cortex,[8] an area that has undergone astonishing expansion in us humans. Working memory may well therefore play a part in consciousness, especially the sophisticated kind of consciousness that adults enjoy. But we cannot say that working memory *is* consciousness. If we do, we inevitably end up with a circular description of consciousness as some sort of inner dialogue.

The psychologist Larry Weiskrantz[9] starts with the reasonable assumption (indeed, one made by Baars, too) that if we could identify the differences between conscious and unconscious processes in the brain, we would have a clue about the critical feature or features related directly to consciousness. However, instead of developing a model founded on metaphor, Weiskrantz lets the brain speak for itself, via his patients, by drawing from his own direct clinical experience with amnesia and *blindsight*,[10] a fascinating condition where a patient with a defective part of his or her visual field quite reasonably denies seeing an object placed in the defective region; nonetheless, the patient can point it out. In both this condition and in amnesia, the damaged brain is still processing information, but the information cannot, for whatever reason, be pressed into service in conscious thought.

According to Weiskrantz, the essence of consciousness is the rendering of some sort of ongoing account, a commentary. By asking the patient to perform diverse tasks, this commentary can be distinguished experimentally from a response that is a mere reflex or guess. While actual experiments might successfully discriminate unconscious from conscious acts, the metaphor commentary is of no obvious added value. In fact, it can be downright misleading: who is, after all, talking to whom? There is, as we saw in Chapter 1, no little omniscient and omnipotent Numskull.

Dan Dennett[11] has scathingly captured the essence of the problem by using the theater metaphor, this time in denigration, to illustrate the fallacy of an inner brain within a brain, no less than a "Cartesian the-ater." After all, the essential function of a theater is that it is there for someone to watch some onstage spectacle. Surprisingly, however, even neuroscientists themselves often refer to the brain as though it was an autonomous little man lurking beyond the neurons. The psychiatrist and sleep expert Alan Hobson,[12] for example, refers with no further elaboration or reservation to "top-down" control in the brain, when one is enabling various events, and "bottom-up" control when one is not in the driving seat. The problem is that, as we saw in Chapter 1, one cannot be separated from parts of one's complete brain. There is no little man lurking behind the chemicals and brain cells to watch any-thing or to set up any kind of commentary or dialogue with different bits of brain.

This problem is encapsulated in perhaps the most famous and cer-tainly one of the most hotly debated thought experiments: the hypo-thetical scenario of the Chinese Room, devised by philosopher John Searle.[13] Imagine the task of translating from Chinese to English. It would be possible to deliver an output in Chinese in response to an in-put in English as long as one has the appropriate rulebook. As far as you, the operator, are concerned, you would not need to understand Chinese to give the illusion, by behavior alone, that you are a formida-ble linguist.

The Chinese Room is a highly successful thought experiment be-cause it is easy to see immediately how behavior can be a good index of learning, yet only in the narrow classroom context of producing an ap-propriate, rote response on demand. The computer chess champion Deep Thought[14] would seem to have a powerful intellect if we use the criterion of specific, correct responses.

It is easy to confuse learning with understanding: it is over this every-day ambiguity that the Chinese Room has been pushed beyond its in-tended limits. Searle's deliberately absurd scenario has attracted criti-cism because people conflate learning—a behavioral change—with understanding—an inner process. If the person in the Chinese Room were really to understand rather than respond in a rote fashion, then the critical debating point would be whether he or she would have to be conscious. But consciousness is not an issue here at all. For the pur-poses of the thought experiment, the simple point that the model makes is that outward behavior is an unreliable index of internal mental events.

So where might consciousness fit in? As I see it, algorithmic agility, a modification of responses due to experience—what we might as well call learning—differs from understanding in that it is independent of any other process. As long as the algorithms are in place, no other facts are needed or used. By contrast, understanding differs from rote learning in that it is predicated on preexisting, additional knowledge of some sort or other, a personal context within which the new fact or process is interpreted and evaluated. If you go along with this idea, then mind and true understanding are inextricably bound, and neither need have anything to do with outward behavior.

This mismatch between outward behavior and inner states is also an important aspect of a very different type of model, in which the issue at stake is indeed the presence of some inner consciousness. Here the idea is to attempt to replicate the bare essentials of the brain and mind in artificial systems. These systems are usually silicon-based computers, although in the future other artifacts might be constructed from other types of material. "Machines," in the widest possible sense, then, are systems that are not the product of a fertilized egg.

Already, machine responses can be contrived to give the illusion of some vibrant inner world. The popular computer pets that respond to care but die if unattended are the latest in a long line of examples, from speak-your-weight machines to our personal computers, all of which are based on the idea that sensitive, seemingly highly personal reactions to our particular inputs are the result of understanding locked into the circuit boards.

Yet one can understand a situation and yet not behave or respond in any way. Such understanding, what amounts to wisdom, is often a non-proactive consolation. "Experience is what you get when you don't get what you want," runs a pithy and, as far as I know, anonymous saying. Wisdom offers a means for an individual to come to terms with something or someone; any additional words of advice to, or any subsequent action toward, third parties is merely a fortuitous spinoff. The primary result of such understanding is that it benefits primarily the individual. Presumably, consciousness is a prerequisite for understanding. True understanding, then, is surely dependent on consciousness. And a truly intelligent machine would, therefore, have to be conscious. Perhaps it is no surprise that consciousness has become the ultimate quest for many proponents of artificial intelligence (AI), who attempt to model the brain in silicon.

But it is very important not to confuse a mind that understands and that is dependent on consciousness with consciousness itself. Just as when we sleep, our brain is personalized by prior memories that will not be accessed until morning, so the functions of a machine could well be modified by experience but remain permanently unconscious. In La Jolla, California, Nobel laureate Gerald Edelman[15] and his team[16] have developed a series of models of how the brain can learn by experience. They are working with "Darwin" machines, robots that have no agenda other than to wander around a confined space on their little wheels. Their behavior changes constantly in response to chance and experience. Edelman uses the term "reentry"[17] to describe the interplay between experiment-related inputs and changes in the brain to groups of cells. This adapted brain is not like a thermostat, where states are generated by mere feedback, but more like an intricate web spun iteratively between one surface and another by a spider.

Edelman's Darwin machines are fairly sophisticated as far as robots go. In terms of behavior, they could be viewed as a series of futuristic infants,[18] crawling around and bumping into the equivalents of coffee tables or TV sets as they learn to navigate their little worlds, literally, by trial and error. This model shows that the biological brain might work like a computer. But it would be the same type of mind that you and I have when we are fast asleep. Not even its most ardent fan, not even its creator, would suggest that a Darwin machine has a brain, or more accurately, an inner life, that is in any way comparable with that of its conscious biological counterpart. No pattern of response, no behavior is an adequate criterion for such an artifact to cross the Rubicon into awareness.

Unlike machines, young children and nonhuman animals have very poor cognitive[19] abilities, yet we attribute to them sentience, a crude portfolio of feelings. Surely when a machine is built that can be happy or experience pain, then there would be a convincing claim to consciousness. Of course, there is the issue of how we would know that the machine was experiencing these feelings, but then the same argument would apply as to how we know one another were conscious, given that we have seen that we cannot judge by external responses. But even if we raised a computer screen to the same status as a human being, with the assumption that it is conscious, then the problem would still not be solved by simply factoring in emotions as an icon on the screen. The whole point is that the machine should possess an inner state as vivid and subjective as that of any biological system, not that it should make outward responses that simply represent such feelings.

We can model learning without thought to consciousness, but no one has yet successfully modeled the more basic property of the brain, feelings. The idea that emotions such as pleasure can be modeled according to certain logical algorithms certainly goes against the grain of the folkloric view of the brain. Quite recently, a colleague of mine finished an extramarital affair. The decision was unilateral, and the woman in question, also a friend, was very upset. Inevitably and ineffectually, I was called in as the hapless mediator. "But I can't explain why I've done it," the man sighed in happy resignation, "it's just an emotional thing." As far as he could see, this intervention of an over-powering feeling conveniently negated any further discussion by trading on that universal, intuitive premise that emotion is not tractable to logic. How odd to think that for the AI approach to help, the brain would have to be plodding through a series of preordained, causally related steps while giving the illusion that there is no underlying logic. "The heart has its reasons that reason cannot know," said French mathematician and philosopher Blaise Pascal. If we are to capture the essence of the brain in computational terms, then first we would need to establish what is different, what very special additional factor is present in or absent from emotions, compared to normal thought processes that are tractable to logic and thus to computer modeling. In this spirit, the pioneering authority on artificial brains Marvin Minsky has admitted that the important question is not to ask whether an intelligent machine could have emotions, but whether a machine could be truly intelligent without them.[20] To date, no AI proponent has come up with a clinching argument.

One contender is the engineer Igor Aleksander.[21] His recently completed MAGNUS (Multi-Automata General Neural Units Structure) uses artificial neural networks to study how real neurons in the human brain operate to underscore the complex functions of which humans are capable. Aleksander starts with the "basic guess," that "the personal sensations which lead to consciousness of an organism are due to the firing patterns of some neurons, such neurons being part of a large number which form the state variables of a neuronal state machine, the firing patterns having been learned through a transfer of activity between sensory input neurons and the state neurons."

So far so good. As long as one is not a pan-psychic,[22] who believes that consciousness can be expressed in all manner of objects, indeed, in the ether around one, or someone who thinks that consciousness is beamed into our brains from the Planet Zog, then few would dispute Aleksander's assertion. In any case, it would be hard to find an alternative way of describing brain activity or explaining brain functions without referring to groups of neurons being activated in certain combinations.

Another advantage of Aleksander's state machine is that it is so abstract that it can easily include all the different factors influencing the brain, along with the interconnections underscoring the heterogeneous organization of the different interactive brain structures. For example, when a brain cell, or neuron, "fires," it generates a tiny electrical signal that can be seen as a blip lasting for one millisecond on an oscilloscope screen. The term *firing pattern,* as used by Aleksander, is presumably meant to encompass the events that can precede the firing off of any single action potential. So, in addition, another factor in the firing pattern would have to be the ceaseless modification that neurochemicals in the brain make to generate electrical signals. These chemicals, which are vital in determining the readiness of neurons to generate action potentials, happen to be related to arousal and biorhythms.[23]

The best test now would be to see how the model can cope with a feature of the human brain that is high on the list of requirements for a truly intelligent machine: emotions. We need to see how we might model pleasure, for example, within the framework of a state machine, according to the tenets of Aleksander's basic guess.

Aleksander sees emotions in terms of planning and coping strategies. He views pleasure, in particular, as "planning representations in large areas of state space which lead to pleasure states." But what is a pleasure state? One answer appears to be that it is an "internalization of instinctive reactions." And yet if a reaction is instinctive, it is still an open question whether one is conscious of it or not. Certain movements in driving, for example, are automatic, performed unconsciously by instinctive drivers.[24]

Of course, according to the MAGNUS model, emotion and feelings could be represented by some constellation of neuronal connections. For example, physiologists can already point to the activity of certain groups of neurons during the sensation of pain,[25] but such revelations do not address the issue of what pain actually is and how only the brain in which the neurons are firing has exclusive access to that direct sensation of severe unpleasantness. For Aleksander's model to be truly helpful, it would need to incorporate a means by which morphine alleviates pain and bestows dreamlike euphoria, and to do that one would need to factor in brain chemistry and brain anatomy. To be sure that some key feature, unknown to us in advance, was not omitted, we would have to build a brain, down to the very last atom. Of course, if we knew in advance what the key feature was, there would be no point to the exercise.

To my way of thinking, Aleksander's approach is not so much wrong as it is lacking in detail, both physical and functional, of the real brain. Because a state machine is devoid of the real anatomy and chemistry that make vital contributions to final mental function, in a way we have yet to discover, it is hard to see how a system lacking those features might truly help us understand the real brain. A biological brain with exquisitely biased, albeit highly complex, links between each of its hundred billion neurons could nevertheless be arguably reproduced in principle in silicon, as some kind of tenth-rate model of learning or memory. But by emphasizing the state machine model, unfettered by constraints, Aleksander concentrates, as do most other AI workers, on physical structure, learning, and appropriate behavior. Although models of this sort are useful for strategic thinking and behaving,[26] neither strategic thinking nor behaving are necessary for a rich inner life, for consciousness and emotions. In short, learning machines are not the same as feeling machines.

The mocking paradox is that somehow subjective consciousness does happen, and so far it appears to be an exclusively biological event. The objective physical brain, so readily modified by mood-modifying drugs, so readily darkened and silenced in anesthesia, can spontaneously allow you to generate an experience that no one else can share firsthand. Neither Minsky nor Edelman nor Aleksander would admit that their current machines, though awesome in their achievements at learning and memory, are in any way conscious. The most important question, therefore, is whether—and if so, how—consciousness might be finally realized, not only in terms of new physical components but more importantly in terms of *phenomenology,* that is, inner feelings and emotions. If there is some underlying principle or algorithm for emotion, it will have to be of a very different type indeed than those by which artificial devices usually operate.

Since most AI models focus exclusively on experience-driven adaptive processes, it is perhaps no surprise that they tell us little about consciousness and emotions. On the other hand, the philosophers' models that do target these interesting questions effectively highlight the problems, rather than offer solutions. For example, another very famous thought experiment involves Color Blind Mary,[27] a world expert on color vision, who has herself experienced only a monochrome environment. Because Mary knows everything there is to know about the objective brain processes involved in the perception of color, is she really missing out? If Mary suddenly acquired color vision, would she discover anything new?

This completely absurd scenario nonetheless highlights very accurately the problem between objective events, the type of physical facts and factors that can be modeled, and the subjective feel of the first-person, personal world. But as it stands, the thought experiment does not inspire any positive way to actually understand consciousness and how it occurs in the brain.

Nonetheless, those who do not deal in real neurons could be tempted by *functionalism,* a general term that covers any approach that concentrates on the idea of systems and their interrelations as being of prime importance.[28] For example, the philosopher David Chalmers uses a thought experiment to fuel his argument that the actual substance of the brain is irrelevant. If silicon chips were gradually substituted for neurons, Chalmers speculates, then the subjective sensations, or "qualia,"[29] would not end up fading, nor would they be working one moment only to be defunct the next, in some kind of biphasic rhythm, "dancing." The problem that I have here is with Chalmers's initial assumption of a simple one-to-one correspondence between particular neurons and particular states of consciousness. Chalmers's assumption rests on the idea that an isolated circuit will be autocratically responsible for a sensation of the color red, for example; but the brain just doesn't work like that.

Another proponent of the functionalist approach, the philosopher Dieter Birnbacher, dismisses the argument of such mere technical impossibility of thought experiments as theoretically unimportant. But as a neuroscientist, my own view is that the technical considerations are after all the most challenging and the most important. In real life, the brain functions holistically, with different circuits and brain regions all making contributions to net function, as instruments do in a symphony. In this spirit it is plausible to imagine that normally we are not really conscious of a disembodied sensation of the color red in its own right, as opposed to the more complex experience of a red flower or even the more holistic quale/qualia of a garden in bloom. Hence it is not realistic to deride, as Chalmers does, the concept of a disembodied fading color red. In any event, clinical observations[30] suggest that consciousness can wax and wane; it can also be reduced gradually with the onset of anesthesia or sleep.[31] Only when modelers successfully come up with a strategy for accommodating, for example, the "technical" but very real fact that the chemical transmitter dopamine,[32] which is needed to make certain types of movement but that in functional excess leads to schizophrenia, will functionalism offer the true prospect of progress.

I personally find it hard to see how AI models will ever really elucidate the most exciting aspects of brain function, understanding and indeed consciousness. At the physical level, imagine that a new component or feature had been discovered as the magic bullet for consciousness. There would be no point in attempting to build a conscious artifact because the problem would have been solved before the experiment began! On the other hand, a mysteriously developed yet guaranteed conscious machine would be of no more help than a biological brain in finding the as yet unidentified factor responsible for consciousness. Such a system would presumably be as ethically constrained and as frustratingly miserly in revealing its secrets as the simplest of animal brains.

We need first to contemplate exactly what we expect of a conscious brain, but then immediately we run into a conundrum. In Homer's *Odyssey,* the wandering hero Odysseus had to sail between Scylla and Charybdis—a monster and a whirlpool. Successful avoidance of one meant a fateful encounter with the other.[33] Similarly, anyone contemplating how consciousness might be generated by the physical brain is in danger of falling into one of two traps, which I shall call the Readout Fallacy and the Thing Fallacy.

Because there is no one in your head as observer, then surely nothing further happens once consciousness occurs. It is not relayed on further, or read out, to anyone or anything else. Obvious though this may seem, it is surprising how the Readout Fallacy can creep in. The easiest conduit for appreciation of consciousness would be a behavior, a misconception that underlies AI models and is lampooned well by Searle and his Chinese Room.

A subtler example of the Readout Fallacy is when we think about what is happening within the brain itself. We have seen already that metaphors of dialogues and theaters are still peppering people's perspectives. Dennett solves the problem by denying that there is any enduring Self, but the fact remains that even without a Self, something remains. Emotions or feelings are felt, if not by a self-conscious individual, then by some passive, characterless observer capable of raw sentience, or feeling. But there is no separate observer. So where does the registration of consciousness go? That is the Readout Fallacy.

Underlying this way of thinking is the conviction that consciousness is a process. And if it is a process, it cannot be exactly synonymous with whatever is generating it, an object. A washing machine, for example, is an object that generates movement. So if consciousness is a process, it must be something that can be discernibly distinguished from other brain operations. But all brain operations, like each brain chemical and each brain region, in themselves are unconscious. We saw in Chapter 1 that consciousness depends on a holistic, interactive, and integrated concert of many brain regions.

The only way to stop the Readout Fallacy from driving you crazy is to admit that the generation of consciousness itself is where the buck stops. But having navigated Charybdis, the Scylla of the Thing Fallacy now looms on the horizon. The Thing Fallacy has to be reckoned with as soon as we begin to use phrases like "generating consciousness." The idea is that something tangible is being given off, like car fumes, waste produce, or bile.[34] Although this fallacy might seem so absurd that it is not worth mentioning, there is sometimes adrift in thinking that consciousness can exist as something in its own right.

The most recent and perhaps the most sophisticated example of the Thing Fallacy has been proposed by David Chalmers,[35] who could see resolution to the frustration of the problem of consciousness only by deducing that it must be a basic property of the Universe, a little like space and time, but above all irreducible. Just as time can exist independently of a brain, a brain nonetheless appreciates time, so perhaps it is with consciousness.

Chalmers's suggestion, though admirable in the fact that it is radical, is nonetheless just a version of pan-psychism, which asserts that consciousness somehow is soaked up or mediated by brains, not actively generated by them. This idea is neither attractive nor distasteful, simply because we cannot take it any further; we are in an intellectual cul-de-sac. The concept does not explain why Prozac makes people less depressed, or why anesthetics suck people into oblivion. If consciousness floats free as some irreducible and therefore separate entity, what are these drugs manipulating in the brain? Chalmers's suggestion certainly sheds no light on the type of consciousness experienced by a rat, nor does it give any new take on the issue of emotions. To me, then, it seems pointless to argue about whether such a scenario is plausible because the concept of consciousness is not unpacked in any way that can help us understand it to any greater extent.

One way to avoid the Scylla and Charybdis of the fallacies entailed in the concept of consciousness is to avoid sailing toward them in the first place. Another class of models do just that. They avoid tackling the nature of consciousness head-on, and instead approach the issue crabwise, from a perspective rooted in real biology. This approach is so down-to-earth that theory plays little part at all, and technique leads.

For example, it is possible to see the brain of an awake human subject "light up" in critical brain regions, during certain sophisticated tasks. The most common methods make use of the fact that the brain is very greedy and consumes enormous amounts of oxygen and glucose.[36] Moreover, the most hardworking brain regions will consume the most oxygen. Hence by monitoring this differential consumption, either with a radioactive tag (using positron emission tomography, or PET) or by observing the difference in magnetism caused by the increase in the oxygen-transporting molecule hemoglobin (using functional magnetic resonance imaging, or MRI), it is possible to observe the conscious human brain at work.

Weiskrantz has argued that if it were possible to use these techniques to view the areas of the brain active in a blindsight patient when he was conscious compared to when he was allegedly unaware of an object, then the difference in images generated by these powerful new techniques would constitute a giant step toward understanding consciousness, using an objective scientific method. It turns out that the prefrontal cortex could be important. As mentioned earlier, this area is related to a host of disparate functions, from character change, to depression, to working memory, to source amnesia (a loss of the space and time reference points to a memory). But Weiskrantz attempts no theory as to how this area, in concert with others, might contribute to different types of consciousness. And the experimental bottom line, once finally discerned, is rather a letdown. Perhaps not surprisingly, no magic-bullet brain area emerges from imaging studies as a center for consciousness. Instead, we find there is a different configuration of working brain parts in conscious compared to unconscious conditions. The big question then is, how might these configurations of neuronal populations, *yet not others,* provide the special means for consciousness?

One candidate phenomenon that would be undetectable in imaging studies is the synchrony that can occur in the electrical signals generated between populations of neurons in different brain regions. Within the cortex and in remote brain regions such as the deeper-lying *thalamus,*[37] much has been made of the concerted activity in the electrical signals of groups of neurons situated far apart from one another. The idea, first advanced by Francis Crick of DNA fame, is that this coordinated activity of neurons in the thalamus and the cortex acts as a kind of searchlight that illuminates part of an otherwise dark, unconscious brain. But the big question remains as to what the light is actually shining on.

Crick and his colleague Christof Koch have now modified their views[38] in favor of multiple loops of circuits of neurons in the thalamus and cortex that are active only during consciousness. But we still need to know what would be so special about the currently unspecified conditions that ensure consciousness at one time but preclude it at others.

Returning to the metaphor of the searchlight, physiologist Rodolfo Llinas[39] has placed his money on an elaboration of synchronicity of electrical activity between large groups of cells in different brain areas. He has recently refined a scheme to suggest that consciousness occurs when not one but two sets of systems linking thalamus and cortex work in conjunction. On the one hand, a nonspecific system provides an energizing context of arousal, while a circuit specific to any one of the senses furnishes the content.

In the past, I personally have had problems with an explanation entirely dependent on oscillating loops of neurons, and my unease is merely doubled now that there are two sets. One difficulty is that although all mammals tested to date display the same oscillatory phenomena, they do not have the same levels or type of consciousness.[40] Oscillations alone, then, could not explain the bat or rat inner world forever denied us humans. Conversely, within any one individual, two such crude parameters offer no room for differentiating one type of consciousness from another (e.g., fear from pleasure) or explaining the mood- and consciousness-modifying properties of, say, morphine. Experimental data can well indicate that such conditions are necessary for consciousness, but that does not prove they would be sufficient. After all, if a thalamus and a cortex were extracted from a young rat brain and grown together in a dish, as is now possible,[41] few would claim that that tissue culture would now be generating consciousness. We would still need to determine what extra ingredient would be needed.

Consciousness might not depend on a magic bullet but on the collective presence of several permissive components or properties within the brain, such as arousal. Arousal is not only a useful everyday term for describing how excited or sleepy we are but a physiological reality.[42] Deep in the most primitive region of the brain, the brain stem, are diffuse groups of neurons that send their connections throughout the rest of the brain to release their transmitters. They act not so much as local specific messengers but more like fountains. These diverse chemicals (dopamine, serotonin, noradrenaline, and acetylcholine) are differentially active at different times of the day and night. But they are always at work, energizing the rest of the brain to different degrees and in different ways. Arousal, then, is important for consciousness, but because biorhythms of arousal can be generated in patients who are brain dead,[43] and thus will never regain consciousness, there must be something additional.

Another obvious factor is input from the sense organs. It is odd that Llinas focuses on a single sense as the only other factor that is needed, because most states of consciousness are throbbing with nature's multimedia input from more than one sense organ. On the other hand, if he is suggesting that consciousness can be subdivided further into isolated mini-states of consciousness, then the same problem remains as to how it is all brought together in that familiar yet astonishing unified state we experience most of the time. Moreover, because we know that sensations can be registered in the brain during anesthesia,[44] we still need to know what else has occurred as *the* crucial condition for consciousness. The suggestion that everything oscillates in synchrony with everything else, be it the retina with specific loops in thalamus and cortex, or arousal systems with sensory ones, is still too vague to be of help.

At a meeting on consciousness in Tucson[45] in 1996, David Chalmers parodied the problem of identifying the ultimate factor for consciousness by producing a hair dryer. Waving it around his head, he suggested that it was a "consciousness monitor," rather like a Geiger counter. All you needed was this device to measure consciousness unequivocally in other people's brains. The scientific community may yearn for such an instrument, in vain. No one has yet identified the magic bullet, the center of consciousness that lights up, the brain property that suddenly starts up, or the special chemical that gets released. There is no qualitative factor within the brain that is both necessary for consciousness and—and this is the crunch—*actually sufficient*. If a chemical or a brain region or the particular activity of a certain set of neurons was indeed all that was needed, then that region or chemical or activity could never do anything else in the brain and not generate consciousness. Such a faithful index of consciousness would be marvelous for the hair dryer or its ilk to monitor, but my own view is that it does not exist. A brain region cannot be simply turned into a mini-brain in its own right; still less can an isolated circuit of neurons or an oscillating loop or two make *you alone* feel a certain way. These neuroscientific models therefore have to date suffered from too much emphasis on one particular feature or process of the brain, that is, the one the experimenter happens to be studying. This problem is the inevitable consequence of being driven by observation alone, not hypothesis.

An alternative, and great favorite among the biological models that do not suffer from the problem of being overly reductionist, is the evolutionary approach. Most recent ideas on the evolution of the human brain have focused on our supposed intelligence. William Calvin suggests that intelligence is all about good guesswork.[46] Whereas lesser brains function in a genetic straitjacket, as we saw in Chapter 1, the more intelligent an animal, the more it can extemporize from one situation to the next. The intelligent can thus muddle through when the crunch comes, although climatic changes in evolution or the closure of all neighborhood food stores would necessitate creative improvisation with whatever remains in the fridge.

Similarly, Dan Dennett[47] has reworked the ancient nature–nurture axis into a question of degrees. In brief, the more primitive the brain, the more predictable the action according to the dictates of prewired instinct (which he rather confusingly refers to as "free floating"). The idea here, as with Calvin, is that our more sophisticated brains will liberate us from single-minded genetic tyranny and allow us to develop individual, ontogenetic agendas as we interact with the environment. The gradual freeing-up of increasingly sophisticated brains from the narrow-minded dictates of species-specific gene commands is not a new idea, as we saw in Chapter 1, but recently, both Dennett and Calvin have attempted to elaborate the telling features of a more idiosyncratic, intelligent brain.

For Dennett, the central issue is that more sophisticated brains are able to see the significance of garden shears and generalize it to nail scissors. This interpretation of understanding the significance of something fits exactly with my earlier suggestion that understanding depends on the extent to which an object, person, or event can be related to other things, that is, to preexisting knowledge.

For Calvin, all objects, actions, and ideas are subsumed under the term *cerebral code*. The concept of a code is slightly tricky, as it implies that the objects, actions, or whatever is being processed in the brain are then decoded into something else.[48] Unfortunately, once an event in the outside world or some change in the inner milieu of the body has wrought a change in the brain cells, then that change will only ever reside, for however brief or long a time, as a neuronal event of some sort—an increase in the generation of the electrical signals, an elevation in certain brain chemicals, or a much more enduring and subtle change in the physical shape of a neuron. But a code is of value only if it can be decoded. The idea that anything within one's brain can be transmogrified into being anything more than mere banal electrochemical phenomena—the release of a few thousand molecules of transmitter or the generation of action potentials some 90 thousandths of a volt in amplitude and some thousandth of second in duration—is a fallacy that strikes at the very heart of the problem of trying to understand subjective sensations.

On the other hand, it is feasible that the brain might contain not so much codes of ideas but some kind of unit of organization; let's call them "mind units." Calvin suggests that such units would be realized in physical assemblies of neurons. The general idea of such groupings of neurons has already fired the imagination of a range of philosophers, psychologists, and physiologists,[49] starting with the "neuronal pools" of the great pioneering physiologist Sherrington in the first half of this century.

Sadly, however, Calvin turns his back on the enticing strategy of relating groupings of neurons to holistic brain function. Instead, he follows the well-trodden path via relatively isolated neuronal circuits toward the prospect of silicon intelligence. Like other AI proponents, he ends up emphasizing problem solving and outward behavior. The human mind may well play chess, and it can respond in certain ways to certain inputs, but it can also feel. Yet the evolution of feelings, the survival value of sensations such as pleasure, is, as with computational models, bypassed here as well.

Dan Dennett, in contrast, is acutely aware that different species have different types of consciousness that cannot be subjectively experienced firsthand, but which he nonetheless can describe objectively in the appropriate, nested setting of the physical body, environment, and lifestyle of the animals concerned. But it is not obvious how the objectively observable behaviors any of us might describe relate to that elusive, subjective feel of the first-person, personal world. If we are mere voyeurs and not actually inside the skin of a simian or feline cousin, then surely we have thrown the baby of subjective consciousness, the actual feel of pleasure, out with the bathwater of unwarranted anthropomorphization.

The nagging contrast between what we feel ourselves and what we can study in others is reflected in the contrast between consciousness, the feel of your first-person, personal world to you, and the idea of mind developed as a long-term, lifelong, personalized brain. In this chapter, I have reserved *consciousness* for the inside-the-skin sensation and used *mind* as an umbrella term for the objective, observable factors that constrain and determine the quality of that firsthand sensation, the personal memories seized on earlier by Baars. If we continue with this terminology, then we could view Dennett's probing into the lifestyles of different species as a survey of mind, a collective of different, objective factors that influence the type of consciousness one might have. But such an approach does not explain the actual experience, consciousness itself.

Dennett focuses on what he—and I—refer to as *mind* and introduces the metaphor of a tower of intelligence. As we ascend the tower of increasingly complex brain design, the seeming irrelevance of the subjective impact of first-person consciousness becomes increasingly apparent, and for me at least, worrisome. Just as with Calvin's scheme, power within the tower is measured in problem-solving agility amplified by language skills, but it is not at all calibrated in feelings or emotions. The very feelings that are arguably present in a conscious yet helpless newborn but absent from even the most sophisticated of computers is not an index here. Unfortunately, as with Calvin's vision, Dennett's scheme of towering brains happens to be based precisely on the very experience-based problem solving beloved of AI, not on depth or subtlety of feeling.

It seems to me that the evolutionary approach lends itself so well to dealing in the coinage of abstract thought and problem solving precisely because it is in these talents where we truly part company from all other mammals. Arguably, humans spend far more time in these thinking and reasoning cognitive processes than any other mammal, even compared to our chimpanzee cousins, whose DNA is only 1 percent different from our own. More than any other species, we can plan ahead, visualize a tool we might see as perfect for a certain task, form hopes about the future, and reflect on abstract concepts. Although the precise terminologies might vary, there is a unifying scheme: the generation of intellectual inner resources.

This kind of abstract thinking, in the absence of any cues from our senses whatsoever, is the province of sophisticated brains. Imagine a rabbit, snug, warm, and safe in its burrow, unable to sleep at night simply for the hypothetical worry that it might be eaten by a hypothetical fox. Only when the rabbit really smells a real fox will its brain instigate a real action. On the other hand, it is easy to see how a worry, if not of being eaten, then of having a mortgage foreclosed, could keep one of us adult humans tossing and turning in our darkened bedroom without any trigger at all from our senses. Such higher-order consciousness, an abstract worry, can grow only as the mind evolves, as cerebral inner resources are marshaled, as associations are built up within the brain in response and retaliation to the relentless assault from objects and events in the world around us. A rabbit will have less of a mind than its human counterpart in that it will be more firmly locked into its immediate environment.

Most brain models, whether inspired by AI or by evolution, have much in common. They focus on certain distinguishing features of the human brain: our ability to think, reason, remember, and employ the benefits of an idiosyncratic earlier experience; in short, to use a mind. Because AI and evolution models are predicated on the same assumptions, they might be more powerful if they were combined. Enter the psychologist Steven Pinker.[50]

Pinker defines *mind* as "what the brain does." Although he has little time for neurons, Pinker does worry about the mechanical level of brain bump and grind, albeit one that is resolutely silicon rather than carbon based. He vaunts the type of model that we looked at earlier, of the brain as a very special computational device. This nuts-and-bolts position is brought up alongside a more theoretical, evolutionary approach, inspired by Darwin's theory of natural selection,[51] combined with the basic concept of genes unswervingly bent on replication.

Pinker's explanation of the mind combines these two approaches to give an inevitable haiku-like conclusion: we are driven by a genetic imperative, realized by an automated series of hierarchical cerebral circuits that function computationally. Although Pinker spends much time in detailing for the AI aficionado the mental processes of converting the visual world into meaningful objects, he actually has very little to say about the really subjective aspects of vision. For example, what is a hallucination? We are merely reassured that an imaginary experience can be attributed to the visual centers of the brain receiving an input not from the usual source, the retina, but from long-term memory. But what is long-term memory? A mere label is unenlightening in the absence of a frame of reference, such as an actual brain phenomenon or process.

Memory for one-off episodes certainly needs to be distinguished from that used for skills, and such distinctions are not really explored within the constraints of Pinker's haiku; nor for that matter is the hallucinatory distortion to our minds that can occur following administration of certain drugs, such as LSD. The truth is that the computational model is, once again, limited to learning and memory skills that can be measured objectively, and which can be performed easily by a machine.

Unfortunately, this approach is of no help at all in understanding the more slippery phenomena that so far seem to be unique to biological brains.

Pinker's model does incorporate emotions, but merely as "adaptations, well-engineered software modules that work in harmony with the intellect and are indispensable to the functioning of the whole mind." Yet surely, as with the issue of long-term memory, he is merely spinning words. As for consciousness, he dismisses it altogether as a mystery that is a topic "not for science but for ethics." Instead, an exhaustive, computational approach to neuroscience and psychology will, we are assured, eventually eliminate the difficulty posed by the question of consciousness. And yet, we are still left in the dark as to how we would ever compute a headache or the exhilaration of first love. Once again, it looks like the computational approach cannot really help with the issue of emotion and indeed the related question of consciousness itself.

Perhaps the evolutionary aspects of his theory could be of more use. Pinker adopts a zealotlike position in the nature-nurture debate, though he reviles the very dichotomy. Although many of his arguments against creationism and anti-Darwinism are indisputable and cogent, Pinker is so keen to send out an unambiguous message that much of the interesting biological detail in the debate is lost. For example, the sliding scale of mindless genetic tyranny as opposed to the flexibility allowed by learning, which we have just seen characterizes most other evolutionary models, such as those of Dennett and Calvin, is given no house room at all.

Pinker has already headed off in an obvious direction: the marrying of (a) automated, computational brain processes with (b) a strong genetic basis points us clearly in the direction of instinct. Here is where he is most comfortable; as with echoes of his previous work claiming that language is a human instinct,[52] he starts to view human thoughts and behavior in terms of that admittedly fascinating topic, atavistic human nature.

Pinker is able to work his way through a gamut of human feelings and thoughts, viewing them, perhaps not with total originality, but with a natural selection twist. But there is a certain unease to this narrative, because he admits that not everything we do is simply reducible to our genetic dictates. For instance, why should he himself choose to remain childless? Because he is happy that way, and "if my genes don't like it, they can go jump in the lake." This admirably honest stance surely pinpoints a truly fascinating aspect of the human mind, where human nature developed over thousands and thousands of years collides like a tectonic plate with what we might call "human nurture," an immediate ontogenetic agenda very much involved with living out life at the turn of the twentieth century. It seems that after all, we have still not escaped the nagging nature-nurture issue. Nor has Pinker offered any new guidelines or principles by which we might analyze the respective contributions of a caveman past and a more immediate, gene-defying lifetime of experience.

Models based on evolutionary considerations might still be of use, however, if they concentrated more on emotions and feelings, rather than cognitive prowess. Darwin himself was the first to acknowledge[53] that expressions of different emotions, such as anger and threat, in animals had survival value in signaling behavioral intentions. But the most important and nagging question here is that of the accompanying, internally generated feeling. After all, a robot could be trained to grin or a computer programmed to display a smiley face. Once again, we return to the big questions of how the subjective feeling of emotions such as pleasure has actually evolved—and why.

It is not so much, then, that a consideration of evolution necessitates concentrating on purely cognitive processes, but rather that many approaches to date have used evolutionary processes only to explain one particular aspect of the brain. But the value of the subjective feel of emotions can also be interpreted in evolutionary terms. All creatures that move from one place to another have a primitive sort of brain. Indeed the term *animated,* to be on the move, shares the same root in Latin with *animus,* everyday consciousness. One value of brains, then, is to enable appropriate and fast reactions to a fast-moving, everchanging environment. In animals with simple brains there would be very little need for understanding to be built up by experience because the nervous system would have screened out unnecessary details already, and the reactions would be, as Dennett describes, reflexive, dictated by the genes. Hence one goldfish, for example, would have a behavioral and cognitive repertoire, and thus a mind, very like another. As we saw in Chapter 1, there would be no great individuality. But the balance tilts more in favor of nurture than nature as species with more complex brains evolve.

The less at the mercy of the genes you are, the greater the repertoire of behavior, and thus the more choice at your disposal. Now, it would be important to ensure that an animal with a choice made a good decision about to what to do. Repetitive rhythmic actions, such as eating and copulation, would ensure survival of the species far more than placing yourself in a situation where the sensory inputs changed rapidly, for example, being chased. The different ways the senses impinge might determine a different "feel" of emotions. In turn, the feel of different emotions might therefore be important in guiding choices and thus in aiding survival. The more choice available, the wider and richer the repertoire, and arguably the greater the diversity and capacity for feeling. In a rat, say, rather than a goldfish, the beginnings of pleasure as a distinct and sporadic state beyond a more homogenous sea of sentience might have survival value.

As the brain becomes more sophisticated as one enters the primate stage, then one's repertoire would increase still further. Skills at interpreting more of the world and of developing technology to achieve one's aims would be developed. The fact that these aims were to attain pleasure would have to be learned by individuals within their own life spans.

Although the ability to think, to express oneself, and to exercise an ever-finer memory—in short, to exercise one's mind—will all be useful for solving primate problems posed in the outside world, the corollary risk now is that we humans could use our highly developed minds to the exclusion of all else. We are in danger of spending all day indulging in an inner fantasy of the future or memory of the past. To combat this very human tendency to escape the here and now, how valuable it is to have a goal, the attainment of a feeling of pleasure, where one will strive to be in situations that counterbalance the mind and revert the individual to a throbbing, sensual present.

In evolutionary terms, we can view emotions as processes where one is highly interactive with the environment. If you are interactive with the environment, then you are focusing on your senses, and the more you are the passive recipient of the senses, the less you are accessing the mind. The more you do this, the more you are letting go of the Self. It could be the case, then, that the more emotional you are, the less the world around you means anything, and the more you have literally let yourself go.

In this way, one may be still conscious but indeed be out of one's mind, but it does not work the other way round. An unconscious mind, a plethora of experience-forged associations that lack that mysterious extra ingredient, merely amounts to a machine of the type that already exists, be it a Darwin robot or my laptop.

To date it seems that nothing else has come along that is like the biological brain in the universe. It would therefore indeed be surprising if it could be modeled in terms of other things—be they theaters, towers, penknives, or silicon chips—and yet retain the most exciting and as yet unidentified properties, too, those that engender the subjective state. On the other hand, the brain must clearly be appreciated as an integrated, holistic system, whereby the awesome abilities it displays are not yet attributable to any single subcomponent or process, be it a chemical, a gene, a brain region, or synchronized electrical activity.

Despite the explosion of ideas about consciousness and the mind that have been presented over the last decade or so, some of which I have briefly reviewed here, it seems to me that we have not yet really moved forward at all. Clearly, we need to know what is happening in the real brain, and yet the big question that scientists are still ducking is how the actual feel of emotions, raw consciousness no less, is accommodated in the physical mass.

A new way forward might be to see what happens in brains where emotions seem to be far more dominant than in adult humans. According to the idea sketched in Chapter 1, emotion, or feeling, is the most basic form of consciousness. The corollary of this idea is that when we experience basic and strong emotion, our physical brains must in some way be temporarily transformed, for a moment or two, to recapitulate a more fundamental brain state characterized by a consciousness bereft of logic or reason, a consciousness stripped of meaning and memories, that is, the brain state of an infant. The next step, then, is to look at exactly what in the brain might have changed at such times, when we are conscious but have no sense of Self, no mind. In Chapter 3, we will turn to what exactly it is that is grown within the brain throughout childhood, only to be turned down, even abandoned, in emotional states. In short, what is the physical basis of the mind?

3

THE CHILD

One day, I happened to catch the quicksilver expression on the face of a friend's three-year-old. His older brother had pushed him over, and as he fell he hit his head on the side of a table. Tears, wails, and sobs were broadcast. But in the middle of the public wretchedness, a glare of pure malevolence was hurled like a dagger at the back of the perpetrator. All in a single moment.

Small children seem to live on an emotional roller coaster. With miraculous rapidity, heartrending sobs give way to gurgles of delight at the sight of a chocolate bar or a cat walking past. Yet at the time the rage—or the laughter—seems so important and so definitive. Were such intense emotions displayed in an adult, they would presumably be assumed to be indicative of some inner state, such as a bereavement, so extreme that it would have to pervade the individual for far longer than the seconds for which it streaks across the face of a child.

Children can more readily abandon themselves to the joys, perhaps it is even the ecstasy, of an amusement-park ride or the sight of the sea, compared to adults, who find it virtually impossible to shake off the dripping worry of the mortgage payments. According to David Warburton, director of human psychopharmacology at Reading University, children laugh on average 300 times a day. By adulthood, this number plummets to 50. But by the same token, a child will be more readily frightened by a creak on the stair, by someone with a white sheet draped over his head, or by a train roaring into the station. Children experience emotions as strongly, perhaps even more strongly, than adults, but seemingly, for less good reason. We may call them "crybabies," not because of the nature of the emotion itself, but because such strong feelings have been evoked by such a feeble cause.

To a much greater extent, children are passive victims of their senses, one-off experiences that have an impact by virtue only of their intrinsic physical quality: the brightness, loudness, smell, taste, or touch of whatever is going on. This exaggerated emphasis on the actual sensuality of waves of sound and light and of clouds of chemicals pervading the ears, eyes, nose, skin, and mouth is because, for the very young, there is nothing else. Children are less equipped to interpret the present situation against the sobering yet reassuring background of past experience, a private collection of memories that tells us that it is only an ordinary person masquerading as a ghost under the white sheet or that there are more significant possessions in life than an ice cream cone that has fallen on the sidewalk.

As we grow up and see the world increasingly in the light of previous experiences, we develop a personalized inner world of private resources that increasingly act as a retaliatory buffer to the assault of the "booming, buzzing confusion"[1] that previously poured into our brains unopposed. And as we continue to live out our lives as adults, more and more associations pile on and around the objects, events, and people among which we are thrown.

This rapidly expanding inner world of personal associations offers an ever-growing framework of reference, an increasing degree of meaning to ongoing experience. The most obvious type of meaning is the culturally and socially accepted identity of objects and people around us. But gradually these objects and people acquire ever more extensive and idiosyncratic associations, and hence ever more eccentric and intense degrees of significance. The more ramifying and multiple the associations, the more "meaning," or "relevance," an object will have.

Think of a cup.[2] A newborn child, even if it could focus on a cup, would not be able to recognize it as such; it would be just a series of curves, shades, and shadows. As time went on, however, the child would begin to associate the different shapes and sizes of cups with the activity of drinking and would eventually learn the verbal label for the general concept of "cup" so that the object could be conjured up in his or her imagination, even when a cup was not there. One cup in particular might become associated with a particular event or be special because it was a present from a special person, in that it, too, evoked a raft of memories. Once the child entered high school, he or she might read Freud and assign a new meaning to the cup (e.g., as a symbol of fecundity). Or the child might become an expert in eighteenth-century porcelain, so that certain types of cups would become even more finely differentiated than snow to Eskimos. Hence the object, the humble cup, would be shot through with a rich range of associations triggering all number of memories, and it would thus acquire a significance it could never have had had the child been reared in some hypothetical environment where people drank only from bottles.

Another example, perhaps the most obvious for those of us brought up in a traditional family environment, is a mother. For the infant, Mommy's face looms into view most often. It is a swimming constant in a shifting world of colors and smells and textures, and quickly it acquires associations of feeding, being warm, being rocked, and being dry. Throughout the child's early years, such persistent involvement in much of one's daily experiences will ensure that some woman whom the rest of us would pass in the street without a glance, a woman who in psychophysical terms makes no impact on the raw senses, would nonetheless be of overwhelming significance to someone.

Following this train of thought, it is easy to see how the gradual forging and trafficking of associations equip us first with a simple, literal meaning for the immediate world around us. As more associations pile up, objects, people, and events acquire differential degrees of importance with corresponding ease or otherwise of recall. A well-known memory trick is to attach as many associations as possible, however contrived, to the object, list, or fact that you want to remember. For example, if you can visualize the items on a shopping list as distributed around a kitchen, or can imagine being back on the playground with those classmates whose names were previously so hard to call to mind, then the whole business of remembering becomes easier. By stacking up associations, it is not so much that our memories get better but that they become more readily accessed through more potential routes.

As we grow, we learn to generalize across experiences, to see common patterns and themes and thus to develop generalizations such as "cat," abstract concepts such as "beauty," and finally to relate these concepts to one another in an original way—to have ideas. But in each case, the constellation of such associations will be as varied as an individual life, and thus the understanding of the world—as we viewed it in Chapter 2—will be different for each individual. Sometimes, associations with certain objects seem to others to be excessive and baffling. When we speak of something having sentimental value, what we really mean is that an object will trigger far more extensive connections than might have been expected on the basis of its physical properties alone. A cheap plastic toy ring might have been the token of love used in a spontaneous marriage proposal when found in a Christmas cracker at a particular party one December. Only two people in the world share that particular memory, and only for them would the subsequent sight of the ring trigger a particular state of mind. For them, the worthless object would mean a great deal at a very private level. This sort of association applies not just to objects of sentimental value. Everything around you will be imbued with a significance that is unique to you because only you have lived your life—had a particular set of experiences.

One object, one word, one glance, will act like a stone cast into a puddle, sending out ripples of memories triggering off one another. Gradually, beyond the generic concepts, the verbal label, we acquire a more sophisticated and highly personalized view, an understanding of the world that is unique to each of us. As we grow up, we are better able to understand or explain an ongoing situation in the light of previous experience and objects, people, or actions with only a modest impact on the raw senses will monopolize our attention because of a far more covert, less tangible, and private significance. We start to register not only the loudest and brightest in each waking moment, but the secret lover's eyebrow raised silently for a fraction of an inch over a fraction of a second across a noisy, crowded room.

Each time you hear a noise, blink at the light, have a conversation, or cut another piece of cake, some small, imperceptible, and unspectacular modification to the configuration of the brain occurs,[3] and we interpret the world in a slightly different way. With increasing frequency, previous associations start to dominate our interpretation and response to ongoing situations. The brain becomes less of a sponge and more of a yardstick in a turning world, retaliating in an increasingly balanced dialogue with the outside world.

The critical issue here, as we saw in Chapter 2, is to develop an understanding, to attach meaning to an event or person by placing it or him or her in a wider, more general context of preexisting facts and memories, however idiosyncratic or misguided it might appear to others. For example, how often do we hear someone excuse the behavior of a friend or colleague as "human nature"? The very concept of human nature is one that will have evolved through a lifetime of dealing with people and seeing recurrent and common ways in how people act and respond. If someone makes a spiteful remark, say, about a friend's new dress, a teenager might be wounded, whereas someone older might react less strongly by placing the remark in a more general context, such as the "natural" tendency for jealousy among peers. Such understanding cannot be simply downloaded from a chip or, more prosaically, taught at the blackboard. It is only as we become older that we stand any chance at all of being described as "wise." But we need to see now how the generic brain can become personalized in this way, that is, how it develops a mind.

Mind. It is a murky concept. It peppers our daily conversation, lurks in idioms and expressions, and yet evades a clear definition. Ask most people to define *mind* and they will probably come up with one of two possibilities, neither of which is satisfactory. The first answer is that somehow the mind is the opposite of the brain. This knee-jerk response is the inheritance left to us more than 300 years ago by René Descartes, whose distinction between mental and physical, a dualism, has clung to Western thought ever since.[4] Nowadays it might seem easy to resort to the reassurance of the material world and spurn anything that smacks of the mystical. However, it is important to remember that Descartes lived in an era dominated by the church, where no theory could fly directly in the face of the religious and thus spiritual perspective on life. How much neater, therefore, to develop the idea of parallel systems, a concept concerned with the bump and grind of banal material things that left the sanctity of the human experience as remote and unreachable as ever. Many still like to think that there is more to our lives and to ourselves than our banal existence in our sweaty and imperfect physical bodies.

This additional but intangible special quality is seldom described or defined, but following this line of thought, it might be regarded as a "soul." Now, let's distinguish mind from soul. What we are dealing with here, in this chapter, is the essence of individuality, the constellation of characteristics, propensities, and prejudices, that make us who we are, literally ourselves, until we die. For those who believe in a soul, the most important aspect is that it is immortal; it would survive the death of the brain. But with death, the mind, as defined here, is finished. We are dealing with the lifetime consistency of development of character that is rooted in the development of your physical brain, and therefore it terminates when your brain does. True, we refer in an everyday sense to someone "having soul," but really we are not speaking literally. Soul, as in "soul music," is a metaphor that encompasses more emotions and sensitivities than gray-suited crowds of commuters or, dare I say it, white-coated neuroscientists. Whereas for Descartes, immortality and character were more easily conflated, from the privileged stance of the twenty-first century, we can place considerations of immortality outside the scope of this investigation of the Self.

So, we are confronting the riddle of a mortal mind versus a mortal brain. Meticulous clinical observation over the last few centuries has revealed how the actions of drugs, head wounds, and strokes modify the state of the physical brain and at the same time how those physical processes modify how people think and feel. The idea of something mental, divorced from the tangible gray matter, has grown increasingly unattractive.

An alternative, more modern way of defining *mind* would simply be to view it as no more than the physical brain. In the 1940s, the great behaviorist movement led by B. F. Skinner proudly brought a new age of reason to the study of the human mind by dispensing with the concept altogether and placing emphasis instead on the inputs and outputs of the physical brain.[5] Final behavior—observable, measurable phenomena—was all that mattered. But it soon became clear that the brain was not just a receptacle for reflex responses to specific triggers, or stimuli. Instead, even laboratory rats showed that something was intervening between the stimulation going in and the response coming out: thinking. So, this stark, mechanistic stance gradually gave way to the cognitive (literally "thinking") approach where, as its name suggests, the importance of the intervening mental processes played a central role. Instead of throwing out the term *mind* altogether, advocates of the cognitive approach, such as Dan Dennett, now instead use it interchange-ably with the term *brain*.[6]

But the old terminology and the need to separate the generic, physi-cal brain from something else endures. Despite the clear demonstra-tions by modern medicine of a causality between tampering with the physical brain, say with drugs, and subsequent changes in the mental world—in one's mood—we still seem to need the two separate words, *mind* and *brain*, in everyday conversation. Even medical textbooks of-ten describe disorders of the brain, the "organic" dysfunctions such as strokes and epilepsy, as opposed to those of the "mind": schizophrenia, depression, or anxiety, with the treatment in each case segregated re-spectively to the artificial, in my view, distinctions of neurology or psy-chiatry.[7] If the mind is indeed tied in with the brain, the nature of that relationship is far from that of a mere synonym. So Descartes's division lingers: we may legitimately reject the idea of airy-fairy stuff, a New Age alternative to matter, but we apparently need—in our vocabulary at least—a term that refers to something beyond the physical brain.

Mind still captures a subtly different concept that cannot be catered to automatically by contemplating the physical lump of tissue between the ears. All our physical brains look pretty much the same, but one's mind is quintessentially one's own. In Chapter 1, we saw that there was no uniqueness in the generic brain and that it was far from obvious where or when the individuality crept in. If mind is not airy-fairy, then it must be reflected in some special physical feature of the brain, devel-oped as we grow up in a world that only slowly we come to under-stand. If our minds take shape over childhood, then we can look at the changes in the brain over this time frame to address the great question, what is the physical basis of the mind?[8]

Imagine a room. When you first move in, you have almost infinite scope in determining what sort of room it will turn out to be. Of course, you will have to make do with its size and the shape, the height of the ceiling, and the number of windows. But the early stages of liv-ing in the room and decorating it from scratch will probably be the most formative. Most likely, you will immediately impose a theme, a general style, be it Art Deco, antique, high-tech, sloppy student, or un-domesticated bachelor. But it is only as you live in the room that you will be able to evolve the most pleasing and practical configuration of furniture, and indeed to discover which items you need most. With changing fashion and changing lifestyle, these needs will, of course, themselves change, albeit in the minor move of an ornament being shifted along a mantelpiece or in a more drastic manifestation, like a new overall color. Then there will be changes that you do not control or anticipate: perhaps a window will be smashed, a rug burned, or items will wear out and need replacing with more efficient or more effective alternatives. But whether dramatic or modest, by accident or on purpose, nothing will remain the same. Few people could be confident that the rooms in which they are currently living would never undergo the slightest modification. So it is with brains, but on an infinitely finer and faster scale.

It is in early childhood that experience has its most dramatic effects in determining our world view. "Give me a child until he is seven," promised the Jesuits,[9] "and I will give you the man." It is self-evident that it is the experiences that occur after birth that will determine the language we speak first, the accent we have, the religion we adopt, the values we live by, and so forth. In my case, I was born in London, the product of a mixed marriage between a Jewish father and Protestant mother. I assumed everyone in the world spoke English and that some invisible line running from head to foot demarcated the Jewish half of me from the Protestant side, though it was unclear which was which. Such is the attempted holistic view of the child, colored wholly by the haphazard and literal inputs of the immediate environment.

Throughout life we constantly modify our outlook and expectations, shifting the furniture around in the room, purchasing new items, and throwing out the old. In imperceptible steps, we become increasingly unsurprised by and cynical about human behavior. Or there may be some dramatic changes in perspective—a bereavement, religious conversion, or indeed the realization that those childhood beliefs should be challenged. Some of these changes of mind will appear to be initiated by ourselves, such as deciding to have a child, having another slice of cake, going to a party, or going to work in another country, whereas others will be imposed upon us, say, a car accident, a death, a lottery win, a chance encounter. Our world view, then, remains highly interactive and dynamic, but increasingly there is a theme, a continuity of style as we grow that is more personalized and more individual than any room—even for clones.

The common perception of science fiction clones is that they not only look alike but have the same personality, and even the same consciousness. Yet having a clone, who is, after all, merely an identical twin, is like having an empty room of identical size and shape as your neighbor, with exactly the same number and size and position of windows. Individual differences will soon creep in. If I had a clone living in the Amazon jungle, even at the physical level, she would only partly resemble me; after all, height and weight would be influenced by diet, and the stress induced by teaching medical students and running a lab might affect the number of wrinkles and gray hairs, and facial muscle configuration, compared to my genetic counterpart luxuriating in tropical vegetation. She would have a host of rain-forest survival skills that I lacked, though her views and knowledge, say, of daily life in Oxford would be zero. Nature and nurture would have interacted to produce two distinct individuals.

In the old days, the segregation of environment from genes seemed quite straightforward. The investigator studied the coincidence of traits (covariance) in human clones, namely, identical twins who had identical genetic portfolios yet had been reared apart. In this way nurture was cleanly separated from whatever cards had been dealt from an oblivious sperm and ovum. But a recent paper in the journal *Nature* (no bias intended) threw a wrench in the works of this dichotomy.[10] Devlin, Daniels, and Roeder, working at the Pittsburgh School of Medicine and Carnegie Mellon University, have highlighted an anomaly over the delicate and much-debated question of the degree to which one's IQ is inherited.

For some time this issue has presented a puzzle to behavioral geneticists. The difficulty arises from different results generated by different types of studies on twins. When the subjects have been identical twins reared apart, it has been estimated that the degree of IQ they inherit is about 70 percent. Yet it is also possible to tease out the genetic component of a trait such as IQ by working with twins living together. In this case, one compares identical twins with nonidentical counterparts. Assuming that any factor arising from a similar environment will be constant for both types of twins, any other difference in ability between identical compared to nonidentical twins should presumably be genetic. Surprisingly, the degree to which IQ can be attributed to genes is much lower, only 50 percent! What is the extra, unaccounted for factor that was inflating the value of an inherited component to IQ, specifically for twins reared apart? Devlin and colleagues have an ingenious hypothesis.

For twins growing up together, the important factor is not whether they are identical: the shared environment, nurture, would be undeniably a constant factor irrespective of whether the twins came from two eggs or one. For twins growing up apart, however, only identical twins would usually be investigated, in order to distinguish the identical set of genes from the variable environment. But for twins living in different homes all their lives, the hitch is that nurture might not be as negligible as one supposed. It is easy to overlook that there is a common shared environment *before* birth. In comparisons between identical and non-identical twins living together, this factor would be common to both groups, but it might not have counted in any final discrepancy. When Devlin and his colleagues reanalyzed previous studies, they indeed found that a staggering 20 percent of IQ could be attributed not to shared genes, nor to a shared home, but to a shared womb.

It seems truly remarkable that the developing fetal sense organs are able to transmit information reflecting specific variations in its uterine environment back to the growing brain, where there is presumably a sufficient influence on cerebral mechanisms to be reflected, ultimately, in differences in some kind of external performance or trait later on in life. So, if there is a wild card, the womb environment, that contributes to our mental makeup, then perhaps we are one step less near *Brave New World* eugenics.[11] But turbulent events are occurring nonetheless in the womb.

As early as four weeks after conception, the human fetus has a recognizable brain. As you might imagine, it is of course very different from the brain that will control its life, effectively *be* its life, for the following seventy years or so. The four-week brain consists of three swellings, like beads on a string, that develop into bulges and in turn become rounded brain regions that enclose a stalk. This is the brain stem, the most primitive part of the brain, which we first encountered in Chapter 1, which is continuous with the spinal cord. As growth gets seriously under way, the cells that constitute the brain will proliferate at the staggering rate of 250,000 per minute. Slowly, this restless mass of tissue takes shape as the future brain cells, or neurons, shuttle back and forth from the innermost core of the brain to its outermost reaches. The newest cells will end up in the outermost layers, so the brain effectively grows inside out.[12]

Once they have reached their final destination, the itinerant brain cells start to set down the neurological equivalent of roots. They will no longer be able to travel back and forth according to a preordained script, but now start more to resemble a spider in the middle of its web. In terms of the real brain, the web is actually a cosseting of support cells that form a delicate cradle for the neuron and ensure that its local environment remains benign, free of debris and harmful substances, yet rich in nutrients. And so it is that with some 100 billion neurons in place, and ten times as many support cells, we make our debut in the world.

Already, we have seen, the experience in the womb might shape certain traits by influencing, presumably, certain circuitry between neurons,[13] but it is from the moment of birth that this process is about to be massively exercised and exploited. Experience now becomes completely unique: no one, however close, occupies the same identical points in time and space throughout your life as you do. And as you live, memories pile up, and this accumulation of past scenarios, all stored within your brain, gives you a unique perspective from which to interpret the flood of sensations that bombard you every waking moment. Memories and mind are, therefore, inextricably linked.

One of the most remarkable differences between us and our closest simian cousins is that our brains undergo astonishing postnatal growth, doubling in size during our first two years, finally increasing by 400 percent, from 450 cc to a maximum of some 1700 cc by the time we are sixteen years of age.[14] But we are born with most of the neurons we are ever going to have, so something else must be going on within our postnatal skulls. It is not the brain cells themselves that change and continue to change, so much as the *connections* between them. These neurons, which are already in place at birth, have no further room to maneuver; they are henceforth static, but the extensions that now grow out of them can be diverted and steered by chemicals. These extensions, some of which are established in the womb, remain highly dynamic. They are constantly strengthened by experience or atrophying through lack of it. The neurons do not increase in number, but the connections between them now become increasingly conspicuous, pushing the main bodies of the neurons ever farther apart, as though they were clasping hands with one another and then unfolding and stretching out their spindly arms. The "arms" in the case of neurons can be tens to hundreds of times longer than their main central body, and some one hundred times thinner.[15] It is via these threadlike conduits that electrical signals buzz at speeds of up to 250 miles an hour along any of 10,000 to 100,000 connections.[16] Only once these connections are in place, networking one brain cell with another, are neurons able to communicate with one another. Only then will the brain be able to work to its full potential and start to interpret the world in the light of experience.

As we develop, as our bodies move around in the world, our brains are working incessantly on the use-it-or-lose-it principle.[17] Just like the muscles of your body, connections in the brain will strengthen and grow as they are exercised. In a general way, this phenomenon can be seen at work in all human brains. For example, the fingers and mouth are capable of highly agile movements and are particularly sensitive to touch. Despite being relatively minor, in purely anatomical terms, it is the fingers and mouth that receive the greater allocation in neuronal territory in the brain compared to, say, the upper arm or the back.[18] But this "neuronal plasticity" is also at work at a much less generic, more individual level. The brain cells that are involved in the activities that occur most frequently will have extensive connections, whereas those that are used less frequently will be pushed out of the way, and their targets will be taken over by their more hardworking neighbors.

One particularly dramatic and extreme example of neuronal plasticity took place in the brain of a six-year-old Italian boy. This child was blind in one eye, but doctors could find no cause for the blindness. Eventually, extensive questioning of the parents revealed that the boy had undergone a particularly incisive and unusual experience when less than a year old—unusual, that is, in terms of what the brain might have been expecting. The child had had a minor infection in one eye, which had consequently been bandaged. However, no one realized that this treatment was administered at a critical period when the connections were being laid down between the developing eye and the young brain. The developing brain was, sadly, highly sensitive to the all-important issue of the eye not working. The unbandaged eye, meanwhile, continued to work actively in the usual way, incessantly relaying in signals concerned with the sight of the outside world. But not only did it establish lines of communication within the brain in the expected manner, it also invaded and colonized the potential target of the occluded eye, too. By the time the bandage was removed, the connections from the occluded eye had nowhere to go. Hence the erstwhile, silenced eye could still not work, even though nothing was now impeding it. Accordingly, the boy has been blind in that eye ever since.

Although this story offers an exaggerated and far from typical example of how the brain adapts as it develops, neuronal plasticity is an everyday occurrence.[19] For instance, kittens trained to lift one paw up and down during special daily sessions actually show a markedly denser pattern of connections in the respective region of the brain concerned with control of paw lifting, compared with kittens that do not selectively exercise that one limb.[20] Similarly, adult owl monkeys trained to use two digits more than the remaining three, by rotating a small disk for an hour or so a day, exhibit an increased allocation of neuronal territory in the appropriate part of the brain, selectively for the two digits that have been working harder.[21] Even more subtle, and more "natural" still, are the changes that can be reflected in the brain by merely living a certain lifestyle. Adult rats who play within a cage "enriched" with budgie toys, exercise wheels, and the like develop a denser number of connections between brain cells than their counterparts in the humane but more Spartan world of a cage with only food and water.[22]

When I give public lectures, I'm asked quite often whether it is possible to observe and measure variations in neuronal connectivity in humans, postmortem, and relate those, as with the rats, to a lifetime of interaction and mental activity. The answer is no. It would be completely infeasible to distinguish those who had led stimulating lives— whatever that means—from those who had not. After all, an enriched environment, in neurological terms, would have little to do with whether one was on a beach in the Caribbean or trapped in a financially compromised position at home. As far as the brain is concerned, stimulation is provided by conversations, experiences, and encounters, irrespective of material wherewithal.

On the other hand, nature has at times conducted her own demonstration of the remarkable plasticity of the human brain. There are frequent stories of coma victims revived as relatives have sat by their bedside, stimulating the brain by endless talk or by playing music. Perhaps less dramatic but, to me at least, equally emotive, was what happened to my own father.

On a cold February day in 1991, my brother phoned from London with alarming news. The snow made travel from Oxford almost impossible, but I had to get home as quickly as I could. Apparently, my mother had returned from a shopping trip to discover my seventy-eight-year-old father sitting listlessly in a chair, oblivious to everything around him, including her increasingly agitated questioning. On arrival at the hospital, a brain scan confirmed that my father had had a stroke. His speech was unimpaired, and he had full control of his movements. It was just that he did not recognize any of us or have any idea where he was or what had happened. He was utterly confused, beached in a world that he did not understand, that made no sense. Of course, my family and I were distraught. What arrangements do you make for someone who is capable of maximum mobility, but who might easily walk across a busy road or burn down the house? The doctors shook their heads and showed me the scans: Part of my father's brain resembled Swiss cheese. But then, a seeming miracle occurred. Within a week or so, the paternal world started to right itself. A few months later, he had made a full recovery, and within the year he had even regained his driver's license. Now, at the age of eighty-three, he has been considering a sponsored bungee jump for charity—an idea quite understandably vetoed by my mother.

In this way I saw with my own eyes how someone I knew and loved well could vanish in an instant, but then gradually reappear. My father's brain could not replace the neurons he had lost, but gradually the ones that remained were able to take on the functions of their deceased colleagues. Even in old age, brain plasticity can occur.[23] The brain, or, rather, its internal circuitry, is constantly restless.

Certain configurations of neuronal connections, then, imperceptibly personalize the brain, and it is this personalized aspect of the physical brain that actually is the mind. This individual mind continues to respond and react by shifting neuron allegiances as we live out our lives. However, as we mature, the dialogue with the outside world will become less one-sided than when we were younger. Instead of processing brute lights and noises as independent happenings, certain consistent combinations of shape, color, sound, and smell that constitute one's mother, for example, will start to trigger connections that have already been stimulated and established by previous experience. The unique concatenation of sensory experience that was one's mother will now mean something as a complex but single entity corresponding to one's female parent. It is this preconceived concept that is so hard for most of us who are not artists to unpick into mere colors and shapes again, for relaying into a painting of what we literally see at the purely sensory level. For most of us, our carefully nurtured, preconceived notions intervene.

Within the brain, certain scientists such as the physicist Erich Harth[24] and the physiologist Semir Zeki[25] are starting to identify circuits that might underlie this interaction between the incoming sensory flood and preexisting associations, that is, the established connections between groups of neurons. In both cases, it is now well established that visual signals are not just relayed passively into the deep recesses of the brain and up into the cortex.[26] Instead, there are also other connections that intercept this incoming stream of information, projecting it back down in the opposite direction to modify the way the incoming signal is relayed and thus how the world is perceived. We see the world in terms of what we have seen already.

The more complex the brain, the greater the potential for variations in the neuronal connectivity that underlies its interpretations. The longer the childhood, the more the brain will be able to forge connections that mirror not just the demands of the species or the immediate habitat, but the particular and peculiar history of the individual concerned. As the brain becomes more sophisticated, particularly in primates, the part played by the environment becomes even more marked compared to the generic, genetic programming seen in, say, the goldfish. Animals that interpret the world in a way that is beneficial and necessary to the stereotyped repertoire and lifestyle of the species rather than to that of an individual would not need to learn from experience, nor would they need a highly developed mind. They would be at the— literally mindless—dictates of their genes.

When we are born and our brain, at last unconstrained by the demands of a narrow birth canal, starts to swell through the establishment of connections, we humans start to learn and remember in earnest. During learning and memory, signaling from one neuron to the next becomes more efficient. This concept is referred to as "synaptic strengthening," and it was first introduced by the visionary psychologist

Donald Hebb almost half a century ago.[27] Only more recently, however, have the actual nuts and bolts of Hebb's idea become clearer.

Think of a warm-up comedy act. Once an audience had been primed to laugh, it will respond much more readily to a joke that might normally have left it cold. Similarly, following the kind of repeated stimulation that might occur during learning or exercise, neurons can be primed to respond more sensitively in the future. In the world of the neurons, *long-term potentiation,* as its name suggests, can last for many hours. Much is now known about how transmitters and receptors contribute to the effect,[28] but long-term potentiation is just the beginning. As the neuron is being primed, changes start to occur inside the cell itself. Eventually these changes might alter the density of connections, or at least the manufacture of further molecular machinery for more effective communication, indefinitely.[29]

But this local cross-talk from one tiny brain cell to another is not all there is to memory and, hence, to mind. Not every experience changes the contact between every neuron all over the brain, like a vast homogenous soup in the bony bowl of the skull, slopping first one way and then the next. Instead, specialized brain regions will change for special situations. Here then is a very big difference between a brain and any artificial device. In Chapter 2 we saw that computational methods might easily be able to cope with a model for synaptic strengthening, for learning, at the level of isolated contacts between the equivalent of one cell and the next. Unfortunately, such models fail to incorporate the additional, macro-level of complex brain regions and their respective diversity of function. And, as we saw in Chapter 1, this further level of organization of specialized yet interconnected brain regions is critical to understanding brain function.

Although memory might seem like a single process in everyday life, the brain treats it as it treats vision[30] and language,[31] for example, as a multitude of different operations,[32] and this is where it becomes important to distinguish different brain regions. One type of memory is known as "procedural memory." It is needed for skills such as playing the piano and driving. These laboriously acquired talents, as most of us know from tedious firsthand experience, require many repeated trials before the brain masters the required coordination between senses and movement for the eventual, seemingly effortless execution. Memory for this type of learned sequence of procedure is organized within the region dubbed the brain's "autopilot," the cauliflower-shaped structure that we saw in Chapter 1, sits seemingly in semiautonomy at the back of the head. It is even referred to as though it were a separate entity, "the little brain," or cerebellum.[33] Processes here have been successfully modeled in silicon.[34] They enable the brain to coordinate inputs and outputs and therefore lend themselves to the algorithmic processes of biasing connections that have been stimulated or exercised more than others.

But the ability to ride a bicycle or drive a car, once learned, makes little intrusion into that special first-person, personal world of our consciousness. These memories for skills can therefore be left within the orderly interstices of cells that make up the cerebellum. Consider instead the other broad class of memory, the type that permeates most intimately our conscious, everyday thoughts and determines our view of the outside world.

Completely separate from implicit, procedural memory is "declarative memory."[35] Declarative memory is explicit, in that we are aware we are remembering something in the first place. But what we are remembering can be divided further. On the one hand, there is memory for facts, such as the French word for *table* or the habits of cockroaches. On the other hand, there is the memory of spending a day last summer at the seaside with Auntie Flo. Initially, these two types of memory are treated in the same way by the brain. Central to operations is the hippocampus, so named because of its supposed resemblance in shape to a seahorse.[36]

The involvement of this particular brain region in the laying down of declarative memory became obvious in the 1950s, when H.M., a severely epileptic patient, underwent a radical operation in which the hippocampus and neighboring tissue was removed from both sides of his head.[37] Although the epilepsy was vastly improved, a terrible side effect soon became apparent: amnesia. H.M. could still perform skilled movements and learn skilled movements. His retention of procedural memory is consistent with the parceling out of different types of memory by the brain because his cerebellum was still intact. On the other hand, interestingly enough, H.M. could not actually remember the event, as such, of learning complex tasks, for example, tracing a star in a mirror.

Over the thirty or so years that H.M. has cooperated with a host of clinical psychologists and neurologists, some valuable insights have been gained for elucidating the mystery of the memory process. An intriguing observation was that H.M. could remember everything up until two years prior to his surgery. This time scale of several years puzzles me, as a neuroscientist. Normally, neurons signal to one another over thousandths of a second; longer-term adaptations in the efficiency of neuronal contacts, such as long-term potentiation, take place over minutes or, at most, hours.

What could be happening among the relevant neurons that takes years to accomplish but that then renders the hippocampus redundant? Abnormally long time scales—in brain terms, those that exceed minutes or perhaps hours at most—are already very familiar: stroke victims often display astonishing recovery of function as other parts of the brain adapt to taking over the functions of the neurons killed off through deprivation of their oxygen-carrying blood supply. And that process can take months or even years.

In some way, the role of the hippocampus appears to be like scaffolding on a building or training wheels on a five-year-old's bicycle: an essential feature during the development/learning/building process but obsolete once the endpoint is established. The vastly longer time scale of months and even years, exceeding as it does more familiar events at the one-to-one cellular level, suggests that for the memory of a complex event, which presumably requires the participation of many banks of neurons, the net activity of those neurons collectively must be consistently in a state of flux for very long periods.

You do not need to practice many excursions to the seaside with Auntie Flo in order to recall a single day trip. The simple model, then, of an increased efficiency between individual neuronal contacts established through repeated stimulation is therefore not sufficient here. One way of explaining why the hippocampus might be needed for such a long time, to lay down a unique memory of a complex event, might be precisely because it *is* a unique memory. Perhaps the hippocampus is acting like some kind of internalized practice device, in turn stimulating and eventually strengthening many types of earlier associations, covertly linked to a day at the seaside: perhaps for large numbers of neurons to be pressed into retaining a well-established memory, the scale of operations is such that the net time taken is much longer than for the strengthening of a single connection between two neurons isolated by neuroscientists under highly contrived experimental conditions, where a thin sliver of brain slice is kept alive in a dish for a few hours.[38]

Internal iterations between hosts of disparate neurons would take time. In any event, during this lengthy period of consolidation of a memory, there would be some kind of cross-talk between the hippocampus and the all-enveloping outer region, the cortex. As we saw in Chapter 1, the cortex has long been associated with higher functions, not only because damage there causes an impairment of memory and language functions but because the more sophisticated the animal, in the evolutionary scheme of things, then seemingly the greater the surface area of cortex that species possesses.

The constellations of associations, finally forged after lengthy activation by the hippocampus, would constitute a single memory. As time goes on, however, the connections might be strengthened by further associations, or weakened or distorted. Biological memories, unlike those of a computer, are highly dynamic and continuously subject to subsequent influences meddling after the event.[39] In any event, little clean clumps of neurons, each corresponding to a unique memory, are unlikely to be distributed evenly over the cortex. Both facts and events need to be placed in a context: in certain cases, most arguably in the controversial "hothousing" program for very young children,[40] emphasis might be being placed on acquisition of facts rather than on idiosyncratic understanding. But in the normal course of events, the growth of associations for disparate objects, people, and events will gradually lead to the linking of certain common features, and hence to the eventual development of more abstract and general ideas. Gradually, we become better equipped with neuronal inner resources to interact with, rather than merely react to, the outside world.

By the end of the first year, the immediate world is sufficiently familiar, and there are enough preestablished associations to elicit fear when a new stimulus impinges. As children start to make voluntary utterances to name objects spontaneously, they could be exhibiting the first early signs of communication—a sign that we know from bone relics preceded the Neanderthals. It is now, as they approach two years of age, that human infants start to exercise the unique birthright of the species, that is, the use of language.

According to the archaeologist Steven Mithen,[41] as we hominids have evolved, so have we been able to accommodate an increasing number of functional compartments within our brains, each of which is responsible for a different aspect of survival. For example, in addition to a general intelligence that presumably would come into play for problem solving, we, along with many other species, also have a social intelligence that enables us to live in a highly organized tribe and to communicate by grooming and a series of signals. In addition, animals such as chimpanzees have a natural history intelligence that enables them to interpret immediately the significance of a snake as danger. Mithen's idea is that these specialized intelligences can be distinguished from the type of general intelligence that we have already seen liberates us from stereotypical, predictable, genetically ordained behavior. Nowhere is this idea more obvious than with language.

Of course, it is very unlikely that language evolved overnight. As one of the first scientific thinkers, Lucretius, pointed out in the century preceding the birth of Christ, "... it was practical convenience that gave a form to the names of objects.... To suppose that someone on some particular occasion allotted names to objects, and that by this means men learnt their first words, is stark madness."[42]

Evidence dating as far back as the Neanderthals some 200,000 years ago indicates that we were already communicating with language. The angle of bones in the jaw can be used to indicate the position of a long-decomposed larynx.[43] A low-lying larynx, just above the windpipe, would suggest ability for speech. Our adult human larynx is positioned low so that we can make a fuller range of nonnasal sounds: the larynx acts as a complex valve for exhaled air to come out in puffs, thus providing the energy for speech shaped by the lips and tongue. In nonhuman primates, and indeed in all other nonhuman animals, the larynx is positioned high so that it seals off the windpipe when food and liquids are being ingested. This anatomy is also characteristic of the human infant, who can thus suckle and breathe without choking to death. By contrast, we humans, as Darwin pointed out, have evolved with the unique ability of choking to death. Bones from the Neanderthals indicate that they, too, had low larynxes: such a risky anatomical move would probably only have been worth it if there was a very great payoff, such as the ability to make a wide range of nonnasal sounds.

The anthropological neuroscientist Terrence Deacon[44] argues that language is distinct from complex avian vocalizations, the often subtle, conditioned responses of intelligent mammals, or indeed from our own emotional sobbing and laughter. Rather, the quintessence of language is the manipulation of symbols in a whole variety of flexible and changeable ways. At the age of around two years, this specialized language module is activated in the young human brain. The human child will suddenly have a specific talent, as starkly obvious in comparison with the chimp counterpart as if I (who am tone-deaf) had grown up with Mozart.

From this very early stage, the difference in agenda is clear: very young children, unlike intensively trained chimps, volunteer information about passing planes, cats, and distant cars even when such observations are not needed for survival.[45] However, both Mithen and the physiologist William Calvin[46] suggest that this language talent could also bootstrap with it other new skills. For example, language might go hand in hand with tool making. Once one has a word for an entity, a way of focusing one's thoughts on an object that is not actually present, then one can design and build, say, an axe head.

Rather than a specialized language intelligence, Mithen suggests that the rudimentary proto-language seen in chimpanzees and small children is a result of a general intelligence stretched to its limit and doing its best. Even primates that have been taught very sophisticated proto-languages, including complex manipulation of symbols, are incapable of copying our ancient hominid ancestors and building such artifacts. The only tool so far that a primate has built is a stick for fishing termites. Mithen, however, points out that such a task is relatively straightforward, given that the leaves are mere fragile appendages and lend themselves to being readily stripped off. The construction of a stick for fishing termites requires very little imagination, compared to an axe head, where the lump of stone itself offers very little inspiration in envisaging the finished product.

Calvin goes along with the idea that we share a proto-language with many animals, namely, the use of symbols and of naming, but that this talent is very different from the seemingly unique human ability to construct meaningful sentences. The task of constructing meaningful sentences is of course far more intellectually challenging than generating single words, but sentences act as a kind of cerebral Trojan horse, via which a host of other very powerful benefits are unleashed. From here it follows that once sentence construction is in place, one can pass from mere labels to whole stories, and once one has access to stories, then one ceases merely to react to the immediate, purely sensory, world around one.

Now, liberated from the present moment, we are thus at a huge advantage over even those other animals that can assign rudimentary labels to objects around them, the proto-language of manipulating plastic letters or computer icons. Along with sentence construction, the argument runs, one can pass from mere labels to whole stories with complex narratives, and once one has access to story lines, one can plan ahead.

The idea of sentence construction inspires Calvin to turn to a "two-for-the-price-of-one" principle of evolution. If we were developing skills to structure and order words, then an analogous structuring and ordering of actions could also be bootstrapped on, or vice versa. Hence increasingly skilled movements would go hand in evolutionary hand with more elaborate verbal relations—what Calvin refers to for both skills and speech as a "structured string." The idea of such structured strings of mental activity makes it possible to generalize still further from words and movements to abstract ideas.

Mithen's metaphorical thought processes, Calvin's structured string, and Deacon's multiway symbols all suggest that language enables the promotion of endless associations between any one object/person/event and another. According to Dennett, too, it is by virtue of language that humans can soar above the rest of the animal kingdom in problem solving, hypothesis formation, and more general thinking.

How is it that our human brains can invariably and inevitably master such skill as language, but only when intensively trained under highly contrived conditions can a bonobo chimpanzee make merely the most modest of starts? Deacon does not believe that our brains have a prewired language instinct, new custom-built parts, or a language center. Nonetheless, the human brain does deviate from the brains of other primates, not so much in the basic theme but in the variations. The gross brain regions might be comparable, but the relative size and hence the degree and directness of their connections with one another, as well as with the rest of the body, have made all the difference. Because our human brains have grown out of proportion to our bodies, there is more scope for the parts of the brain that are not immediately concerned with the processing of individual senses to dominate and prosper.

But a human brain so readjusted is not automatically better off for catering so effortlessly to the use of symbols. Deacon's route through the perils of chickens and eggs is to suggest a bootstrapping co-evolution. It is an attractive idea to envisage a brain adapting its functioning, and hence the organization of its constituent parts, to the changing demands of the organism toward use of symbols. However, Deacon's reason for this rapid and disproportionate growth in the brain is far more speculative and less obvious: the conflicting demand of pair bonding and meat eating. Only by devising symbols for demonstrating the exclusive relation to a specific female within a group would a male be able to ensure that her offspring, for whom he was hunting and providing meat, did indeed carry his particular genes.

Deacon does not pursue fully the origins of meat eating beyond its obvious immediate relation to our ancestors' unique ability to make stone tools. Mithen, on the other hand, cites meat eating as the link between language and proper tool making and contends that both would have evolved as a consequence of bipedalism. Some six million years ago in Africa, when we were competing with other primates for survival niches, a great efficiency evolved in reducing the effects of solar radiation by standing upright.[47] Once upright, our hands were freed and thus we were able to fashion tools, which improved our skills at catching prey and butchering their carcasses. Once we were eating a meat diet, it became more economical to live in larger groups. Once in larger groups, it turned out to be very time consuming to communicate by touch and by grooming: hence it became increasingly valuable to communicate with sounds. The ability to talk and make tools would, in this way, empower each other.

In addition to the generic primate penknife model of different types of intelligence modules, Mithen suggests that the Neanderthals would have been equipped with a further language intelligence and a technical intelligence. Only once a natural history intelligence, such as interpretation of hoofprints, combined with the social intelligence of intentional communication, and yet again with the technical intelligence of producing artifacts from inner mental templates, would the modern human mind be able to communicate via the final creation of artifacts and images that are effectively symbols for other objects, events, and people—that is, art.

This penknife imagery is useful in this line of reasoning because it provides a way of comparing the human brain through the ages with that of other primates. On the other hand, like all metaphors, it has its limits. If the brain were really to work in a literal way in the modular fashion of a penknife, then we would be left with the problem of who chooses which module to use, that is, who controls the knife itself?

Another consequence of taking the penknife imagery too literally is to fall into the ever-waiting trap that the brain is literally organized into strict compartments. There are no literal modules corresponding to specific functions, but rather a readjusted and reemphasized organization of the same brain regions that are present in other mammals. Mithen, as far as I can see, is not trying to suggest that we have more centers for this or that in the brain, but rather that the enhanced functions at our disposal have led to cross-fertilization between these functions.

As well as enabling us to create art and, perhaps less glamorously, to use symbols, the cross-fertilization afforded by language also enables us to have a grasp of that ultimate abstract concept, the Self as different from others. For example, although vervet monkeys can communicate that a snake is present and that it is dangerous, they will communicate in the same way irrespective of whether another vervet is present or not.[48] Similarly, although chimpanzees may undergo stereotyped behaviors, such as hiding an erect penis from rival and superior males, the actual improvisation of strategies where the relevant objects are not already present eludes them.[49]

By contrast, from the age of four onwards, human children realize that their thoughts are unique.[50] If a child over four is shown that a box of candies actually, and surprisingly, contains a pencil instead of the expected goodies, he or she realizes that that knowledge will not be shared by a friend who comes in later and observes the candy box all closed up. The belief as to the contents of the candy box will be different according to the earlier experience or the lack of it. A very small child, and indeed autistic people of all ages,[51] cannot grasp that different people are just that, people with their own sets of ideas, their own inner universe—a separate mind that is comparable yet different from their own.

In evolutionary terms, this individual milestone would be matched with our very recent Cro Magnon development over only the last 40,000 years, when we began to display different behaviors to other primates in the use of bone artifacts or of teeth from carcasses serving as food by using them also as decoration—a necklace of teeth, for example. Only then did we start to indulge in art. Once we established language and were able to escape the immediate here and now, then not only were we able to plan for the future and remember the past, but to indulge in scenarios that have never been, to imagine magical entities and mystical, mythical scenarios. This is the time, too, when religion became practiced, in that our imaginations were powerful enough to extend belief to nonphysical entities, just as young children universally believe in magic.

It is in early childhood that the imagination is most fertile for most of us. Young children start to see links between objects, albeit frequently superficial or idiosyncratic ones: because these associations will be the result of relatively few experiences, they may well be suppressed later because more frequent associations become dominant or because the original pairings turn out to be supernumerary. On the other hand, at this early stage, thanks to language, connections are agile enough to be formed in the absence of external sensory cues, yet sufficiently unconstrained by inner resources rigorously cross-checked against endless variants of reality. At this stage, a child has a robust enough mind to become engrossed in a comic, with its visual prompts, but not mature enough to conjure up pictures entirely from words alone, as in adult novels. Their need for sensory stimulation is decreased sufficiently in urgency to listening to stories, where the narrator adds tones of voice and interacts, but not to read a story undistracted on their own. And before these censoring inner resources are so firmly established, how much easier it is for a large cardboard box to become a car or a house, or to believe that Teddy really is alive like you are. It is this ability to see something in terms of something else, to use one's imagination, that Mithen points to as the apotheosis of human achievement over that of the other primates.

But as we grow further, we stunt our imaginations. Gradually, one screens out the instinctive fear of the dark, the sensual joy of a sunset, or the awesome impact of the sheer size of the sea. Whereas Mithen offers the final stage of human evolution as the stage at which we can actually use our imaginations, I would argue there is one more stage, where the attainment of an individual adult mind matches the true civilizing of our ancestors. Wisdom and understanding replace magic and superstition.

Perhaps the modern lifestyle, emphasizing as it does the immediate multicolored universe of the CD, the in-your-face technology that requires little conceptualization and still less imagination, is breeding a generation that cannot use their minds sufficiently to get engrossed in a book. Instead, the new generation more readily ricochets from one moment to the next as outgrown and misplaced prisoners of the here and now, a here and now so heavily overexperienced that it is easily bankrupt of sensual novelty and impact: a gloomy prospect indeed.

For the moment, however, we live in a society where most people have minds that have developed sufficiently to allow them to daydream, to think, to remember, and to hope. The delicate ebb and flow between raw feelings and thought processes becomes apparent in the adult only when one or the other dominates in the extreme. Most typically, an outburst of temper or a surge of desire will make us feel "emotional," and to a lesser extent, a long spell concentrating in a library can, on exiting into the sunlight, bring about a realization of an erstwhile numbness, an alienation from the immediate outside world.

Let me remind you again of the central idea: this carefully nurtured wisdom and understanding is lost during a state of strong emotion. At parties, on the ski slope, on the dance floor, and at the table, we chase the sensational and the sensual, literally the stimulation of our senses: after all, we are still able to experience strong emotions on occasions, even as sophisticated and cynical adults. This undeniable fact would suggest that our brains can transiently reconfigure in some way, to revert back to the state where our carefully controlled life, our personal reality, increasingly fades out in favor of the moment, the context-free, meaningless sensation where we have quite literally let ourselves go.

Now that we have an idea of how mind is represented in the physical brain, we need to see what happens in the brain when that mind is temporarily out of commission. We need a scenario where we know something is changed in the brain and can match that physical change with a change in subjective feelings. We need a physical agent that has observable actions on the physical brain but that will also induce feelings, say, of "blowing your mind" or "losing your mind." I'm talking, of course, about drugs.

4

THE JUNKIE

Drugs. Whisper the word and immediately you are in smoky opium dens, or face-to-face with the brutalized alcoholic, or peering over the shoulder of the adolescent glue sniffer, or cross-legged on the student floor, beatifically passing around the pungent cannabis joint. Thousands of images can crowd in at the mere beckon of this one word. Of course, there are the images, too, of the terminally ill patient mercifully relieved of all pain, of the aspirin giving absolution for the hangover headache, of the sobbing, keening depressive converted back to some dry-eyed standard by Prozac.

Drugs are a bridge between the objective, physical events in the brain and the seemingly contrasting, subjective inner state. In this chapter we explore the actions of different drugs that have undisputed effects on emotions. For the first time we test the idea outlined in Chapter 1: if emotional states are indeed characterized by an abandonment of the mind, the neuronal baggage of a personalized past and future, then there should be some final factor that is common to the way that the vast range of drugs taken by otherwise healthy people temporarily "blow the mind"—prevent the brain from using the personalized connections between brain cells.

Recreational drugs are self-administered to change consciousness in a dramatic way, to create a sustained and different sensation. Despite their very distinct modes of action, these drugs presumably all have one final effect in common—the subjective emotion, presumably, of some sort of pleasure.

The most commonly abused drug of all time is alcohol. The process of fermentation, whereby yeast cells convert sugar to alcohol, has been practiced since the earliest agricultural civilizations.[1] And virtually everyone, at least in Western societies, has witnessed, even if only secondhand, the effects. Already after one drink, say, a glass of wine or a single shot of spirits, the drinker experiences a mood elevation: he or she laughs a little more loudly, contributes to the conversation a little more eagerly, and generally seems more involved in what is happening around him or her. This enhanced preoccupation with the immediate world, the gradual abandonment of the inner world of the mind in favor of the here and now, also hints at a return to the mentality of the child, unencumbered by regrets of the past or anxieties for the future.

Such greater intimacy with the immediate environment need not always be a happy one. Sometimes, the drinker turns out to be far from the hearty back-slapper, and embarks instead on a one-person campaign of hostility and aggression to those around him or her. In any event, for the drinker, the outside world can no longer be so readily understood or explained. Increasingly, the irrational starts to dominate. As still more alcohol is consumed, immediate surroundings become still less relevant as, after three or four drinks,[2] coordination and balance become difficult, speech becomes slurred, and mental functions become massively impaired. Even everyday objects start to lose significance as they disintegrate into abstract noises and colors, as overladen with sensation and as bereft of significance as for a very small child. Thought processes, as for the very young, break down; confusion increases. All that is left is that building block of consciousness, raw feeling. Eventually, between ten and fourteen drinks, consciousness itself recedes, and one is well on one's way to a coma: the state of the brain has regressed so far that it cannot even support the most basic state of sentience.

Just as the initial use of alcohol is buried deep in the history of mankind, so intoxication through inhalation seems to stretch back into comparably misty origins: primitive tribes such as those in South America used to inhale incense as part of religious rituals, a practice still in use today with the religious sectors of Native Americans.[3] On the other hand, routine solvent abuse in current civilization is, compared to alcohol, a comparatively new phenomenon. One of the first reports in the United States was in 1951, when two boys were discovered sniffing gasoline. Other volatile solvents in demand nowadays include paint thinners, glue, and lighter fuel. In addition, however, aerosols, the anesthetics in grease dissolvers, and the ancient remedy of amyl nitrite ("poppers") for the heart condition angina[4] all fall under the heading of solvent abuse.

Although they invade the body not through the mouth but through the nose, solvent molecules are destined to have the same effect on brain cells as alcohol: the main difference is that the effects are shorter, and the onset of action is very rapid. Reality becomes blurred. Just as the drinker does, the sniffer, or "huffer," will experience a brief high, a moment of positive emotion. Like alcohol, solvents go to work on neurons in the most general way possible, undermining the structure of their delicate outer walls.

Think again of the child's brain, where there is only a modest degree of connectivity between neurons. Although lines of communication might be potentially available in the adult brain, they can nonetheless be temporally out of service, like telephone lines that actually are in place but are simply not being used. The brain equivalent to an activated telephone line would be the process of synaptic transmission, whereby the transmitter chemical released from the initial neuron could cause the generation of a new electrical signal in the receiving neuron.

Alcohol and solvents interfere with this process in the most basic way possible, by preventing the phone call in the first place. The key action in both cases is that communication between neurons is generally impaired. The walls of brain cells themselves are kinds of oily sandwiches, made up of two parallel barriers of molecules with fat in the middle.[5] The stability of the molecules that make up this two-layered structure will determine how readily the electrical signal, the action potential, will be conducted along it. Alcohol and solvents, by a process that is still not completely understood,[6] destabilize the molecular configuration of the wall of the neuron. And once the parallel barriers in the wall start to buckle, then the electrical signal will not be able to be sent as normal. Alcohol and solvents therefore make it more difficult to access the multitude of associations, reflected in the dense neuronal connections that, as we saw in Chapter 3, could imbue the outside world with meaning.

§

Although alcohol enters the brain easily, it requires at least 7,000 mg (slightly less than half a pint of beer or one small glass of wine) to have a perceived effect on one's consciousness. But another notorious and ubiquitous drug, cannabis,[7] offers an interesting contrast. Cannabis, inhaled in a reconstructed cigarette, has a harder time gaining access to brain cells, yet it can have effects at doses as low as 0.3 mg! The reason cannabis acts so efficiently has been attributed to the existence of specialized molecular targets, the receptors, on which the drug can exert a custom-made action. Hence, instead of having to spread out and work along vast stretches of membrane wall, the effects of cannabis can be realized at strategic molecular hot spots, where its effects can be concentrated.

So, molecules of cannabis, more specifically the active ingredient, delta-9-tetrahydrocannabinol, fit first into their custom-made molecular gloves, their specialized receptors: the net effect on synaptic transmission is subsequently similar to alcohol and solvents. Now neurons will generate and propagate their electrical signals, or action potentials, much less readily. Once again, the net effect of cannabis smoking would be one of a reduced accessing of the personalized neuronal connections that give the world meaning—the mind, no less.

The subjective, psychological effects of smoking cannabis can be compared with the pleasure of alcohol: a disconnection with the ordinary world of worries and expectations, a pronounced sense of amusement, the ability to laugh more, as well as an impaired cognitive reasoning ability. In short, we see again a drift away from abstracted logical reasoning tendencies that characterize the human mind in favor of a more emotional perspective, one focused on the immediate here and now, the very features that we have seen already characterize the perspective of the small child.

And the parallels between child and cannabis smoker, both trapped in the present, continue. Just as time passes slowly for a child, so a feature of cannabis abuse is a slowing down of time.[8] As the dose increases, the consumer actually feels depersonalized, a loss of the sense of self. The senses impact more and more: Colors shimmer as the stimulation from the outside world regains suzerainty over the carefully nurtured inner mind. Although its actual molecular action might vary from that of solvents or alcohol, cannabis nonetheless exerts a comparable inhibitory action on neuronal signaling, and the end result is the same: a retarding of neuronal communication and, hence, restriction on exploitation of individual, idiosyncratic associations.

But the pleasure resulting from all these dampening drugs is not, actually, very extreme. At most, when someone smokes a joint or has several drinks, that achingly elusive, active zap of sensual thrill seems only to occur as a rare and transient spark. As the dose increases, it seems that a far more likely consequence will be a shutdown from the world altogether: unconsciousness. The much sought-after state of euphoria is only ever a brief stopover on the journey into oblivion. But then one of the critical features of pleasure is that it *is* transient. The forging of many neuron connections into a large, working conglomerate to constitute a memory, building into constellations of memories and hence into the human mind, is, I suggest, a fundamental tendency of the adult human brain. It is easy to imagine that if there is now an opposing tendency, a drug-impaired signaling between neurons, then it will be naturally offset by this inherent feature of adult neurons to communicate with each other. The actual feel of an emotion at any one time would therefore normally be fleeting, as the mind gradually yet persistently regains lost cerebral ground.

And yet, there is an ancient and powerful substance that also dampens down signaling between neurons but which gives a far more enduring high. In contrast to the brief whiff of pleasure in a solvent, this substance transports the recipient more reliably and for a longer period, way beyond the realms of the mind into a dreamlike state of allegedly unadulterated euphoria. That drug is morphine.[9]

Papaver somniferum, literally the "sleep-bringing" poppy, grows on rarified uplands in long hours of sunshine. It seems to have been known to centuries of generations for its powerful properties: the gods of sleep of ancient Greece and Rome are both shown carrying opium seeds, and a 6,000-year-old Sumerian tablet depicts it as a "joy-plant."[10] In the previous two centuries, the British encouraged the import of opium to China, hence the familiar scene of the Chinese opium den, replete with glassy-eyed clients propped up on couches, living only for the delectation of the long pipe.

In England itself, however, the fashion for such easy and potent escape into bliss also caught on. The most documented of addictions, that of Thomas de Quincey, provides a faint insight into what kind of pleasure the smoking of opium might bring. "That my pain had vanished was but a trifle in my eyes: happiness could be brought for a penny."[11] And "In Xanadu did Kubla Kahn/A stately pleasure-dome decree: where Alph, the sacred river, ran/Through caverns measureless to man/Down to a sunless sea." Such lines in the famous poem "Kubla Khan"[12] — with its surreal and dreamlike visions of a magic, sensual world so remote from the alternating foggy and sunny worlds of the little fields of England — capture vividly the state of mind of Samuel Coleridge, a contemporary of de Quincey and another famous addict.[13]

But opium as a drug belongs to those earlier times of empires and horsepower. During the 1800s, the use of the purified active ingredient of opium, a ten-times-stronger compound known as morphine, became increasingly prevalent. Morphine actually takes its name from Morpheus, the Greek god of dreams, yet its action is not really one of a mere sleeping pill, but rather of a trigger for a particular state of consciousness, one detached from the harsh reality of real life. And although it is morphine that is still usually found within the confines of the clinic, used to alleviate the pain of the severely ill, the street has another preference.

The most ubiquitous derivative of morphine, heroin, is so named because it was initially regarded as a "heroic" drug[14]: it is a form of morphine treated by a relatively simple chemical reaction to be more freely soluble in fat, and thus to gain access from the bloodstream through the tight barriers of fatty cells that isolate the brain from the rest of the body. Addicts prefer heroin, quite simply, because they do not have to wait so long for the rush of pleasure that washes over their minds.

But whether it is opium, heroin, or morphine that finally gains access to the brain, the basic action is the same. Like cannabis, the "opioids" have their own specific molecular target, again, a receptor in the brain specialized for opiates. But why should the brain be equipped with a molecular lock for which these artificial, external agents are the only key? Why should the brain be designed to be sensitive in such a highly specific way to the actions of a drug that only a minority of humanity might ever happen to consume?

It was arguably one of the greatest discoveries in neuroscience within the last few decades that the brain contains its own naturally occurring opiates, "enkephalins" (literally "in the head").[15] Enkephalins work within our brains as chemical messengers, just like other transmitters, to enable the electrical signal to have an effect beyond the synapse that separates neurons. We saw back in Chapter 1 that transmitters are a vital intermediary for neurons to function in a circuit. The electrical signal may well hurtle down the fine connecting fiber of one neuron at speeds of up to 250 miles per hour, but it is stopped dead by having nowhere further to travel. However, the actual invasion of the extremity of the neuron by an electrical impulse itself acts as a trigger to release a chemical transmitter, in this case, enkephalin. Enkephalin molecules then glide into their custom-made molecular dock. This docking—or to use another more well-known metaphor, the insertion of the key in the lock—acts as a further trigger to cause a new wave of electrical signaling in the target brain cell. In this respect, then, at the molecular level, our naturally occurring opiates are no different from other transmitters in the brain.

But this transmitter action of the enkephalins might provide a valuable bridge linking the objective events in the physical brain and the more subjective and elusive sensations of the junkie's personal consciousness. Enkephalins play an important part not only in pleasure but in the normal relief of pain. Volunteers who take a drug (naloxone) that blocks the docking of enkephalins with their receptor report that the pain of dental surgery is heightened.[16] Similarly, this same blocking drug, naloxone, can diminish the pain-relieving effects of acupuncture.[17]

Such an observation suggests that the actual basis for the analgesia seen in acupuncture might be, at least in part, through large amounts of the naturally occurring enkephalin, the release of which is stimulated mechanically by the needles. This scenario would explain the lengthy time of onset of some twenty minutes for the analgesia to come into effect, as well as the time lag seen as the relief from pain continues even after the acupuncture needles are withdrawn. The time taken for the analgesic effect to appear and disappear, respectively, would parallel the actual presence of the enkephalin molecules, released and ready for action.

Just as the artificial compounds morphine and heroin can bring active pleasure as well as relief from pain, so can the naturally occurring opiates. "Jogger's high" is triggered by the process of strenuous exercise, which in turn induces the release of enkephalins in the body.[18] So why are we not all junkies? The critical issue is one of degree. When chemicals are released by neurons in the brain, they are let loose into the synapse in minuscule quantities that are rapidly removed from the site of action. Moreover, they are released only from certain neurons in certain places, according to the functional state of the brain at the time. With drugs, on the other hand, the spatial niceties of specific location cannot be respected, as the drug is not administered directly to target brain regions.

Instead, a drug has unfettered, promiscuous access to the entire brain. As long as there is a receptor to act as a molecular dock, or a lock to its key, it will bind to it and have an action. Another big difference is that a natural chemical already within the brain will be active for only a brief period of time and present only spasmodically, whereas an artificial substance will not be degraded by naturally occurring enzymes and other mechanisms, and will therefore continue to have protracted effects.[19] Here we come to a very important difference between the natural enkephalins and the drugs derived from opium, and it is at this point that both the lock and key analogy and the docking comparison start to fall down.

Irrespective of the number of times a key is inserted into a lock, the properties of the lock and the effectiveness of the key remain the same. On the other hand, if a receptor is bombarded over and over again by a transmitter, or as is more likely, a drug molecule, then the handshake eventually becomes less effective at triggering an ensuing electrical signal. Imagine the numbness you would start to feel in your hand if you were running for president, pressing the flesh over and over again. In the end, your handshake will be quite limp and less effective. As the combining of drug and receptor becomes less effective, more effort will be needed to achieve the same effect: more drug will be required to produce the subsequent electrical signal.

As the brain demands ever-larger quantities of drug that vastly exceed the levels of enkephalin produced by the brain itself, so the receptor becomes less sensitive, and ever more drug is needed to achieve the original result.[20] Hence addiction ensues. However, whether it be heroin addiction or jogger's high, the intriguing question is: how might the simple action of a small molecule alleviate pain and at the same time cause such euphoria?

Interestingly enough, the effect sometimes reported by patients taking morphine medication is that the pain is still present, but it simply does not matter any more.[21] This "mattering" could be viewed as the interpretation of one's experiences in terms of previous experiences and ideas, using one's mind. Perhaps the more we are able to see something in terms of previous references, the more it matters, and *the more subjectively painful it can be*. Witness that we often refer to pain in terms of other experiences such as pricking, stabbing, and burning. Moreover, if pain is anticipated—in brain terms, if more associations are activated—then the pain itself, when it comes, is perceived as greater than if it were inflicted unannounced.[22] The breakdown in neuronal communication that might be encouraged by the naturally occurring enkephalins, and in caricature proportions by heroin, would reduce the ability to incorporate these associations into a moment of consciousness: the result, therefore, would be an ongoing state where the inner mind has receded in favor of the impact of incoming sensations. The reason that opiates bring both relief from pain and pleasure as well might be because anxieties of the future and worries of the past, the baggage of the mind, are no longer, at least for a brief while, so readily accessible.

Like cannabis and alcohol, the opiates too are depressants within the brain: the term *depressant* here has nothing at all to do with one's subjective mood, but is a neurophysiological term describing a reduction in the number of electrical signals neurons will generate. Opiates cause certain brain cells to generate far fewer than normal action potentials: in fact, the most common reason for death by overdose with heroin is that the cluster of neurons in the primitive brain stem region of the brain that controls respiration can become so dampened by the drug that the addict simply ceases to breathe.

But opium, morphine, and heroin will wash away the mind way beyond the foothills of contentment reached with alcohol or cannabis. Opiates are undeniably far more powerful in the extremes of pleasure they induce, and indeed in the degree to which they can alleviate pain. Why?

Let's return to the gray world of the neurons. Unlike alcohol, and even unlike cannabis, the regions where opiates can work, the siting of their receptors in the brain, are much more restricted to the basic region, deep below the cortex.[23] Because of this highly selective positioning of the opiate receptors, the action of heroin and enkephalins alike may have less to do with a generalized depression of local associations between neurons in sweeping banks of brain, as is the case with alcohol and cannabis. Instead, they can exert a more effective action by seizing control of fountainheads of powerful chemicals released from neurons in the core central region.[24]

In a revolution, it is far more effective to seize control of the central radio station than to gain dominance by a series of local hand-to-hand fighting engagements. The opiates, similarly, might erode away at neuronal networking, not by a direct action themselves throughout the myriad local contacts in the brain: instead, they could work indirectly in a highly concentrated fashion on naturally occurring chemicals that, in turn, have very widespread and potent effects by spraying on to large tracts of neurons in the cortex and other sophisticated brain areas. These outreach targets of the brain are the sites for the flexible and dynamic formation of neuron connections underlying previous memories, and, accordingly, for how much significance is attached to the incoming sensations. Indirectly, then, the opiates modify the widespread release of marinating chemicals that could, in turn, affect wholesale the connectivity that underpins the personalized brain. Temporarily, such connections would be out of service on a very large scale indeed. With opiates, nothing matters, literally: the mind is not operating.

Perhaps this rupture with one's individual inner resources might be the common factor linking the two actions of the opiates, pleasure and pain relief. If, as I am suggesting, emotions are more prevalent when the mind is nonexistent or nonfunctional and if, as I have argued, pain accrues in intensity as neuronal connections build up, then the common factor would be the degree of active neuronal communication within certain idiosyncratic networks occurring at any one moment. Perhaps this factor, degree of neuronal networking—or lack of it—might be the first clue as to how to link subjective feelings with what is happening in the objective, physical brain.

Another chemical route for escape from the anchoring reality of one's mind is a drug that, unlike opium and alcohol, is a relative newcomer. It was synthesized by a Swiss chemist, Albert Hofmann, working for the drug company Sandoz in Basel, Switzerland, in 1943.[25] Hofmann was working on chemicals derived from ergot, a fungus that grows on spoiled rye grain and that had proved useful in stopping bleeding within the womb after childbirth. The story goes that somehow Hofmann must have contaminated himself with a very small quantity of one of the samples, lysergic acid diethylamide (LSD), which was nonetheless of sufficient potency to bring about a profound hallucinatory experience lasting several hours. The next day, Hofmann deliberately gave himself more LSD, and again went into a hallucinating state.

By 1965, some 180 people a year were admitted into psychiatric emergency services with adverse affects following illicit use of LSD, with an additional three to five calls of inquiry concerning LSD for every patient seen.[26] Such statistics are hardly surprising. LSD produces a complete reorientation of consciousness. Colors may appear to glow, and nonexistent objects move in one's peripheral vision, whereas erstwhile inanimate objects pulsate, and perception of depth is transformed. "Trippers" might feel disembodied and depersonalized: they have "blown" their minds. As might be expected, such experiences, where both the environment and oneself are experienced as a slide back into the meaningless and uncontrollable sensations of childhood, can, as in childhood, be very frightening: the bad trip. LSD is not so much an infallible passport to pleasure, but a trip back to the swamp of emotions in all their diversity.

If strong feelings are linked to a breakdown in normal neuronal communications, then LSD should have a dampening effect on the accessing of neuronal networks. But unlike morphine, alcohol, and cannabis, LSD is not, as it happens, a brain depressant. If it is to restrict the degree and efficiency by which neurons can communicate, then it does so by another mechanism. The LSD molecule actually resembles another naturally occurring transmitter in the brain, serotonin. Because of its similar shape, the drug will act as an impostor and occupy the receptors that would normally be used by serotonin molecules to instigate the next electrical signal in target neurons. In this way LSD can fool the brain into reacting as though serotonin had been released. However, there is an important difference: LSD is not as potent as serotonin. In effect, therefore, LSD prevents the normally far more potent, naturally occurring serotonin molecule from gaining access to its normal target.

Serotonin belongs to the important group of chemical systems that travel to the outer reaches of the brain from its most basic core.[27] In the core, the brain stem, brain cells stretch out in a line, the so-called raphe nuclei, so named from the Greek for *seam* because the nuclei straddle the midpoint of the brain, like a central seam. From this concentrated region, as befits such a fountainlike arrangement, the fibers that spurt serotonin will target vast areas of brain, stretching from the spinal cord right up to the cortex. It is perhaps not surprising then that this transmitter, in keeping with its pervasive distribution, has a suitably generalized function within the brain.

Serotonin plays a key role in generalized states of consciousness, such as sleep and mood.[28] Indeed, it has been known for many years that less serotonin is used by the brain during sleep, so sleep could be viewed as a way of conserving the supplies of serotonin molecules. Sleep deprivation will therefore lead to a depletion of stores of serotonin: sleep deprivation also leads to hallucinations, reminiscent of those experienced under the influence of LSD.[29] A hallucination, like a dream, could readily be described as the slipping of the anchor of the carefully developed inner resources: one is back yet again to the irrationality and magic of childhood. Perhaps the tripper experiences a feeling of unspecified pure euphoria, but as with children, it is equally likely that that euphoria will dissipate for the most banal of reasons, such as the transient disappearance of the sun behind a cloud.

Serotonin can certainly, in normal circumstances, help neurons to generate more electrical signals.[30] Perhaps a reduction in serotonin action throughout the brain, be it through LSD or sleep deprivation, will result in a decrease in neuronal networking. Once again—this time because the drug is blocking the full force of normal serotonin—connections between neurons will work less readily and hence less rationale and meaning will be attached to raw sensations. Again, then, there is a loosening of the constraints of the mind. Time is of no consequence and one becomes trapped in the present. Just as in dreamlike states, where the illogical can regain the dominant position it has in childhood, so once again under LSD, nightmarish experiences can produce the same irrational fear, inviolate from the sobering power of adult reason. LSD is not necessarily a drug of euphoria, but rather a drug that opens up to the consumer all the thrills and terrors of an interaction with the outside world because the brain has been denied its full inner resources, a mind.

A thread is emerging here that links LSD with other drugs of abuse: a state resembling childhood, where one is upset or excited by minor, meaningless events, and very vulnerable to suggestions and to literal images, without the ability to buffer experiences with reason. By contrast, another substance, similar in its chemical targets to LSD, suggests by its very name that extreme pleasure is guaranteed: Ecstasy.[31]

Ecstasy also works primarily on the serotonin fountain, where it causes an explosive gush of the transmitter. Although the drug produces less hallucination, many of its effects are similar to those of LSD. The taker of the tab of Ecstasy will again be lost in the present moment, and time ceases to be of relevance. Instead, the relentless beat of literally meaningless music and flashing lights of raves will ensure that raw sensations dominate. The fact that the music is a thudding rhythm stripped of all cognitive content and that the user will probably pulsate in rhythmic and repetitive activity to the music would again suggest a state where the mind is, with all its personalized and specialized memories, not playing any part at all. Instead, there is a characteristic sublimation of a sense of individuality. Not only is the user the passive receiver of sensory experiences but of sensory experiences frequently shared with many of the other ravers as a collective: all are engaged in similar rhythmic motion, and all are able to share the same, purely physical properties of the world—its sounds, smells, and lights.

At a rave, under the influence of Ecstasy, chances are no personalized interpretation is taking place at all: the brain is now a mere passive receiver of the incoming senses, devoid of all the buffering internal resources, even the flimsy, superficial, and bizarre links of early childhood. The very word, *ecstasy,* derived from the Greek, means to stand outside of yourself. Interestingly enough, the first name thought up for the drug was "Empathy." It was subsequently discarded because the word would not feature as obviously in everyone's vocabulary!

Ecstasy has different effects than LSD: on the whole, Ecstasy is nowadays regarded as a more likely way to experience an extreme pleasure, whereas LSD carries with it the serious risk of a "bad trip." But both drugs work on the serotonin fountain. The difference between sheer pleasure and dicey hallucinations can, perhaps, best be explained in brain terms.

When serotonin is normally sprayed on banks of brain cells, it influences their networking not as a simple chemical messenger with a unique signal, but rather by helping brain cells generate action potentials. Instead of triggering an electrical signal, an action potential, as a simple, unique event that is over and done with, the action of serotonin can be more subtle. Think of a telephone analogy: if a rumor of a pay raise spreads through an organization, the telephones would be picked up with greater alacrity than otherwise. Of course, the rumor itself would not mean that anyone picked up a silent phone. Only once the ringing started would the effects of the rumor be apparent. Neuroscientists refer to this phenomenon as "neuromodulation"[32]: in brain terms, neuromodulation is a little like a rumor, in that it puts cells on red alert so that they have the *potential* to generate electrical signals more readily. So, during wakefulness, when the availability of serotonin is highest, networking between cells is easiest, and the mind is most readily activated and exploited. During dreaming or under the influence of LSD, when the levels of serotonin have dropped, fewer connections can be brought into play, with the consequent lessening of the influence of the mind. The fragile, irrational, fantasy world comparable to that of the child is the result.

In the case of Ecstasy, the action of the drug on the serotonin system is very strong: there is an explosive release, followed by a depletion of the transmitter.[33] With abnormally high levels of serotonin, we might now expect that communication between neurons would be optimized and that the mind would grow and grow—the outside world be shut out completely. In fact, the very opposite happens: the sensuality of the outside world rushes in, and the mind closes down. Why?

We have to get technical, but it might help to consider the rumor analogy again, even if it means stretching it to breaking point. Imagine that the rumor was circulating too loudly, wildly, and frequently, so that you put in earplugs to shut out the din. The situation would be worse than ever because you would not only have excluded the rumor, but all other normal sounds would be silenced as well. In the case of Ecstasy, the very high levels of serotonin unleashed would have a crudely comparable affect on the channels through which ions need to pass, so that crucial ones closed up completely.[34] Perhaps more than for any other drug, far fewer connections between neurons would now be working: the state of the brain would enter a configuration much like that of a very young infant before full connections are forged, where the world consists of completely meaningless sounds and shapes and colors.

By contrast, the effects of LSD may well not be as dramatic on the serotonin system. Hence, the LSD tripper will be more likely to make at least superficial associations, and the chance of a more differentiated range of emotions would thus be more likely. With LSD, the feelings will be as irrational as for a child; but with Ecstasy, as with an infant, the mind will be more diminished still—unadulterated feeling with no thought whatsoever.

Another drug of abuse, similar in molecular structure to Ecstasy, is amphetamine, the most potent upper, or stimulant, known.[35] Amphetamine was first synthesized at the beginning of the twentieth century when it was used in a range of situations from combating obesity to preventing fatigue in warfare. Although the user aims to increase alertness, the enhanced excitability can all too easily result in restlessness, and high doses can produce paranoid hallucinations comparable to those of schizophrenia.

How might uppers fit into the current model of emotion? Yet another stimulant that is far older than Ecstasy or amphetamine was first purportedly used by those slaving high in the Andes of Peru for the building of Machu Picchu. The workers needed to combat the exhausting effects of low oxygen levels. The drug they took was a natural compound derived from the leaves of the coca plant that gives it its name: cocaine.[36] The effects of cocaine are similar to those of amphetamine, although they may be more intense due to the route of administration: unlike amphetamine, which is taken by mouth, cocaine is traditionally snorted or "freebased," dissolved in a solvent such as petroleum, and then evaporated so that crystals are formed, which are then smoked in a cigarette. Because it is spared the route through the digestive system, the rush of this drug into the brain is thus much faster than amphetamine.

Like LSD and Ecstasy, amphetamine and cocaine work on the fountaining groups of modulating neurons that nestle in the base of the brain. This time, however, the main target is not the serotonin system, but sibling molecules with widespread alerting actions: dopamine and norepinephrine.[37] As with serotonin, the effects of unnaturally large amounts of dopamine and norepinephrine could also be likened to a rumor being shouted so loudly and persistently that everyone puts in earplugs so that no sound at all could be heard. So once again, certain drugs, this time amphetamine and cocaine, could act to reduce the extent of neuronal networking, yet because they increase the availability of norepinephrine, they also do something else.

One of the most primitive mechanisms in our bodies enables us and other mammals to switch from a peacetime mode, when all is well with the world, to a wartime body economy for dealing with situations when immediate action is required. The portfolio of changes that occur in the body at this time have been collectively dubbed the "fight or flight" response.[38] It is at such times that we will describe ourselves as "aroused": the heartbeat quickens to increase the flow of oxygen carrying blood to the vital organs, the luxury of digestion ceases, and sweat breaks out to cool the body as it runs. Many of these changes are brought about by norepinephrine acting as a chemical messenger not only in the brain, but as the indirect intermediary between nerves in the spinal cord and vital organs such as the heart itself.

Therefore, any drug that acts, as do amphetamine and cocaine, on the transmitter norepinephrine will not only have direct effects on the brain but will also induce an aroused state of fight or flight throughout the whole body. This is why people taking these stimulant drugs are restless and excitable. As a result of increased activity, they will interact at a much faster rate with different aspects of the outside world, once again inducing a state of mind more like that of a small child. So stimulant drugs have a direct action on the chemical systems of the brain and reduce the ability of neurons to exploit their connections. At the same time, these drugs also have an indirect action, as the feedback comes into the brain from the rest of the body that there is a rapidly changing situation that requires immediate reactions.

Interestingly enough, a wide range of substances that are chemically very diverse in what they actually do to the body are taken for pleasure, but all have one factor in common: to greater or lesser extents, they increase the level of arousal. In a far gentler fashion and to a much lesser extent, we might all be selecting foodstuffs in our everyday nonjunkie lives that produce small blips of enhanced arousal. The sheer indulgence locked in the innocent chocolate bar, the balm of an ice cream cone in the hot street, the petit fours after a grand meal—these are all examples of eating for pleasure, as opposed to reducing a genuine hunger drive. How interesting that such eating is invariably of something sweet and not infrequently, chocolate. The appeal of sweet tastes might be because of the surge of energy that can immediately accompany glucose consumption. Glucose, as far as your body is concerned, is the most immediate form of food. Carbohydrates such as pasta and potatoes must first be broken down into sugars, of which the simplest is glucose. Only let a morsel of bread dissolve on your tongue and discern how in the process you can start to taste sweetness.

Sugar and oxygen are the most basic requirements for the cells of your body to stay alive. These two commodities are used to make a chemical called adenosine triphosphate (ATP) that can store energy, just like a wound-up spring.[39] More than any other organ, the brain is greedy for this basic fuel and uses ten times more than any other organ at rest. Even though the brain is only about 3 percent of our total body weight, it consumes some 20 percent of all oxygen and glucose. So, taking a taste of something sugary will result almost immediately in a surge of energy, a readiness for arousal. In addition to sugar, chocolate also contains a chemical called theobromine,[40] which is derived from the cocoa bean (not to be confused with the coca plant from which cocaine is made) and can also act as a brain stimulant.

Chocolate is particularly effective at making us more aroused. Perhaps that is why it is so welcome after a large meal when the more banal processes of digestion compete with the brain for energy. In certain children, chocolate can actually make them so hyperactive that they become out of control.[41] This particular arousing effect of chocolate might well make an important contribution to the special pleasure that it brings, above and beyond the strong stimulation that would be provided by the tastiest foods.

Theobromine belongs to the same group of drugs (the xanthines) as that famous stimulant caffeine, as well as theophylline (literally, "divine food"), an extract of tea leaves. Thanks to xanthines, drinking not only coffee but tea offers a mild form of brain stimulation. Interestingly enough, the drinking of tea or coffee was placed highest of all in a list of some thirteen activities in a 1993 UK national poll where participants were asked to list their chief forms of pleasure.[42]

But now let's explore just why all these different agents that enhance arousal, from amphetamines to coffee, from cocaine to chocolate, give the emotion of pleasure. When we are aroused and interacting more readily with the immediate environment, we are far more easily distracted. Hence instead of a stimulation of the senses being particularly strong, we treat a modest stimulus *as though it were* strong. It is far more difficult to retreat into contemplation of the future or past or to retreat into our own inner world. Hence heightened arousal would prime us for an immediate sensual experience. It follows then that any agent, be it chocolate, tea, or coffee, that made us even slightly more excitable might also predispose us to respond more quickly to sensory stimulation, and hence to experience stronger emotions. The actual stimulation of the warmth of the liquid or the texture of the chocolate, as well as the taste of these substances, might also, in addition, provide in itself a direct and vivid stimulation of the senses, a further sinecure for the sensuality of the present.

Another more pernicious agent much sought after as a path to pleasure is the cigarette. Although the actions of nicotine on the body are well documented, no one has as yet come up with a convincing theory as to why these actions might be perceived as pleasurable.[43] Smoking, of course, entails far more than the mere administration of nicotine. When, over ten years ago now, I eventually managed to give up smoking, I did not even bother to try nicotine patches: I knew that something clamped to my upper arm would be a poor substitute. There is, after all, the ritualistic removal of the cigarette from the packet, the kindling of fire, the lighting of the cigarette, and then the sight and smell of the smoke rising in translucent blue clouds above and around one's head. Moreover, the cigarette must be constantly tended by lifting it to one's mouth and flicking ash into an appropriate receptacle, only to be followed by the final grinding down of the butt and the termination of the glowing end. By the same token the rasping smoke hitting the back of the throat provides additional stimulation. All these gestures, acts, and events could be regarded as a means, once again, of focusing an individual in the here and now, of ensuring that by going through certain stereotyped and common motions, one is unable to wander off into one's own inner reality.

However, by far the most basic effect of smoking is due to the action of nicotine itself on the vital organs. The dreaded weed can fool many of our vital organs into acting as though a certain transmitter (acetylcholine) has been released and is working at certain target sites that, when activated, can cause a concatenation of effects,[44] including activation of the fight or flight response. As epinephrine is unleashed into the bloodstream, the body is geared for immediate action at the nicotinic command, albeit as a hoax. Hence cigarettes might be seen as yet another route whereby arousal can be heightened and thus, indirectly, the chances of pleasure increased.

These domestic and familiar sources of delight are hardly the launch pad for the wild thrill and abandonment that might characterize, say, Ecstasy. But the smell of freshly ground coffee or the light-headedness of the first cigarette of the day still offer transient little stabs of pleasure that might prick into our morose train of inner worries, if only for an instant. But a heightened arousal is surely not the whole story when it comes to emotion. After all, high arousal can be linked to fear and paranoia, not pleasure, whereas low arousal states, such as those associated with alcohol, cannabis, and heroin, could also have the effects of inducing great pleasure. Heightened arousal then, on its own, would not be the bridge we seek between linking the chemical actions of drugs in the physical brain and feelings of pleasure. Certainly, opiates have a global effect on certain parts of the brain that dampens arousal, thereby inducing the dreamlike stupor familiar in junkies. On the other hand, we know that after intense activity, athletes can experience jogger's high, associated with a spurt in release of the opiate chemicals. The jogger is hardly underaroused, and yet he or she experiences the same feeling of euphoria so sought after by the junkie.

So, arousal in itself is not the prerequisite for pleasure. Rather, the critical factor must be something that chemicals such as dopamine, released during high arousal, can do to brain cells, which opiates can also do, *independent* of a high arousal level. Opiates and dopamine, two very different types of molecules, must be having some similar common effect on brain cells as the final common pathway of emotion. The trick is, of course, to discover what this essential, final common action might be. My own suggestion is that it involves limitation of neuronal connections activated at any one moment. But then you might immediately ask how reduced neuronal networking—if indeed it is linked to a more emotional state—can occur in states of both high and low arousal.

As I see it, the overarching framework is just that, an arch. Many years ago two psychologists, Yerkes and Dodson, described how human performance was related to arousal.[45] They plotted performance efficiency against arousal level. Instead of a simple line climbing upwards and showing, as one might have imagined, that the greater the arousal, the better the performance, Yerkes and Dodson described an inverted U shape, an arch, relating levels of arousal to effectiveness of performance. Low arousal levels were associated, perhaps not surprisingly, with low levels of performance. As levels of arousal increased, performance improved to an optimal level, from which it then started to decline as arousal levels continued to mount. On reflection, this observation makes perfect sense. You only have to imagine a distracted or distraught or excited state of mind to realize that anyone experiencing such a sensation would not be able to concentrate on any one task for very long.

I am arguing that this inverted U of performance and arousal might also apply to the ease with which constellations of neurons, the mind, can be activated. Alcohol, solvents, cannabis, or opiates would induce a dreamlike state detached from excessive cognitive activities, due to relatively poor communication between neuronal groupings. By contrast, drugs that generate states of high arousal also would be associated with only modest neuronal networking—albeit by a different mechanism—generating an overdose of serotonin, dopamine, and norepinephrine that therefore dampen potential networking in neurons. If these intermediary chemicals are in such abundance that they overshoot their alerting action and silence the neurons instead, then again, the connectivity that gives meaning to the world and constitutes the mind will not be realized. Bliss will ensue, shading ultimately into almost meaningless, mindless oblivion, enhanced indirectly by intense and immediate interaction with the literally sensational outside world.

Throughout our daily lives we blunder between the two extremes of two types of oblivion that can be caricatured by drugs: the dreamlike stupor of opiates or alcohol and the vivid sensuality of Ecstasy or cocaine. But in normal drug-free life, our brains will still be in a constant state of flux, sometimes surrendering to sensuality, but often buffering it with the mind. The key final factor linking a subjective state of mind with the press of events in the real brain might be the degree of neuronal connectivity, of mind, accessed and activated at any one time. Drugs can shift the balance of power in favor of the more passive, the more immediate, the less self-conscious, and, according to the original outline of the idea from Chapter 1, the more emotional. But if emotions, as I am suggesting, are an abrogation of Self, and if the abrogation of Self is achieved by only modest neuronal networking, then the next big question to sort out is how we manage to experience different emotions. How does pleasure, say, differ in physical brain terms from fear?

5

THE NIGHTMARE

In northern Queensland, Australia, there is an ingenious new way of seeing the tropical rain forest without setting foot within it and thereby disturbing the fragile ecosystem. Instead of carving up this ravishing, wild region with roads, and thus inviting the inevitable human detritus, a cable car takes you up over the dense, dripping green canopy. You swing near to the treetops over a vista that reaches for miles. Slithering and jerking along on the fragile wire in my goldfish bowl, I felt a great thrill, but at the same time I had not been so afraid for a long time. Fear: that same sensation when you wake up alone in the house and know you heard a creak on the stair. Your heart punches against your rib cage, you are bathed in sweat, your mouth is dry—your brain is on red alert, waiting for the next, almost imperceptible change to register in the senses. Fear, like pleasure, is an emotion. We are now at a stage where we can explore what actually might be happening in the brain when you are afraid and how that particular experience can be distinguished from any other emotion, such as pleasure.

It is hard to imagine being frightened without also being aroused. The mechanical changes in the body, of increased heart rate, of shallow, fast breathing, of excessive sweating and dry mouth, are the body's cave-man defenses [1] that we visited in Chapter 4. These changes prepare us for action by increasing circulation of the blood to deliver more oxygen (the fast heart rate), while remaining as cool as possible (the sweat).

At one stage, this heightened arousal seemed to be the key to understanding feelings. There is an old, and now discarded, theory of emotions, formulated a century ago by the American William James and the Dane Carl Lange.[2] Working independently, these two psychologists came to the same conclusion. The James-Lange hypothesis suggested that the mere sensation of the turbulent operations within the peripheral organs would constitute the feel of an emotion: it was the feedback of all the chemical upheaval going on below the neck that was effectively all there was to an emotion. But this idea has run into problems.

A few years ago Christopher Reeve, known to everyone as the actor who played Superman, fell from a horse, severing his spinal cord at the level of the neck. This tragic accident meant that the nerve motorways coursing down within the spinal cord from brain to muscle were now completely nonoperational and that muscle contraction, which underlies all movement, could no longer occur. Not only does such injury result in paralysis, but it also blocks information about the state of the body that is transmitted in the opposite direction, up the spinal cord to the brain.[3]

If the James-Lange hypothesis was valid, then patients with spinal cord injuries, such as Christopher Reeve, should no longer feel any emotions. Yet Reeve allegedly contemplated suicide, such was his understandable despair, before deciding to go on with life, in large part because of his feelings for his children. In a recent article in the British press, Reeve was reported to have adopted an impressive and highly courageous campaign to help others like himself from simply giving up on life. This type of positive attitude and will to fight back surely testifies to emotions at full throttle. Such patients, who have no direct contact with the machinations of parts of their body other than their heads, might, if anything, actually be experiencing more feelings compared to those with an intact spinal cord and the neuronal wherewithal for registering in the brain that the heart is beating faster.

A further problem is that an arousal response could not, in itself, account for the singularity of each different emotion. The body can be put on red alert for anger and fear alike, as well as for positive emotions such as pleasure. High arousal characterizes all of these very different emotions. As you sway suspended from a wire above a tropical rain forest or pause at the top of an expert-level ski run, what draws the neuronal line in the brain between fear and pleasure? Certainly not arousal level.

Just as arousal is a common factor in seemingly antithetical emotions, so it does not seem to be a prerequisite for any single particular emotion, such as pleasure. As we saw in Chapter 4, pleasure can come packaged in a dreamlike, heroin-laden calm as well as in the hotwired, highly charged Ecstasy-suffused rave. A state of heightened arousal is absent from the former yet commandeers the body in the latter. Raised levels of arousal might, as in bungee jumping, be just one of several conduits to pleasure, but arousal cannot constitute an explanation or even a description of the feeling itself. We need to look more deeply into the physical brain.

I have been arguing that emotions are with us all the time, with only their degree varying. In extreme measure, emotions entail a temporary yet complete abandonment of the Self, the cerebral inner resources developed through life. If so, then it should be possible to trace how this Self, the mind, can be gradually unpicked as emotions increase in intensity. Let's start with scenarios of pleasure.

With formal dancing, for example, you remain in control of what is happening to you. Although you might be very much aware of the events, objects, and people around you at a particular moment, the core of a personal reality remains beyond the glancing blows from your senses. You are aware of the identity of your partner, the meaning of the words of an accompanying song. Carefully cultivated values and facts still hold, even though the sensuality of the outside is starting to blot out the private inner world of promotion scenarios and reiterated grievances. You are thrust completely into the present moment, albeit a present perhaps rather like that of a six-year-old: a firm sense of identity, even though it may no longer be an identity defined by abstract values, assumptions, and hopes. After all, no one really enjoying a dance with his or her partner is that concerned about the mortgage; the activity, literally, takes your mind off of inner, private issues.

Now dim the lights, disengage from your partner, and start instead to dance not so much according to the rules, but according to the beat of the music itself. Now the status-dependent well-being that comes from being seen dancing with a good-looking partner might start to recede. Instead of a sustained feeling, which is under your control and derived from values and associations attributable to your particular life history and culture, the surge of a more direct sensation, a stronger pleasure, will start to overwhelm you.

The pleasure of music may be, at least in part, that it is more easily abstracted from a rigid meaning of a world that for us humans is predominantly visual. A cup of coffee and most objects around us can be seen as little else by the time we are adults. Their meaning is locked into the pattern of color and form dancing on the retina. Sounds, however, are not usually so tightly linked to a specific meaning. Obvious exceptions are the sound of a lavatory flush, the cork pulled from a bottle, the shriek of a braking car. But sounds can far more easily remain abstract than can visual images—at least, they can retain a far looser range of associations.

As the dance gathers momentum, you are aware only of the music and the movements of your body in perfect synchrony. It no longer matters whether anyone is watching, whether you will win a prize. All that matters is the immediate sensation, the flashing lights perhaps, and the certain beat of the music. Even the lyrics of the music no longer have relevance. Your personal inner world no longer matters. You have, literally, let yourself go.

In a similar vein, at the end of the film *Zorba the Greek,* the worldly wise yet philosophical Zorba, played by Anthony Quinn, faces total disaster in a project shared with the effete and innocent young Englishman, played by Alan Bates. As the complex edifice for transporting wood to the beach collapses, Zorba, the happy-in-his-skin Greek peasant, slaps his thighs and roars with laughter at the spectacular nature of the failure. With a twinkle in his smile he then extends an outstretched arm to the pusillanimous Bates character and invites him to dance. The film fades as the camera pans back, with appropriate zither music, as the unlikely pair pace out the traditional Greek dance steps, silhouetted alone on the beach.

When I first saw this film, it was so easy to identify, laugh, and wish, trussed up as I was in my carapace of twentieth-century Anglo-Saxon inhibitions, that I could be a little like Zorba. Although we might not usually dare to dance in the face of disaster, the message is unambiguous: escape from anticipating the future or regretting the past, a luxury afforded only for a moment for our mature human brains. Instead, escape back into an immediate, literally sensual, sensational present, a present normally much more familiar to a child. In extreme cases, the world can be pared right down, as it must be for very young children, to sounds, colors, textures, and shapes denuded of all context, of no meaning whatsoever. The entire impact would be derived only from physical properties stripped of all cognitive content.

For any adult who is not an artist, it is usually hard to unscramble the visual world back into what we actually see, to reproduce on canvas a cascade of colors and shapes. Instead, the all too familiar problem for adults trying to paint an object is that it is shot through with meanings and significance that are virtually impossible for us to disentangle from the literal, abstract, sensory properties of an object. In order to paint literally what one sees, one has to view the world again as a baby might, a daunting task. But in the throes of an ecstatic dance, there you are, back in a meaningless world; and if your consciousness is derived entirely from your senses—only on what is flooding into your ears, up your nose, over your tongue or through your retina—then you must be entirely caught up in the here and now. You are trapped in the ultimate present.

This is the world, it seems to me, of the dancer at a rave, high on Ecstasy. The external stimuli that keep you in the immediate present are so strong that there is no danger of slipping away inside your mind to your own private, personal world, to a personalized past or future. You are out of control, your movements dictated by the throb of the music, your personality unexpressed, unappreciated, irrelevant. The raver is "at one" with all the rest of the heaving humanity around them.

Although raves, with or without drugs, are scorned by the majority of society, the extremes of dancing to an extent that one loses oneself, lets oneself go, is neither new nor restricted to our modern culture. Plato wrote of how young children were always on the move and believed that the gods harnessed this natural tendency by teaching us dance. The Bacchae of Euripides, whom we met in Chapter 1, could be viewed as achieving the same oblivious state attributed to many present-day ravers. Similarly, many tribal dances, often fueled by drugs, aim to induce a state removed from reality, perhaps even claiming to lift the dancer to a higher plane. A higher plane of pleasure can often be identified with joy and, in turn, with religious experiences. Such removal from a physical world laden with meaning and significance can, perhaps not surprisingly, be equated with the obvious alternative to the material, that is, the "spiritual."

In a sense, sex and sport, like music and dance, reverse the tendency of the adult human mind to experience private scenarios that have not actually occurred or to conjure up personalized events from the past without any external clues. And even when we are not locked exclusively into the inner world—when we are daydreaming, reminiscing, or fantasizing, for example—we are still interpreting the world around us in the context of our idiosyncratic experiences and subsequent values. Unlike a small child, a sunset is for very few of us merely a glaring orange globe, but rather a romantic vista. Then again, a sunset could be viewed with bitter cynicism if it evokes memories of a lover's broken promise. Rarely as adults are we normally able to take each moment as it comes and isolate it from previous associations. To do so, we have to sledgehammer the senses.

An extreme example, where one is in the thrall of the here and now, is bungee jumping, along with its distant, more insipid cousins, downhill skiing, whitewater rafting, and free-fall parachuting. In these cases, the snow, the water, and the air will no longer evoke elaborate, personalized memories, but are encountered simply as elements with which one interacts—coldness, wetness, noise, and speed. At the very limit, even such reactions will be redundant. In bungee jumping or free fall, one is the completely passive recipient of urgent sensations: you are utterly out of control. When I was recently in northeast Australia, I saw many ads for this type of "extreme" sport. Often the sales pitch emphasized the promise that the participant would be "totally out of control." I pondered why exactly a loss of control would be pleasurable and eventually realized that only when you are out of control can the senses really dominate because "you" have been swept away. Pleasure is, literally, a sensational moment of life.

Another intriguing selling point in the persuasive blurb to try bungee jumping in Queensland was that "time stands still." That really made me think. Often in films such as *Chariots of Fire,* the moments when the athletes are truly performing at their best are depicted in slow motion, as though the pure sensation is everything, beyond the cultural and personal context of winning and acclaim. In a less well-known biopic shown on British TV about the first man to break the four-minute mile, Sir Roger Bannister, the crucial moment of finishing the mile was also slowed down. Extreme pleasure leaves one oblivious to the passage of time.

If lack of control and a slowing down of time are crucial cornerstones of extreme pleasure, and if, as seems to be the case, children can more easily succumb to pleasure than adults, then lack of control[4] and an unawareness of time[5] should also be features of a child's mental state. All of us can remember the long, hot days of the summer holidays when each day was indeed an eternity. As for being out of control, one only has to watch a child shriek with pleasure as he or she jumps into water, or cries in complete abandonment when pushed in a swing. A favorite game I used to play with my much younger brother when he was a few years old was to bounce him on my lap and at an unexpected moment, without warning, scissor open my knees so that, supported of course, he ended up dangling head down in empty space. He loved it.

It seems then that diverse activities that give pleasure do have a common ingredient: a here and now so strongly dominated by the senses that abstract thought, dwelling on a past, a future, and in extreme cases even a Self, is impossible. But we still need to pinpoint the final factor that determines a particular sensation of pleasure, rather than of fear. After all, fear, like pleasure, is a state where one is vividly aware, indeed interacting with the immediate world, living in the immediate present. When you wake up sweating from a nightmare, you are frightened *now*. Fear is not a worry about what might happen in the future, it is an immediate sensation signaling immediate danger. The nightmare is so awesomely different from our everyday adult reality precisely because we cannot sublimate, control, suppress, or rationalize the course of events.

Just as with pleasure, the degree of fear is determined by an absence of the personal inner resources garnered from experience to rationalize or make sense of the situation. When he was about four years old, my brother was convinced that there was a dragon in our bathroom. Even though he was intellectually robust enough to understand all the words we used, and indeed to follow the argument that dragons did not exist, least of all in bathrooms in West London, the persistent fear remained. At a similar time, perhaps a little earlier, he often expressed a terror of "funny noises" without being able to elaborate what one would sound like or where it might come from. In essence, like many childhood terrors, to us adults his fears were without reason and plain crazy.

As long ago as the 1920s, the psychologist C. W. Valentine[6] observed his own children in a similar, albeit more methodical way. His intention was to document the development of fear over the first six years of life. In the very young, seeming fear was elicited by abstract, intense intrusions on the senses, such as loud noises, pain, light flashes, or loss of support. Strange objects also frighten the very young, though presumably the child would have had to experience something of life, even a few days of exposure to its mother's face, for example, in order for an alternative visual pattern to qualify as strange. Earliest fears, such as a simple strangeness in physical pattern of a face or an unexpected noise or shift in body position, are more abstracted and have less meaning. They would thus require a minimal connectivity between constellations of brain cells.

Beyond some two years of age, however, Valentine documents how these fears give way to a more specific fear of robbers, the dark, bodily harm, and indeed, as in my brother's case, of imaginary animals. Surely the key here is with the imagination—the ability to conjure up objects, scenes, and people in the absence of any assistance from the senses, or to overinterpret a meager input such as a funny-shaped cloud or a creak on the stair. Just as an infant does not have the infrastructure that, we saw, develops astonishingly in the first two years of life to enable experience-based associations with animals and the dark, so such objects very early on in life would, literally, have no meaning. Only when the child was slightly older and had acquired certain associations, a certain degree of neuronal connectivity, would an object be of a sufficient significance to elicit fears.

As the sophisticated and personalized connections are forged in the brain, young children will be able to appreciate that the world is filled with many strangers and that sudden noises can emanate innocuously from all manner of objects at any time, but at the same time, the cerebral machinery is still not sufficiently extensive for the indisputable proposition that the dark bedroom *cannot* harbor dragons. Children's inner resources, their reality, can take them far enough to give meaning to the abstract sensory stimuli—to recognize a snake as such, for example—yet they will not realize that the snake is harmless if it is seen behind the walls of a transparent cage in a zoo. The personalized conglomerate of associations, memories, and experiences is still insufficiently developed to place those meaningful objects and ideas into a consistent and rational setting.

But there is still a puzzle to be explained. In early life, children with no prior experience of snakes or any bad experience of the dark seem nonetheless to have innate fears, among them snakes and the dark.[7] Yet very new babies do not act frightened when presented with a snake.

Such behavior does not appear until after two years or so of age. So, whatever might be the genetic factor, it cannot function autonomously in isolation but needs to be realized as some property of the brain that takes some time to develop. One possibility that conveniently exploits a combination of nature and nurture is that some neuronal connections in the human brain are not forged by experience. Rather, in these instances, the process unfolding in the brain would be more analogous to those in the brains of animals with a more restricted lifestyle who, as we saw in Chapter 1, are at the mercy of "instinct," complex behavior patterns based on genetic programming. Scenarios of potential harm to us humans, such as poisonous snakes and predators hiding in the dark, might, over the years, have evolved a built-in defense. We are instinctively frightened of snakes and of the dark because of a neuronal connectivity that has taken about two years to grow within our brains, but the connections for it are primarily preprogrammed by our genes, as opposed to reflecting an individual personal experience. In most cases, however, the inexorable burgeoning of ever more extensive neuronal connectivity resulting from experience will mean the eventual sanitization, the rationalization of those fears. The instinct will be eventually nested within the far more complex and extensive connectivity reflecting individual experience. In this way, instinctive reactions, what we might even call more generally human nature, can be accommodated within the overwhelming agenda of each individual adult life.[8]

Although it is hard for us adults to regress as far back as a very young infant, of being scared once again at the mere intrinsic quality of an abstract sound, we are able to unpick our inner resources to a certain extent. The terror of the irrational world is there as a constant threat in a nightmare. The overwhelming, flooding fear deep in a dark night is an all-consuming state. There is no time to reason, reflect, or introspect. Even when you awaken, for those few long seconds, the world remains tilted in the darkness. The sensation is pure fear.

Normally, however, as the nighttime seconds tick on, the inner resources start to regain ground. Rationalization starts to seep in. But for some, this happy retaliatory measure of the inner resources, the mind built up through life, remains too fragile and for a much longer time scale. When we wake sweating from a nightmare, afraid of the dark, we may not only be revisiting our childhood but gaining some insight into the alarming world of the schizophrenic.[9]

For schizophrenics, as for children, fears cannot be rationalized so easily. As with children, the individual is the passive recipient of events with little control over what is happening. Hence a frequent feature of schizophrenia, paranoia, where one feels one is being controlled by nameless, external forces. The outside world rushes in with its full impact of raw, literal sensations. Colors glow, and as a result, schizophrenics may start to think of themselves as divine.[10]

Another feature of schizophrenic thinking is "bizarre" associations. However, these associations are frequently merely the most literal possible, such as rhymes, for example, "Hey day, May day," or simplistic, superficial links, such as "My Professor August A had gray eyes; there are others who have blue eyes."[11] Once more, this type of thinking might be indicative of only a flimsy, operational neuronal connectivity, as with children. Of course schizophrenics are not to be likened in every regard to children, yet there are certain similarities.

In both cases, the state of mind is disconnected and highly labile.[12] In both cases, one focus of awareness will readily be displaced by another, like some variety show of diverse, unrelated acts, where a rapid succession of neuronal groupings rapidly succeed one another with no attempt at a continuing theme. Another similarity in the mental state of child and schizophrenic is that there are no abstractions:[13] instead, a kind of raw experience dominates where consciousness devolves not around ideas or theories, but on immediate objects, unique events, or a particular person. This emphasis on the literal, sensory world would account for another feature of both schizophrenia and childhood, the inability to interpret the general meaning of sayings and proverbs, beyond the overt significance that, for example, a stone that rolls does indeed gather no moss.[14]

Again, the associations are too sparse to allow any but the most obvious, primary links to be made with an object, in this case, the stone. Given that the original focus had no real meaning, triggered no substantial inner connectivity, it would be readily displaced by competing stimuli. For child and schizophrenic alike, then, any intrusive sound or sight in the outside world can readily supersede an earlier one. A candy or perhaps even the sight of a bird flying past usually pacifies a crying child. Similarly, a schizophrenic reacts to the world in a literal way: objects have an intrinsic value not according to their significance but in relation to their simple physical properties, such as how bright or noisy they may be.

A schizophrenic will thus be more readily distracted by what would seem to the rest of us to be neutral events. Most usually, healthy human adults will ignore stimuli in the outside world to which they have previously been exposed, a phenomenon known to psychologists as "latent inhibition."[15] In schizophrenia, latent inhibition is suppressed, a characteristic that has often been interpreted as a heightened curiosity.[16] Perhaps instead it is simply that nothing in the outside world has sufficient deep significance to be the center of attention for very long.

The world of the child and schizophrenic is one of immediacy: there is no nostalgia for the past or anxiety for the future, no subtle symbolism, and no metaphors nor elaborate internalized theories. Another important point is that for children, many things in life just "happen" outside of their control as they may seem to for schizophrenics.[17] In fact, one of the cardinal symptoms of schizophrenia is the paranoia that the patient feels, that he or she is being manipulated by external, usually hostile, forces. As with the Queensland adventure sports, the schizophrenic is out of control.

If schizophrenia has much in common with childhood and intense interaction with the outside world, and if childhood and intense interaction with the outside world are characterized by strong emotions, then the schizophrenic, too, could be predicted to experience unusually strong emotions more frequently than the rest of us who can access our inner resources more readily. One sign of schizophrenia is indeed "inappropriate emotion,"[18] where the patient will spontaneously laugh or act frightened in an unpredictable way. The schizophrenic may giggle at a funeral or be overly concerned about a picture on the wall. Such behavior could be, and often is, written off as irrational, much like the fears and laughter of children: inexplicable, illogical responses within the constructs of a reality that most of us have constructed for ourselves, along the lines appropriate for our particular society and culture. The schizophrenic, like the child, is emotionally far more mercurial. Above all, like the child, the schizophrenic is trapped in the present.

But how can an adult brain end up like this? With its extensively worked connections between neurons, which we saw in Chapter 3 characterize the adult human, how might a brain be reconfigured into a state with a mentality that has so much in common with a child, for whom the brain is serviced by far less established lines of communication between neurons? There are two possibilities.

The first way in which a schizophrenic brain might recapitulate childhood would be for the carefully developed connections to become gradually disconnected, but if this were the case, it would mean that schizophrenia was always irreversible and that it always deteriorated, neither of which is true.[19] Alternatively, some other factor may be at play that can affect not so much the actual physical existence of neuronal connections but their functional operations. Neurons communicate via their connections using transmitter chemicals. Moreover, as we saw in Chapter 4, drugs can modify the availability of these transmitters, and so modify emotions. The core problem with the radical upheaval of emotion and thought that characterizes schizophrenia may not necessarily be the literal presence or absence of neuronal connections. Instead, the disruption might lie in the chemistry of the brain, which enables those connections to function properly.

In particular, the transmitter dopamine has for many years been associated with schizophrenia.[20] The idea behind the Dopamine Hypothesis is straightforward enough. Drugs such as amphetamine, which enhance the availability of dopamine in the brain, can, on occasion, give rise to the paranoid train of thinking that characterizes certain forms of schizophrenia.[21] Conversely, drugs that appear to tranquilize and calm the patient, such as chlorpromazine, primarily act by blocking the molecular target (receptor) with which dopamine would normally interact. It makes sense, therefore, that the underlying problem factor in the brain of a schizophrenic is an excess of dopamine.

In more recent times, this simple idea has run into problems. For example, if the theory were correct, one would expect higher than normal levels of dopamine in the brains of schizophrenics postmortem. With the possible exception of one brain region (the left amygdala), however, dopamine levels do not differ spectacularly from those in the brains of nonschizophrenics.[22] On the other hand, it is important to remember that most patients receive medication that targets and changes the brain's dopamine systems, so the levels of dopamine measured after death will not necessarily be those that gave rise to the psychotic symptoms in the first place. Moreover, drugs that increase the availability of dopamine will, in both animal models and human volunteers, result in behavioral responses that are to a certain extent reminiscent of schizophrenia.[23]

Most likely, the Dopamine Hypothesis is only part of the story. After all, it would be hard to accept that such a complex and sophisticated disorder of human thought and feelings could be attributed in its entirety to one simple molecule, irrespective of any other prevailing factors or predisposing features of the brain. Just as there is unlikely to be a behavioral profile such as "gayness" or "criminality" lurking autonomously in a few strands of DNA, it would be crazy to expect dopamine molecules to contain all that was needed to produce the complex mental upheavals that characterize schizophrenia.

A more feasible scenario would be that dopamine plays a part in some discordant cerebral symphony. The transmitter interacts with other transmitters in a multiway chemical cadence, which can become unbalanced. If so, then it need not be dopamine itself that has to be in excess to create a problem. Rather, an opposing chemical, Transmitter X, might be *reduced* in availability, thereby giving the normal amounts of dopamine more sway, more relative weight on the seesaw than normal. Hence agents that reduce the power of dopamine, such as the powerful and popular phenothiazines (e.g., chlorpromazine[24]), would have the net effect of working even though the dopamine levels themselves are normal.

In any event, dopamine might still point the way to understanding the long list of subtle and complex problems that characterize a schizophrenic's thoughts and behavior. Unlike its sibling transmitters, serotonin and norepinephrine, dopamine systems do not pervade vast reaches of the cortex.[25] Instead, the fountain that sprays dopamine on large brain regions is mostly confined to the inner regions below the outer layer of cortex. Yet there is one zone within the allegedly sophisticated cortex itself where dopamine does reach—the prefrontal cortex. It seems reasonable, therefore, to surmise that the prefrontal cortex could play an important part in schizophrenia. Moreover, the chemical specificity of dopamine combined with the site specificity of the prefrontal cortex might well be relevant.

In Chapter 1 we saw that in the 1950s, many patients with untractable aggression were subjected to psychosurgery, where the frontal lobes were rendered inoperative. These people consequently became passive and emotionally listless. One idea is that the prefrontal cortex plays an important part in extinguishing emotional associations that are no longer appropriate.[26] On the other hand, I also cautioned back in Chapter 1 that this same region has been credited with a variety of other functions, too, such as working memory, an ability to retain information relevant to an ongoing situation. Yet another problem can be "source amnesia," an inability to impose correct space and time frames of reference on past episodes.[27] A further function associated with the prefrontal cortex is working memory, the ability to access certain rules and paradigms for an ongoing task.[28] It is while engaged in such tasks that the schizophrenic brain seems to show less activity in the region of the prefrontal cortex, when compared with those of nonschizophrenics.[29] The prefrontal cortex need not be the "center for inner resources" nor the "center for inhibition of schizophrenia." Instead of being an independent mini-brain, its significance will depend on its interaction with other brain areas.

Both schizophrenics and very small children have trouble being aware of other peoples' minds as distinct entities from their own. This otherwise natural adult human ability, to attribute thoughts to others, or "metarepresentation," has actually been identified as one of the core characteristics impaired in the condition.[30] If the ability to attribute different thoughts to others is lost, one is returned to a childlike world of literal objects, where there is no abstract meaning and no meaning in the actions of others. Similarly, there would be no way to interpret the world in a rational and consistent fashion, and one would sink back into the passive receptivity to outside forces and staccato sound bites of consciousness that are features of schizophrenia. Somehow, dopamine systems operating within the prefrontal cortex might, if overweighted on the seesaw, be able to reconfigure brain states, and so cause these sophisticated impairments.

To understand what actually might be happening within the brain of the schizophrenic, we will need to compare two very different conditions: first, phobias, which I shall argue counterintuitively are the opposite of fear; second, pleasure, which again counterintuitively I shall try to prove is similar, in brain terms, to fear.

The term *phobia* has its origin in the Greek *phobos,* actually meaning "fear." To the phobic, the experience of seeing, for example, a spider or of leaving the house is one of pure terror—not simple anxiety. One of my close friends, an otherwise highly intelligent woman who was to end up a successful hospital physician, suffered from a spider phobia. One evening I was able to observe firsthand someone who was in a clear state of pure fear. Her face went white and her expression rigid as she stared fixedly at the harmless house spider that happened to have found its way into our kitchen. The spider was the clear epicenter of my friend's consciousness. "Get it out, just get it out," she said in a monotone. I was so amazed at the unraveling of this normally rational adult that I remember the incident vividly from when we were both students, more than twenty-five years ago. An otherwise normal adult human being had been turned into a frightened child for whom no rational explanation would have worked. But frankly, I would find it hard to describe such behavior as neurotic. My friend was displaying all the signs, albeit for that instance alone, of a schizophrenic: an inability to access her inner resources to rationalize her way out of an emotion.

However, it is relatively rare for someone suffering from a phobia to actually be in that position, because sufferers usually go to great pains to avoid the naked fear that will strike them. My mother, who has mild claustrophobia, will avoid elevators at all costs. The agoraphobic avoids leaving the house, the individual scared of heights will not go mountain climbing, and so on. In these cases, the phobic is projecting himself or herself into an unfortunate and undesirable future. This abnormally extreme departure from the present, I would interpret as "neurotic."[31]

The neurotic is usually pitched into a future that is inevitably gloomy or dwells inappropriately on a past that has long gone. Even in the present, a passing remark can be given *too* much interpretation, *too* much significance or meaning. Actions can be given a significance they do not deserve, such as not stepping on cracks in the pavement. A more social example might be overreacting to a friend's turning up late, not admiring or noticing a new dress, or even making an off-the-cuff remark. "Be careful what you say to her, she reads too much into things" is a common word of warning when dealing with a neurotic. So, I am arguing that psychosis is, in a very basic way indeed, the polar opposite of neurosis, which is an overzealous use of one's personal inner reality.

In true neurotic fashion, phobics worry about an *imagined* outcome and are not immersed in the moment of terror. Unlike psychotics, such people do not behave inappropriately. Their construct of reality chimes with that of those around them, with the one exception that they are limiting their behavior in anticipation of an idiosyncratic scenario of imagined events. If, however, an agoraphobic were to be suddenly swept up by some supernatural hand and placed in the middle of Times Square, then perhaps his or her immediate reaction of pure terror, as my friend displayed at the sight of the spider, might qualify as psychotic, in that one regard more similar to the schizophrenic. Phobias lead to neurotic behavior, to overindulgence in the personal inner world of inner resources, but the actual, albeit rare, naked realization of a phobia could be a situation reminiscent of psychosis, where a pure sensation overrides all sense of environment, all sense of hopes, fears, and dreams—all sense of Self. This way of looking at phobias could also be used to interpret the efficacy of the prevailing methods of therapy.

Treatment for phobias does not consist of simple reasoning, of pointing out the logical absurdity of, say, a fear of spiders. The neuronal connectivity, the projected scene of unformed terrors, is just too entrenched. Behavior therapy[32] does not manipulate a patient's thoughts, but merely places him or her in a certain type of environment and lets the brain do the rest. The two main types of behavior therapy are *desensitization*[33] *and implosion*[34] *therapy*.

Desensitization, as its name suggests, is a way of progressively accustoming the patient to the object of his or her fear. One explanation for the effectiveness of this approach takes inspiration from Pavlov's famous conditioning of a dog to salivate at the sound of a bell associated with food: by gradually allowing a patient to be exposed to, say, a picture and then a model of a spider, and to appreciate that they experience no harm, then gradually the inappropriate associations between the spider and the imagined effects are weakened.

But let's think about what exactly would be going on in the brain. The incessant sessions of exposure to increasingly realistic images of spiders allow an increasing number of associations to be set up in the brain and thus allows for the neuronal infrastructure to be in place for the larger constellations that are at work in typical adult memory, and which eventually would be pressed into service for rationalizing fear.

Implosion therapy is the opposite of desensitization in that the patient is subjected to the worst-case scenario, a sort of saturation bombing with the feared object. The argument goes that once the individual realizes that no harm has come to them, despite the occurrence of the worst that can happen, then a cure is effected. Entering a room full of spiders would be the therapeutic equivalent of teaching someone to swim by throwing them in the deep end. Such a unique event, with very evocative, strong stimuli, would create an almost instant constellation of many neuronal connections because it would mean much to the individual to experience an event that had featured so frequently in fantasy.

Just as phobias might be viewed as the opposite of fear, so a seemingly opposite emotion actually equates with fear very closely. In "frustrative nonreward," as its name suggests, an unpleasant sensation of frustration will arise when one is expecting some favorable, pleasant event, but it simply does not happen.[35] Now, a variety of ingenious experiments have shown that if rats do not receive an expected reward, they respond exactly as though they had been actually punished.[36] A situation of frustrative nonreward is, by its very nature, something unexpected and new. This similarity between frustrative nonreward and fear thus could be sending out an enormous clue regarding an important ingredient in fear: novelty.

You might object that you do not see why something new should be relevant for fear specifically, yet not, for example, for pleasure. After all, the sudden taste of burgundy, the orgasm, or the unexpected thrill of the ski run could all be regarded as new. Not quite. For the direct hit of pleasure, we usually need a powerful sensory stimulus, a taste or touch or turbulent body sensation. But a strong sensation that gives pleasure usually does so by giving way rapidly to a subsequent one, a further touch from a lover, our own laughter, another sip of wine. Although these subsequent sensations are strong, they are not altogether novel.

Now think about whitewater rafting, bungee jumping, or indeed, the roller coaster, where the appearance of the next trigger is particularly fast or often unexpected. It is just those scenarios that although pleasurable, could also be said to contain an element of fear. I am suggesting then that pleasure shades into fear when stimulation is just *too* fast and *too* novel.

In brain terms, speed and novelty of stimulation might amount to one and the same process. A novel stimulus that meant nothing would trigger fewer existing associations, fewer neuronal connections would be accessed, and thus be more readily displaced. Namely, the turnover rate for processing a novel stimulus would be faster. The next step is to work out how, in brain terms, the rate of turnover for processing each stimulus might be controlled. A good place to start might be with dopamine, the transmitter that plays a key role in both the pleasure of street drugs as well as in the fear that we have seen might contribute to schizophrenia.

Remember that dopamine is a mere molecule. In order to understand the effects it may have, we need to scale down our expedition into the brain, from subtle behavioral disorders through malfunctioning brain regions, passing unbalanced chemical seesaws. And so we arrive at the basic building block, the encounter between a single molecule of dopamine and its receptor in the wall of a single neuron. In itself the chemical interaction about to unfold might seem light years away from the level of wholesale emotions such as fear and pleasure, but let's see if we can trace the cerebral story line.

Within the brain, everyday ions (atoms that carry a charge), such as calcium, sodium, chloride, and potassium ions, play an important part in generating a steady, continuous voltage, a potential difference in each cell. In certain neurons, dopamine can change this status quo. Once dopamine reaches its receptor, a molecular switch is thrown, and a protein portcullis is raised on tiny channels in the wall of the neuron. Only now can potassium ions flood out from the interior of the neuron. Because potassium carries a positive charge, its mass exodus will make the inside of the neuron more negative. A neuron that is more negative with respect to the outside generates more of a potential difference, that is, an enhanced voltage.

So far, such an action of dopamine[37] will not seem very spectacular, but the enhanced voltage (hyperpolarization) that ensues can have two alternative, yet equally important consequences. We are now about to unpack the actual brain workings behind the analogy of the rumor, introduced in Chapter 4. Just to remind you: certain transmitters (serotonin, norepinephrine, and dopamine) can, in modest amounts, act like a rumor in influencing the alacrity with which someone picks up the phone, or the ease with which action potentials are generated. On the other hand, if the levels of these transmitters are too great, the opposite effect occurs. Far from helping a neuron generate more electrical signals than it would otherwise, the neuron is silenced altogether, just as though the noisy and oft-repeated rumor had forced people to stop up their ears altogether. The critical factor in distinguishing pleasure from fear is exactly how much dopamine is present: let's now see how this occurs.

In moderate amounts, the dopamine would cause just enough potassium to leave the neuron to reach a particular, greater voltage (hyperpolarized). This event, in itself not very remarkable, would nonetheless open up the possibility for a powerful change in the neuron. Imagine a bolt being drawn back from a door. You do not necessarily go through, but you can if you wish. To go through the door, you would have to push it. Similarly, once a certain type of cell has been hyperpolarized, a push is needed, in this case, a signal from another cell. Only when the hyperpolarization and the push signal occur together[38] will the cell become more excitable, and accordingly fire off a whole salvo of electrical signals, or action potentials. Thanks to the enabling action of dopamine, the response of neurons onto which it is spritzed will be far more vigorous. Dopamine can be said to have "modulated" the sensitivity of a neuron to incoming signals.

On the other hand, if the amounts of dopamine were very great and the degree of hyperpolarization therefore very marked, the whole situation would be reversed, just as we saw was the case for serotonin in Chapter 4's analogy of excess shouting having the counter-effect of someone's putting in earplugs. What really happens is that when dopamine levels are very great, the degree of hyperpolarization is very great, too. When the voltage is very great like this, then the ion channels that we met in Chapter 1 become firmly shut. If no ion carrying a positive charge can enter the neuron, it becomes impossible for it to become depolarized, to generate an electrical signal, an action potential: In functional terms, the neuron is no longer working. Yet another image is that of an accelerator pedal. An accelerator pedal, if depressed a moderate amount, will enhance the speed of a car, but if it is pressed too vigorously, it can stall the engine. Too much dopamine will effect the molecular equivalent of a stall. Not only will there be no facilitation, but the electrical signals will be even more difficult to generate than usual.[39]

So, dopamine could affect the ease with which neuronal connectivity is accessed in two opposite ways, depending on its prevailing quantity. If present at moderate levels, it could facilitate the effective communication within constellations of neurons. But because networking would be so easy, one half-formed constellation would be readily displaced by another. The initial impact of an external stimulus will depend less on memories, on internal resources, than purely on its sensual impact—its size, noise, color, or smell. There would be no time for inner meanings to be realized. The turnover would be rapid enough to keep you bombarded by your senses in the present—you would experience pleasure.

If, on the other hand, dopamine was in greater functional excess, as in schizophrenia or with amphetamine, then communication would be impaired, as we have just seen: the neuronal engine would stall. Once neurons can no longer network together properly, inner processing of stimuli will be more minimal, and hence the turnover of inputs flooding the brain will be more rapid still. Pleasure will increasingly shade into fear: a meaningless, sensual, and nightmarish world looms. In an ultimate scenario, a series of highly novel, rapidly occurring, and completely unexpected events, where the degree of stimulation of the senses was very strong, would occur: accidents.

In our adult brains, where there is already a powerful, sensory stimulus, and sufficient neuronal connectivity, the deciding factor between fear and pleasure ultimately will be competition, the *rate* at which one novel stimulation jostles out the previous one. If nothing further occurs to impact on our senses, the emotion of pleasure will fade in the resurgence of the ever-present inner resources of your own mind. One counterstrategy open to a jaded junkie might be to marinate the brain in dopamine, but thereby risk the amphetamine-evoked lurch into the present at too high a dose, thus allowing the exciting, sensual throb of the present to give way to the confusing and frightening world of a psychotic attack.

Alternatively, one could arrange to be stimulated in a strong, sensual way that nonetheless contained no surprises: the insistent rhythms of sex, of music, and of dancing would all fit the bill. Within these obvious paths to pleasure, the stimulus is strong, rapidly displaced by the next, but in an existing context that lacks the shock of the completely unexpected. Despite the loss of self-consciousness, and the loss of future and past, a sensational experience is usually operative within certain constraints: one musical note follows another, or one touch follows another. In the brain, the most resilient and modest of connections that remain in a pleasurable experience are those relating to each of the senses, which are actually in place in the newborn brain.[40]

In conclusion, here is a paradox: in brain terms, the only means of pure pleasure would be the seemingly impossible strategy of sustaining only very modest working connections between neurons that will not be displaced rapidly—as in fear—by a novel rival stimulation, nor allowed to spread their networking in the normal way into an ever greater neuron constellation—the rational mind. An important implication of this idea is that pleasure is the most basic of all our emotions: it occurs in the brain when there are no rapid changes in inputs and no significant inherent neuronal connections. It is a state that we are constantly trying to regain, where consciousness is reduced to abstracted senses, to touches and tastes and shadows and softness, and where such sensations are *not* rapidly replaced by novel ones.

Sadly, however, our healthy adult brains are so configured as to prevent such a state for lasting more than a trice: the feeling of pleasure inevitably fades into thinking. Let's revisit the brain of the newborn infant, with no mind as yet in place. Here, a stimulus, such as the sweet taste of milk or the warmth of a cuddle, might serve as a strong, sensual trigger. But even now, that unadulterated pleasure is in jeopardy. With a sudden—in effect novel—shift in support or a loud noise, a new feeling, fear, enters the young life.

In brain terms, then, fear and pleasure are not very different. The degree of novelty in conjunction with levels of dopamine in key brain regions will determine when one fades into the other. More generally, emotions can be regarded not so much as things in the brain, but as continuous brain processes that enable particular configurations of the brain at any one moment, like a kaleidoscope. For both fear and pleasure, at least one brain mechanism seems to be that high levels of dopamine operating from the prefrontal cortex would enable a ready aggregation of neuron networks beyond the boundaries of the prefrontal cortex itself. Whether fear or pleasure occurs would depend on the extent to which high levels of dopamine-enabled cells are recruited into networks so easily that they succeed each other in rapid succession. This Jeykll and Hyde action of dopamine, depending on the momentary vagaries of level, would account for why people shriek with fear on the roller coaster—why the line between fear and pleasure is frequently so smudged.

Also, we can see that one way of differentiating emotions need not be by different brain regions nor by different chemicals "for" fear or pleasure. Rather, at least three factors will be not so much qualitative but rather quantitative: the *degree* of neuron connectivity active at any one moment, the *rate* of turnover of each constellation of neurons, and the varying *amounts* of brain chemicals. But if these parameters govern and differentiate strong emotional states such as fear and pleasure, we now need to find out what is happening in the brain when you feel the opposite—drained of any emotion of any sort.

6

The Depressive

The world seems gray and remote. You cannot be bothered to eat. In the empty, early hours of morning you awake before it is light and wait for a dawn that promises nothing. Everything in your life seems to be too much, and too much for you to change. You are powerless and a failure. There is no point in washing or dressing, no point in even getting out of bed. It's all too overwhelming. And this feeling inevitably disrupts, in turn, your basic body rhythms of eating and sleeping, and influences how you think of yourselves and others. You are in a decline that is not just a problem of emotion, but one of thought processes and core body physiology.

However, along with the problems of healthy housekeeping, the lethargy and low self-esteem, there is one all-important and telling feature of depression, *anhedonia*.[1] This is yet another term hijacked from Greek, which means, literally, a lack of enjoyment. Those suffering from anhedonia take no joy in a pay raise, in a sunset, in a fine meal, or even in sex. The depressive cannot jump through the complex social and economic hoops that lead even to that pallid cousin of pleasure, a state of contentment. For these individuals, there is a marked feeling of numbness, a lack not just of pleasure, but of a whole spectrum of emotions. Perhaps depression then could, in some way, by virtue of its quintessential lack of pleasure, hold a clue to what emotion, in general, actually is.

One of psychiatrist Peter Whybrow's patients described her condition:[2]

> It is a state of nonbeing; there is no cure, there is no illness. I was convinced that I was dead, emotionally dead. I have no words to describe this thing that was totally alien to my life experience. I see it now as comparable to the astronomer's discovery of black holes. My compulsion to give it description and a name is very strong but the closest I can come is that of a living void; of being condemned to life.

This piece illustrates how a feeling of helplessness does not arise from a simple reaction to the outside immediate world, but rather through the depth charges that that reaction sends reverberating through the mind. Thanks to the intricate inner interstices of our neurons, built up after years of networked experiences and memories, we can finally dwell obsessively on the past or project into a nonexistent but troubled future. Depressives lock themselves away in a highly personalized inner world, a neuronal ivory tower. It is a colorless, muffled world, cut off from the outside. It is the complete opposite of the, literally, sensational world with its bawdy brightness, sounds, smells, and flavors, which we have seen overwhelms the child, the junkie, and the schizophrenic.

According to the model developed in the previous chapters, the depressive's world, therefore, could be interpreted as the product of a brain with an exaggerated mind, an overextensive buzzing of neuronal networks, where memories and events have too much meaning and significance. Whereas in childhood or under drug influence, such associations between neurons would be sparse and superficial, in depression they would be the opposite: overdeveloped and overused. Whereas the inner resources of the child, the junkie, or the schizophrenic are overpowered by the onslaught from the outside world, so in depression the scales have tipped the other way. This time, the inner resources, the mind, filter out the outside world, put up high walls of thought and memories against the simple, sensual sensations. Now the outside world has far less impact than usual. Hence everyone and everything could appear, as indeed it does to depressives, colorless and removed from the real throb of the senses, remote from the individual who has been transported far beyond the here and now. Just as strong emotions characterize a mind where brain connectivity was underworking, so the depressive trapped in his or her own mind feels the opposite—no emotions, a numbness.[3]

Although in an everyday sense, *depression* is an umbrella term, the psychiatrist can recognize different forms.[4] The most understandable is reactive depression, so called because it is triggered by an obvious event, such as the death of a spouse. The new widow does not need to look at a photo of her deceased husband in order to be plunged into the vortex of blackness. Rather, the cause of reactive depression will simply be an ordinary memory, but an ordinary memory where in nonneuroscientific, subjective terms, the object or person in question has a strong, personal significance. If we go along with the idea sketched in Chapter 3, that a memory is served by a constellation of neuronal connections, then the concept of a husband would be very powerful. The newly dead figure might dominate the prevalent brain state not because of any strong external input from the outside world, but because an established, idiosyncratic network happened to be very extensive.

The death of a spouse would ignite vast arrays of neuronal connections. As the fire glows, there would then be a persistent, abnormally sustained brain state for that one scenario alone. One would not be able to stop thinking about one's deceased husband, indeed it would be impossible to "get him out of one's mind." The activity within these connections would be so vigorous and extensive, it would be hard to dislodge, even in the face of the sensory impact of bright sunshine, exhilarating music, or heady food. Round and round instead, in obsessive and enslaving circles, one's thoughts would be unable to move on.

To understand what is really going on in the brain, drugs might yet again provide a suitable bilingual link. This time, however, we will be dealing mainly with prescribed, rather than proscribed, substances. Reactive depression is treated with the same class of drug that is given to combat excessive anxiety, Librium or Valium, the so-called minor tranquilizers.[5] Librium and Valium work by aiding and abetting a commonplace transmitter that works all over the brain. This transmitter is a reliable workhorse in endless circuits of neurons: gamma-aminobutyric acid (GABA). One estimate is that GABA operates at as many as 30 percent of neuronal connections.[6] In any event, the primary effects of this chemical will be to dampen communication between brain cells, to put the chemical brakes on an otherwise persistent and stubborn circulation of neuronal chatter.

Anxiety, as most of us know from draining, firsthand experience, is a persistent worry, a compulsive iteration and reiteration of a suite of events that have not actually happened. So, if anxiety, as reactive depression, is all about an abnormally extensive and enduring neuronal constellation, then any drug retarding such a process will perforce reduce the anxiety or depression arising from a particular scenario created by the mind. Librium and Valium, therefore, by enhancing the action of GABA, will put the chemical brakes on the overly extensive and persistent communication between certain local neuronal connections. Hence the success of Librium and Valium. Doused in GABA, fewer neurons are recruited into a dominant constellation so that the bereavement literally, for the period that the drug is working, means less.

A distinctly different state of depression has been labeled *endogenous*. Endogenous depression is a spontaneously occurring condition that cannot be viewed, in brain terms, as one particular, stubborn constellation of neurons. There is no ready cause in terms either of the brain or of its mind, the collective accumulation of individual experiences. But if the central feature of depression in general is a mind that self-perpetuates and shuts out the usual dialogue with the outside world, then perhaps this overworked, overly dominant inner world could be brought about by other factors.

One obvious candidate is genetic makeup. After all, a tendency to depression does appear to run in families.[7] But just as there is no "gene for" criminality or homosexuality, so it is hard to imagine that a gene, or even a group of genes, would be able to generate a depressed state, completely independent of the particular prevailing context within the brain. Although one might inherit a genetic predisposition, it is still a complete mystery as to exactly what the gene or genes in question will actually be doing in the brain. The genes of the depressive might express some essential protein that in turn makes up an ion channel or a receptor that subsequently leads to a malfunction in the conversion of an electrical signal to a chemical one across the synapse. Alternatively, a gene might be responsible for the action of a rogue enzyme in increasing or decreasing the availability of a powerful transmitter. But just as we have seen how crazy it is to ascribe to a molecule of dopamine the ability to generate schizophrenia single-handedly—or pleasure, for that matter—it is just as hard to imagine how a single molecule, all on its own, could cast the massive shadow that is clinical depression over one's entire outlook.

We need to search on a more macro scale in the brain to discover something more complex than a single gene or a single chemical. Remember, the problem is one this time of a tilted balance in favor of inner resources over the sensuality of the outside world. But now, there is no single dominant factor in one's inner world, no single dominant and all-powerful neuronal constellation. In the case of spontaneously occurring endogenous depression, we will not be able to point to a clear constellation of neurons activated so vigorously that it precludes all else.

Instead, I suggest that endogenous depression involves a more generalized problem in the organizing of brain states: the problem would be that, as a rule, abnormally large constellations between neurons are formed. What might be the critical and pervasive factor?

We have already seen that for drug-induced pleasure, one decisive factor can be increased levels of certain transmitter chemicals known as the "amines"—dopamine, norepinephrine, and serotonin, which are sprayed from bases deep within the brain to its outer reaches. Perhaps it is not surprising, then, that depression has been linked to a shortage of these very chemicals. Indeed, all forms of medication that alleviate depression increase the availability of one or more of the amines.

In the early 1950s, the first drugs used to treat depression were originally used to treat tuberculosis. As often happens in the discovery of agents that turn out to modify mental states, what followed next was pure serendipity. Patients suffering from tuberculosis were given the drug iproniazid. As a result, they seemed to develop a particularly curious side effect: happiness.[8] When iproniazid was administered to depressed patients who happened not to be suffering from tuberculosis, the effect was the same—an elevation in mood. Iproniazid was blocking the action of an enzyme with a jaw-breaking name, *monoamine oxidase*.[9] Hence iproniazid and related drugs such as pargyline and phenelzine became known as the monoamine oxidase inhibitors, or MAOIs.

MAOIs were the first generation of antidepressant drug therapy, and they worked by blocking the enzyme (MAO) that would otherwise have removed the amine transmitters from the site of action. The drugs were therefore increasing the availability of these transmitters and at the same time making patients less depressed. A sensible deduction, therefore, was that depression was related to a lack of amines in the brain. But there was one problem: the MAOIs had certain side effects that were only prevented by demanding dietary restrictions—cutting out, for example, cheese, red wine, and herring.[10] The second generation of antidepressants, such as imipramine and amitriptyline, did not invite such restraint, because they worked in a different way.[11] This time the enzyme MAO was allowed to function as usual. Instead, another mechanism was targeted, one that helped mop up the amines after use by recycling them back inside the brain cell, a process known as *uptake*. Although the biochemical action of the drug differed, the net effect of these uptake blockers was effectively the same as for the first generation of antidepressants: to increase the availability of dopamine, norepinephrine, and serotonin.

As time and science have marched on, antidepressant drugs have acquired more pharmaceutical sophistication and have become more selective to one or other of the amine transmitters. The latest generation targets serotonin systems specifically, and are thus known as selective serotonin reuptake inhibitors. They include citalopram, zimelidine, and of course the most famous of all, fluoxetine, or Prozac.[12] But to persuade you of the value of the model that I am promoting, I will have to come up with an explanation of how a Prozac-enhanced increase in levels of serotonin could combat a general tendency in the brain to network overzealously. We saw in Chapter 5 that transmitters do not always send a simple, unique, local message across a synapse. In certain cases, they put the neuron on red alert so that it generates more electrical signals than it would otherwise—if it is activated by a neighboring cell. The end result of modulating neurons to be more sensitive to one another's signals in this way is that working networks of neurons are helped to grow more readily. So, as we saw in Chapter 5, the net effect of serotonin, as for dopamine, would normally be to facilitate the formation of working groups of neuronal networks. Only when these transmitters ended up inactive due to a neurochemical stall would brain states result that correlated with the subjective sensation of fear—abnormally small constellations.

But now imagine that the preexisting constellations of neurons are abnormally large: depression results. No one would wish to inactivate the alerting amines completely, thereby switching to the other extreme size of neuron constellations, and thus risk a schizophrenic-like state of fear. However, one strategy would be to combat the ease with which preexisting constellations of neurons could be activated without risking a neurochemical stall.

One huge clue to understanding how modern medication can accomplish this goal is the very well-established fact that antidepressant medication, such as Prozac, takes some ten days before it is effective therapeutically.[13] Curiously, however, this scale is in vast excess of the time the drug takes to flood the neuron networks with serotonin. So, clearly, the important factor is not the mere physical presence of the serotonin molecules themselves. Instead, another factor comes into play, the actual molecular handshake between the serotonin molecule and its custom-made protein target, the receptor. Just as repeated handshakes will render the hand numb—less sensitive to a handshake—so high levels of serotonin will make the receptor less sensitive. Hence, as the Prozac-induced overload of serotonin continues, paradoxically, the transmitter will actually become less and less effective.[14]

Now if, over time, Prozac has actually made the action of serotonin less effective, then indirectly, the drug would have dampened the ability of neurons to network easily. As a result, there would be a reduced chance of any existent network, where the signaling is already under way, growing unopposed, to expand. In this way, drugs such as Prozac prevent the mind from exerting a greater sway over the raw impact of the senses: cynicism, familiarity, and prejudices would have less chance of triumphing so readily over the thrill of the moment.

Both endogenous and reactive depression could be interpreted as problems of overly active inner resources. In reactive depression, the problem is caused primarily by an all-powerful inner scenario laden with a deep significance and is correspondingly reflected in a particularly stubborn and extensive constellation of neuronal connections. This persistent constellation would be best disbanded by drugs that slow up the intrinsic, local activity of the constituent neurons, such as Librium and Valium. By contrast, endogenous depression requires a more generalized mechanism to control the ease with which potential neuronal connections are formed in the first place. The rationale for medication in this case would be to curtail, with a drug such as Prozac, the modulating action of serotonin and other transmitters, which pervade the brain.

Sometimes depression is so severe that medication offers little help. In such cases, a mysterious yet powerful treatment still might be considered: electroconvulsive therapy (ECT). ECT has been in use since the 1930s.[15] Its introduction as a treatment was founded on a serendipitous observation that schizophrenic patients who had seizures sometimes temporarily showed signs of improvement. Although initially attempted as therapy for schizophrenia, these deliberate convulsions appeared to be of more value in treating depression. At first, seizures were induced by drugs, but later a small amount of electric current passed across the temples proved to be the optimum procedure.

ECT sounds barbaric. On the other hand, as psychiatrist Peter Whybrow has recently emphasized, the procedure is very valuable as a treatment:[16] In the United States, nine out of ten patients with severe mood disorder show improvement with ECT. Yet the fact that no one really knows how ECT works is obviously a matter for concern—and conjecture. Whybrow's own idea is that the process is analogous to the use of a defibrillator during a heart attack. Just as the heart can shiver, or fibrillate, such that it no longer beats properly, so large groups of neurons can shiver too. ECT, like cardiac defibrillation, would interrupt this pernicious state of affairs. Graphic and attractive though the analogy is, however, the concept of the brain shivering is hard to develop any further. Hence, the ECT-as-defibrillator hypothesis does not explain exactly why ECT is effective in depression. Let's try out my model of depression-as-overly-extensive-neuronal-constellations.

The highly generalized and widespread process of stimulation used in ECT could also lead to widespread release of all number of local transmitters, which in turn could conceivably generate new, less extensive neuronal networks while disrupting the preexisting larger ones. Interestingly enough, a side effect of ECT is amnesia, which would be consistent with this interpretation of neuronal connections being reconfigured. On the other hand, where there is such a persistent and extensive single constellation revolving, say, around loss of a spouse—reactive depression—then perhaps such minor rivals as new, small configurations in the brain would be of relatively little value. ECT, as it turns out, is more effective in treating endogenous than reactive depression.

There is yet another type of depression. We saw in the previous three chapters that in the child, the junkie, and the schizophrenic, respectively, flimsy functional neuronal connections might precipitate the individual into the heat of the moment. The child, the junkie, and the schizophrenic all stand in their heightened emotional states at the opposite pole of the numbness of depression. But in certain brains, it seems that both poles, both types of states can prevail at different times, yet alternating quite rapidly. Quite distinct from both reactive and endogenous depression, this is a most baffling disorder, where the patient oscillates between the listless hopelessness that characterizes depression and forms of mania.

In the early stages, mania might seem to be a highly desirable condition, characterized as it is by leaps of imagination and boundless energy. Sadly, however, this highly creative phase gives way to a progressive loss of judgment leading to antisocial behavior that finally spirals into deep depression.[17] Mania presents as a profile of hyperactivity, grandiose ideas, and impulsive behavior. It has virtually all the features—as for the child, the junkie, and the schizophrenic—of being trapped in the present: reactivity with the outside world, ready distractibility, and hyperactivity. As with children and schizophrenics, manics can also be egocentric because they lack the ability to relate ongoing events to more general, abstract ideas and frames of reference.

It is possible that the core problem underlying manic depression is again one of inappropriately sized neuronal networks. But this time the heart of the problem is an unusual instability in the factors that control the formation of working neuron networks, veering between being too modest and then too extensive. Perhaps there is a stage when the assemblies formed are too small (mania), and then some compensation intervenes such that they rebound to become too large (depression), and so on.

This interpretation of manic depression could go some way toward offering the rationale, in brain terms, of the most common and highly effective medication. Manic depression is best treated by a drug that is totally different from antidepressants such as Prozac: lithium.[18] Lithium is not really a drug at all but simply a salt. Its use was pioneered some forty years ago, again quite by chance, by an Australian psychiatrist named John Cade. Cade was working on a totally different theory of madness, which he believed was caused by some aberrant chemical that would be detectable in the urine of manics. Accordingly, he injected the urine of manic patients into guinea pigs, with the result that the animals sickened. Cade concluded that his theory was vindicated:

the next step was to attempt to identify the offending substance, which he suspected was uric acid.

Cade needed a way to dissolve the uric acid before it could be given to his animal subjects. Lithium did the trick, and indeed, the preparation had a calming effect on the guinea pigs. It is now known that this calming was due to the ill effects that the guinea pigs suffered when treated with lithium: in fact, the urine of manics is chemically indistinguishable from that of nonmanics. Despite Cade's mistaken rationale, lithium, when administered to manic-depressives, proved to have a surprisingly beneficial effect. Serendipity had triumphed again.

In terms of neuronal networking, lithium could put the chemical brakes on the over-easy displacement of competing neuron networks that, as I suggested in Chapter 5, also characterize schizophrenia. Primarily, lithium acts as an impostor to its atomic neighbor on the periodic table of the elements, sodium. In this guise, it manages to replace sodium, which usually enters neurons as part of the electrical signal, the action potential. However, once inside the cell, lithium will not be pumped out again as readily as sodium, and the normal process of generating the action potentials will cease. As a result, neuronal networks will not be able to form as readily, and there will be a reduction in competition, whereas any preexisting network will not expand very easily. Perhaps this is why lithium is effective. It reduces the competition of neuron constellations in mania, just as it slows down the growth of the abnormally large constellations of neurons that characterize the depressive phase.[19]

In a recent survey of depressive illness, the psychiatrist Peter Whybrow has suggested a triple assault in treatment, which can actually be interpreted in the terms used here, of aberrantly extensive neuronal connections. In the short term, he dubs the ideal strategy "perturbation," or as his ex-manic friend favors, "prodding," for example, with a short course of ECT. Hence, sluggish, slow neuronal networks grown overlarge would be disbanded in favor of smaller, newer associations that compete with one another for durability. Second comes the longer-term approach, a slower-acting therapy of antidepressant drugs that work more slowly to change the sensitivity of specific receptor targets to certain transmitters, such as the modulating amine fountains. As the longer-term endpoint Whybrow advocates modification through more cognitive therapies—a change of mind-set through reevaluation and self-education. This cognitive approach, in my particular terminology, is literally a new mind-set, a more established and extensive neuronal connectivity that would nonetheless be more flexible in interactions with the senses, the outside world.

All types of depression share an intriguing common factor: increased sensitivity to pain.[20] Of course, it is hardly surprising that anyone in pain would be depressed, but it is less obvious why someone who is depressed should feel pain more acutely. This observation suggests that the mental anguish of depression might be linked in a very basic way to physical anguish—pain.[21]

According to the brain model of emotions that I am suggesting, pleasure is associated with unusually modest associations between neurons. As mentioned briefly in Chapter 4, it is possible that pain, along with depression, might be the opposite in brain terms, too, and it might be linked to overly extensive neuronal constellations. If so, then the common experience of feeling pain, which we take for granted almost as a reflex sensation, could actually be another indication of a highly individual mind at work.

The physiology of pain processing, as recorded in most textbooks, would certainly not arouse suspicions that the sensation of pain varies from one person to the next or from one moment to the next. Following damage to the surface of the body, the damaged skin and muscle leaks chemicals such as potassium ions or larger molecules such as histamine. These in turn trigger a red, swollen inflamed response in the vicinity of the injury.[22] This swelling and redness are actually due to an enhanced flow of blood through the local blood vessels to carry away any harmful toxins. Meanwhile, the chemicals from the damaged tissue and from the cells that react to inflammation trigger responses in the most delicate, most slender nerve fibers in the body, which are devoted to the transmission of pain signals.[23] This excessive thinness and the lack of insulation from the myelin, the fatty sheath that covers all other nerves, mean that the pain fibers will conduct electrical impulses relatively slowly.

This difference in speed of relaying the incoming electrical signal, incidentally, accounts for the bizarre phenomenon of "double" pain.[24] If you stub your toe, you might feel a well-localized and immediate pain, followed a little later by a dull, aching throb. The immediate pain is actually an exaggeration of the normal sensation of touch and is carried by the fast-conducting fibers that can send their signal to the brain quickly. The same signal carried along the slow-conducting, custom-made pain fibers will arrive later, but when it does arrive it is considered to be far more unpleasant than the fast, short, sharp jolt.

There might be no reason, so far, to think that pain would vary from one individual to the next. After all, as the electrical signals buzz up the spinal cord, it would seem unlikely that the physical specifications of these fibers would vary to any significant degree or—even more far-fetched—that it might vary within an individual at different times. But somehow pain is just that, intensely subjective and variable.[25]

A 1959 study reported that 70 percent of patients admitted to the hospital with severe injuries did not complain of pain, whereas more recently Ronald Melzack found that as many as 40 percent of patients entering the hospital as a result of the usual civilian accidents apparently have reported no pain at the time of the accident.[26]

The intriguing reality is that actual perception of the severity of pain does not depend solely on the electrical signals traveling up the spinal cord but on what happens subsequently within the brain itself. Somehow, the prevailing circumstance will be reflected in the brain, and in the subsequent translation of the arriving signal, into a perception of pain of varying degree. We usually refer to pain in terms of some other associated experiences, such as "pricking," "stabbing," "burning," or even completely imagined experiences such as "excruciating"—literally, the pain experienced while being crucified.[27] Perhaps pain is felt metaphorically, in terms of something else, and depends on established, extensive links between neurons.

If too much is happening in the outside world to allow these individual neuronal constellations to grow unopposed, then the pain will simply not register. The more time available to forge and exploit any associations from one's previous experience, the greater the pain might eventually be: hence, anticipated pain is greater than if the same treatment is inflicted unawares.[28]

A similar interpretation can be applied to an otherwise counterintuitive finding. Alternative, nonnoxious stimulation—for example, intense cold, acupuncture, or electrical stimulation—if it occurs simultaneously, can alleviate pain. This is called "hyperstimulation analgesia."[29]

As I see it, these effects are further examples of strategies for ensuring an otherwise unlikely outcome in the balance of power between the incoming senses and the residual neuronal constellations. If the senses are activated in an abnormally intensive way—rubbing the skin hard, for example—the resultant formation of small, rapidly displaced constellations of neurons would compete with the formation of a large, dominant network that would otherwise have been the source of unpleasant degrees of pain.

Another example of the subjective element of pain is phantom limb pain. This phenomenon is well-established and relatively common among amputees, who often report a sensation of burning pain in the missing limb.[30] Careful studies have revealed that, contrary to what one might expect, the cause of the pain is not due to injury of nerves in the stump. Various means have been devised for intercepting any unwanted pain signals from the stump or indeed the spinal cord, yet the pain often persists.

One imaginative and compelling explanation has come from the pioneering physiologist Ronald Melzack, who suggests that the brain itself has a kind of "neurosignature" that corresponds to each limb, which he sees as a matrix between neurons.[31] It is tempting to draw parallels between this neurosignature and the large constellations of neurons that, according to the current model, constitute the personalization of the brain.

Normally, signals are coming in from all parts of the body all the time, so the brain has a constant and dynamic read-out of the position of different parts of the body from one moment to the next, all in accordance with the activity of the neuron matrix. The neurologist V. S. Ramachandran has recently shown that this matrix of neurons, previously the brain territory for the limb, can be taken over by another part of the body, whose own neuron territory lies adjacent to it. It is this body "map"[32] in the brain, corresponding faithfully and exclusively to the affected part of the body, that enables the illusion that the pain is indeed localized in the injured region. In effect, it is the fact that the signals originate from a specific location and thus register in the brain's body map that usually endows it with such a clear and apparent site—most usually prompting withdrawal, or attempted withdrawal, of the injured part of one's anatomy from the source of the damage.

Ramachandran has shown that, for example, the face and the arm have adjoining maps in the brain. When an arm is lost, a certain part of the face, if touched, will elicit a sensation, seemingly, in the missing arm. An even more intriguing example is the feet and the genitals. In certain cases following sex, entailing inevitably stimulation of the genitals, sensation could be felt in a missing foot.[33] Fascinating and insightful as those cases are, Ramachandran nonetheless offers no explanation for why someone with a missing arm does not always feel a sensation in the phantom limb when the face is touched—for example, when shaving. Similarly, he offers no reason why pain, rather than the mere presence of the limb, should be the overriding experience. However, the activity in neuronal networks corresponding to a missing limb might start to become so vigorous that in 70 percent of cases, the patient does not just feel the limb but reports severe pain.

Melzack suggests that when the brain is deprived of normal signals from a limb, monitoring that it is there and in a certain position, then the neurons in the corresponding matrix retaliate by actually becoming far more active. My own suggestion would be that ordinary touches to the face, as in shaving, are usually insufficiently strong or are of insufficient significance to trigger the larger constellation of neurons in the adjacent, adopted territory to a sufficient extent to register at all, and certainly not to register as pain. But in an examination with a doctor, such as Ramachandran, clearly the act of someone's touching the face would seem important, so even a slight touch might be imbued with a "significance" as described in Chapter 3, when we saw that not just physical severity of stimulation but its idiosyncratic meaning could be represented by an extensive number of neuronal connections.

Another link between an overly extensive neuronal connectivity and perception of pain might come from looking at what we know about general anesthetics.[34] The action of anesthetics has long proved a puzzle. Different anesthetic substances do not respect any particular chemical transmitter system in the brain or any particular population of neurons in any single brain region. An important clue is that, irrespective of their precise mechanisms, all anesthetics have a basic action in common: to cause a swelling of the oily interface of the two layers of molecules that make up the outer wall of each neuron. The immediate effect of this swelling is to prevent the passing of electrical signals from one cell to the next.

If this action was all there was to it, however, one might expect that anesthetics would kill people straight off. The vital neurons responsible for controlling breathing, for example, would be shut down as readily as any other neuron in the brain. Normally, of course, the anesthetized, unconscious patient remains able to breathe. Anesthetics have a non-specific action on neuron membranes, yet key clumps of neurons are—except in overdose—unaffected, so it is unlikely that anesthetics abolish consciousness uniformly at the micro level of the generic, single cell.

The first stage[35] in general anesthesia, before the patient loses consciousness, is one where pain is nonetheless already diminished. This effect could reflect a correspondingly diminished neuronal connectivity caused by the impaired neuronal signaling that is the characteristic of all anesthetics. And if anesthetics gradually reduce the extent of operational neuronal connections, the bizarre prediction follows that during anesthetic induction, there would be a transient configuration modest enough to correspond to the states associated not with the inner mind but with the depersonalized and sensual here and now. Patients undergoing anesthesia will, according to this haiku, actually experience a transient feeling of pleasure or of madness before losing consciousness.

Nowadays, anesthetics are designed to bring the patient to an unconscious state as rapidly as possible. However, in previous eras, "ether frolics" were held precisely to induce a state of euphoria.[36] Indeed, the introduction of nitrous oxide some 200 years ago was initially promoted as a fairground entertainment. It was billed as "laughing gas" that induced euphoria, loss of pain, and only finally, unconsciousness. More recently, the drugs ketamine and phencyclidine,[37] which can induce anesthesia and analgesia, have been taken as drugs of abuse because of the distorted and presumably exciting, deliriumlike sensations they bring, before they are at full consciousness-robbing strength. Hence the seeming difference in quality between drugs for analgesia, which abolish pain, and those for anesthesia, which abolish consciousness, might be one actually of quantity, that is, the degree of neuronal connectivity remaining.

Another factor in determining the degree of pain felt is time of day. Seemingly crazy volunteers willing to have shocks or cold stimulus applied to their teeth report that more stimulus is needed in the middle of the day than at night before the shocks cause perceptible pain.[38] Obviously, the ability of the nerves from the teeth to conduct electricity remains constant, in that the physical size, the dimensions of the nerves, and their myelin insulation do not change on such a casual and cyclical basis. But the availability of different amines pouring out from their fountains from the core of the brain are associated with arousal and biorhythms.[38] The cyclic variations in pain could readily be attributed to the cyclic variability of these modulating chemicals, which in turn contribute in a highly dynamic fashion to the final configurations of neuronal connections, the mind, at any one moment.

If pain is indeed associated with the extent of active neuronal connections at any one moment, then diverse factors could affect the extent of such dynamic networking, and hence the degree of pain actually felt at any one time. Either the degree of neuronal signaling can be modified by creating rivals (as with hyperstimulation analgesia) or by restricting the communication efficiency of the chemical or electrical components of the neurons signaling in a potential constellation (as with morphine or anesthesia, respectively). Alternatively, the degree of pain will also be regulated by the ability of the amine fountains to modulate the readiness of any group of neurons to be entrained in a working network. Hence people with disorders such as schizophrenia, which are characterized by an excessive availability of functional dopamine, will display reduced levels of pain perception.

Given such a close relationship between pain and depression, it is not surprising that the respective treatments for pain and for reactive and endogenous depression treatments are, to a certain extent, valuable in the other condition. If someone in pain is excited or hyperaroused, he or she will be more distracted and thus effectively change the balance between the sensual outside world and the inner mind. Similarly, if a depressive is distracted by an alternative stimulus—music, for example—then it is possible that a persistent and overly large assembly could become, even if temporarily, displaced.

None of these treatments are wholly satisfactory. Eradication of pain by counterstimulation is simply not practical, predictable, or controllable. As for drug therapies (e.g., morphine for pain or Prozac for depression), the same arguments might apply for their undesirability as for drugs of abuse. Drugs, whether recreational or therapeutic, always have side effects due to indiscriminate actions in diverse regions in the brain. Moreover, in both cases, there is the risk of addiction, both at the level of modifying the actual nuts and bolts of neuronal communication as well as at the more organized level of creating the habit of self-administering these powerful compounds.[40]

Nonetheless, if pain and depression are both linked ineluctably to overly extensive neuronal networking, and if that was all there was to it, then pain and depression would be effectively interchangeable and therefore a completely identical experience. But most of us would claim that although both states are unpleasant, they are nonetheless distinct. In brain terms, then, there has to be a matching distinction, a corresponding, distinguishing physical property.

One obvious difference is that pain is usually felt in a specific part of the body: hence the matrix activated in the brain, as with phantom limb pain, will be far more circumscribed, corresponding to the body map with its disproportionate allocation of neurons of, for example, the mouth and hands. Since the stimulation during pain is damaging to body tissue, and is indeed triggered by the chemical consequences of that damage, then the degree of activation would be very strong. Hence there would be a very extensive activation of neuronal connections.

As with pain, we have seen that the extensive network underscoring reactive depression would be specific and attributable to a certain configuration of neurons rather than being a predisposition of the brain. However, it is reasonable to assume that an internally spontaneous, albeit persistently active, hub of neurons would not recruit as many satellite neurons as a matrix activated by powerful incoming signals from damaged tissue. Moreover, we have seen that endogenous depression need not be attributable to a single, extensive network, but rather to factors that predispose neurons to form extensive networks. In depression, therefore, the distinguishing factor from sensation of pain would be one of sheer numbers—that is, the net size of the overly large neuronal network. Although in depression, the abnormally large network of neurons would not be as extensive as in pain, the depressive could experience pain more easily than his or her happy counterpart, for whom the constellations would have to grow far more before pain was felt as such.

Just as depression and pain might have much in common, so fear and pain, according to the scheme I have been sketching, would counterintuitively be very opposite states associated, respectively, with large and small neuron networks. Remember that fear is a feature of small neuronal networks when they turned over very rapidly. Two predictions follow. First, that states associated with modest neuronal networks, for whatever reason, are associated with a reduction in pain. Second, fear and pain would have to be mutually exclusive. It turns out there is evidence in favor of both predictions.

Patients given morphine feel less pain and, according to the reasoning outlined in Chapter 4, have less extensive neuronal networking. Such individuals often say that they can still feel the pain but that it no longer matters to them. Again, it is the mattering, the significance, that would be associated with extensive neuronal cross-talk. Perhaps morphine then exerts its well-known and potent analgesic effects by restricting neuronal communications that give rise not only to states free of pain but actually to feelings of living in the present and sensual pleasure—the euphoria so sought by the junkie. Similarly, that other state I have associated with sparse functioning neuronal connectivity, schizophrenia, is indeed characterized by a reduction in pain sensation.[41] Similarly, in multiple personality disorder, the patient appears to be oblivious to pain during the manic type phase of breezy personality.

What about my second prediction, the mutual exclusivity of pain and fear? Once a large assembly of neurons is operative for any particular moment, then, according to the model, both fear as well as pleasure would recede. This is counterintuitive because normally we might associate fear with something that was also to be avoided, like pain. Although one of the reasons for feeling fear is the threat of pain, the very sensation of pain itself does actually turn out to be mutually exclusive with fear. For example, the anecdotes of soldiers insensitive to wounds on the battlefield suggest that although they are experiencing the fear of the moment, they are insensitive to any pain. More convincing still is that inhibition of pain by fear has been formally demonstrated in the laboratory.

If rats are exposed to an inherently neutral stimulus that they have nonetheless learned to associate with fear, their reaction time to pain, as assessed by licking the forepaws free of an irritant, is reduced.[42] The adaptive value would be that one only concerns oneself with pain once one has escaped from the source of the danger. Moreover, because these effects can be mitigated by an opiate blocker (e.g., naloxone), it would seem that the naturally occurring enkephalins would normally be released in the brain during fear, and that they would act as a merciful, natural analgesic—an advantage of sorts if you were being eaten by a lion, slowly.

Because the reaction to pain is frequently a reflex exerted either at the level of the spinal cord or, as LeDoux has shown, at regions in the brain not participating in consciousness,[43] the survival value of the conscious perception of pain is not immediately obvious. But let's reverse the situation and ask what the survival value of pain might be. Imagine a situation that is a bit back to front, that starts not so much with a stimulus that causes pain, and thence a large neuronal network, but rather with the formation, for whatever reason, of a large neuronal network, where pain is the inevitable corollary. Because I have argued that small networks ensue when we vigorously interact with the outside world, and because interaction with the outside world is needed for feeding and copulation, it would follow that for survival of the species, overly large networks are to be avoided. The subjective sensation of pain would be a good way to encourage the organism to change whatever situation is resulting in a mind-set with such negative survival value.

I am arguing then that pain is not so much an emotion. Rather, it is an extreme state of mind that, along with depression, can be interpreted as the antithesis to feelings at full throttle. Just as fear and pleasure would be bedfellows, characterizing the emotionally charged states of childhood, dangerous sports, drug taking, and schizophrenia, so, too, pain and depression would be closely associated.

We still need to confront the problem of how the overly large constellation that conceivably characterizes the depressive's brain forms in the first place. Conversely, one can often feel highly emotional without taking drugs, going out of one's mind, or interacting, as a child does, with the outside world. Emotions can often be driven by internal machinations that are not dependent on any strong sensory input, but on news softly spoken that has only a private significance. Alternatively, why are nightmares, mere figments of one's internal world, so frightening? Most studies of emotions have taken the obvious example of an external agent, a tiger, say, causing an obvious reaction of fear, where the mechanical, outward behavior of running away is emphasized at the expense of subjective states. And yet we have just been looking at how feelings can influence thoughts. The next step is to reverse the situation and ask a question that is of great importance to those of us who frequently have strong feelings but are rarely confronted by tigers: How might mere thoughts influence feelings?

7

The Human Condition

It takes only the softest whisper telling you that you have cancer, that you have failed an exam, or that you have been cheated on by your spouse to throw your whole body into a turmoil of feeling. How can mere words stir up so much emotion? There is no ski slope slithering rapidly beneath your feet, no psychotic drenching of neurons with dopamine, no pharmacological chicanery scoring direct hits on the brain, nor even the excuse of childhood. No current theory of emotions can yet account for this everyday occurrence[1] — that, in a human adult, mere mental activity, thoughts, can trigger a state primarily characterized by strong feeling.

After all, it is hard to see how grief at a partner's death might be described in MacLean's terms, as an emotion slipping free from the grips of the rational, or in Freud's scheme, as the reduction in some caveman drive. Similarly, LeDoux's model cannot explain the gut-gripping fear that occurs before a driving test, before surgery, or in a quiet house at night, when no snakes — indeed, no triggers at all — are lionizing the senses.

Let's look again at the alternative that I have been proposing: Emotions sweep away all sense of the Self. The emotional behavior of children, the ecstasy of ravers, the mercurial, extreme terror and rage of schizophrenics could all be described as instances when the Self is forgotten in favor of a — literally — sensational experience. The more we feel, the less we are, literally, ourselves — the less we are encumbered by previous, idiosyncratic associations that personalize the brain into a mind. These dynamic connections between neurons enable reason and thought, those cognitive phenomena that have already been successfully modeled in artificial systems, and which normally develop with age along with the growth of neuronal connections. The basic feature of such a process is that associations are established between components that can be modified, where the net performance can be changed according to prior outcomes.

The big problem to solve, then, is how raw feeling might arise, not from direct manipulation of brain chemistry by incoming signals from the sense organs, by drugs, or by disease, but merely through the very workings of the brain itself, a large constellation of these ordered, buzzing networks. If my idea is correct, I must now somehow come up with a way to explain how a large, working constellation of neurons—a thought—might trigger a series of very small neuron networks—an emotion.

The most familiar example of an adult brain left entirely to its own devices is the logic-free, literal, and sensual experience of a dream. After all, in a dream, we are normally dominated by vivid, unique processes and events. We do not generalize, think, or reason, but merely observe and react. As with drugs, childhood, and schizophrenia, I am now suggesting that dreams, too, can be interpreted as a failure to generate and access the large neuronal assemblies that give rise to the adult human mind.

Take drugs, for example. We saw in Chapter 4 that with drugs such as alcohol or morphine, erstwhile active lines of neuronal communications fall dormant once their ability to propagate electrical signals is depressed. In these situations, arousal levels are low, just as they are in sleep. I am bringing morphine back into the discussion here because a common sensation of morphine takers is that they feel as though they are "in a dream."

Not only can dreamlike states be brought on by drugs, but in any event, the naturally occurring chemicals in the brain, the transmitters, will be playing a key role. Of the fountains of different chemicals that we have seen are so important in arousal, certain transmitter systems appear to predominate in certain states. The amines (norepinephrine and dopamine) operate during wakefulness, whereas acetylcholine, a compound that is structurally similar, peaks during dreaming. From here psychiatrist and sleep expert Alan Hobson[2] has gone on to express the normal and abnormal processes that occur in the brain almost exclusively in terms of the actions of these two major chemical systems.

But remember, a transmitter is only a banal, small molecule! In itself it contains no magic property. The secret of the power of transmitters lies in their interaction, the molecular handshake with a custom-made receptor on a target brain cell. There are even subvarieties of receptors for particular transmitters, giving rise to a complex repertoire of diverse potential effects in the modification of electrical signaling within the target neuron.[3] It is hard to discern the precise role that the amines and acetylcholine actually play in the different net states of sleep, wakefulness, and dreaming. We still do not have enough information about how and where each amine acts in the brain, and what kind of effects are possible. And even when the different effects of the different amines all over the brain are eventually known, the old problem we encountered in Chapter 1 will surface: how do we extrapolate, at a micro level, the molecular actions of different amines at different types of receptors in different brain areas to the macro functional level of shifts from wakefulness to dreaming?

Even less accurate and more perilous still is to lump the amines together as a monolithic chemical factory. For example, consider dopamine. According to sleep expert Alan Hobson, dopamine is suppressed, along with its amine siblings, during dreaming. But then there is a paradox. Dreaming has many traits similar to schizophrenia that might be summarized as loss of a grasp of reality. Hobson himself admits that in both cases logic and reason are compromised, while emotions are "just fine."[4] And yet schizophrenia has been linked not with decreased dopamine but with excessive levels of the transmitter. We saw in Chapter 5 that schizophrenia is combated by drugs that actually antagonize dopamine, whereas drugs that raise levels of brain dopamine lead to symptoms resembling those in the disorder. This anomaly—that dreaming is associated with low dopamine levels, and schizophrenia with high—does not invalidate the interesting and reasonable suggestion that schizophrenia and dreaming are similar,[5] but rather shows that neither state can be explained solely in terms of a single chemical such as dopamine. Just as it is impossible to explain schizophrenia in terms of an autonomous transmitter, it is impossible to interpret dreaming simply in terms of dopamine levels.

Nonetheless, let's look at the similarity between schizophrenia and dreaming a little more closely. The psychiatrist's mental status exam has been an established procedure for more than a century to ascertain, by simple question and answer, how someone is feeling and thinking. More specifically, the test identifies whether there are any problems with memory, orientation, perception, or language. Hobson documents how the content, the experience of dreams, can be very similar to the accounts of the schizophrenic. For both the dreamer and the schizophrenic there are "visuo-motor" hallucinations. Both move through a world that no one else inhabits, that is much more a product of the inner brain than of real physical objects in the outside world. Then there is distractability, where attention veers from one focus to the next, with no continuity of narrative. As might be expected of someone so caught up in the present, memory impacts little in both cases, whereas the view of the world is devoid of insight and self-consciousness, and is frequently characterized by delusions. Emotions, however, are, as we have seen, "just fine"!

So far, this profile bears a striking resemblance to the state of mind of the schizophrenic. However, Hobson maintains that a critical difference lies in the fact that dreamers do not display the paranoia frequently seen in schizophrenics, nor does the mismatch of thoughts and emotion that can characterize schizophrenic behavior occur. My own view, however, is that these two discrepancies are not fundamental ones. Consider the alleged absence of paranoia in dreams. An offshoot of the generic dream condition could well be that not only are you helpless but that, after all, here was a particularly malign consequence of the passive state—people were working to harm you. Moreover, in many dreams the idea of evil lurking in a darkened room or at the end of a tunnel is not uncommon.

Similarly, the disparity between thought and emotion is more apparent in schizophrenia because the mismatch is more striking when the standards of the real world are expected to apply. No one sees you behaving in your dreams, although they do see you behaving in the real world. Laughing at a funeral, for example, is aberrant only because of how other people view behavior on such solemn occasions. In a dream, no one else is there to tell you that your behavior is inappropriate. The disparity between thought and emotion is a disparity only for others, not for the schizophrenics themselves, operating upon the flimsy and superficial connections rooted not very deeply in a sound and robust fund of inner resources. However, Hobson prefers to liken the dream state to the delirium states seen during overdoses of or withdrawal from drugs. Personally, I can detect no real difference between the state of the junkie, as interpreted in Chapter 4, and that of the schizophrenic. The key factor is that both lack the inner resources, the mind, built up in extensive neuronal networking.

Another important feature common to dreams, schizophrenia, and morphine use is the reduction in or complete absence of the sensation of pain. If, as I suggested in Chapter 6, abnormally large assemblies can be associated with the sensation of pain, it would be consistent with the idea that all three of these otherwise disparate states are associated with abnormally modest neuronal constellations.

However, I think the most important similarity between drugs, schizophrenia, and dreaming is the focus on emotions. Hobson claims that the emotions in dreams are "high-side" (e.g., anger and joy) as opposed to the "low-side" emotions (e.g., sadness, shame, or remorse). Low-side emotions could be reinterpreted as being dependent on a residual connectivity indicative of the more sophisticated mind, states that are no longer pure emotion. Small children, like nonhuman animals, are unable to show remorse or shame if they cannot understand the significance of their actions. The low-side emotions are perhaps a misleading distinction because they are predicated on the existence of a mind. For the moment we are dealing with the most extreme example, the most basic emotions. For my money, the critical factor in schizophrenia, as in childhood, with drugs, and arguably here in dreaming, is that one is the passive recipient of incoming sensory forces—and that state is emotionally charged.

It is all very well to claim that these states share an important common factor (i.e., abnormally small constellations of neuronal networks), yet quite another to say where in the brain these networks are actually banding and disbanding. Of course, certain transmitters, such as dopamine, must play an important part, but they will also interact with other transmitters, much as people do with one another in a city. Most important of all, as we saw back in Chapter 1, just as people operate from different rooms in different buildings in different blocks and metropolitan districts, so transmitters operate in different ways in different brain regions. The next question we have to address, then, is how the strong emotional states—according to my idea, the most basic states—are expressed in the holistic, physical brain.

In Chapter 5, we saw that in schizophrenia the large area at the front of the brain, the prefrontal cortex, was underactive. Interestingly enough, classic depression has been linked to the opposite, an overactive prefrontal cortex. Using imaging technology that monitors the degree of blood flow, and hence of hard work, in different brain regions in conscious subjects, it is possible to see the prefrontal cortex literally lighting up much more in depressed patients.[6]

The prefrontal cortex, as I mentioned in Chapter 1, has already been linked to modifications to emotional disposition, but it would be a mistake to think of it as the "center for" emotions. No brain region works as an autonomous mini-brain; moreover, the imaging data suggest that the prefrontal cortex actually plays a part not in emotions themselves, but in states with less emotion, the numb absence of feelings.

More usually, the prefrontal cortex is active in the kinds of pursuits that we adults are good at, compared to children and nonhuman animals, namely, being depressed, thinking abstractly, and reasoning. This link between the activities of the prefrontal cortex and all the features that I have suggested profile the mind certainly fits with its disproportionately larger size compared to other animals. Our prefrontal cortex is excessively large for our body weight: it is actually more than 200 percent the volume that one would expect in a primate of our weight, and indeed, it is double the size and out of proportion with the more basic parts of our brains.[7]

The prefrontal cortex is also involved in other functions that are the very essence of the personalization of the brain—the most sophisticated type of memory. Damage to part of the prefrontal cortex can thus result in source amnesia.[8] Source amnesia is a very specific problem. Memory for facts generally, or semantic memory, such as that which enables the recall of the French word for *table,* is not impaired. On the other hand, memory for unique events is markedly affected. What makes the difference between a memory of an event, such as a day at the seaside with Aunt Flo, and the French word for *table*?

The answer is that the former requires a time-space frame of reference whereas the latter does not. A memory for an event robbed of its time and space specification becomes a fact, a statement that has become generalized because it no longer occupies a unique slot in one's personal history. Because source amnesia is essentially a problem in pinpointing a memory in time and space, patients retain only generic memories that float free of a particular date or location.

Some fifty years ago, Canadian neurologist Wilder Penfield[9] was performing neurosurgery on epileptic patients and, in the course of the operations, studying the effects of electrical stimulation of the exposed surface of the brain. Macabre though such an exercise might sound, it is important to realize that the brain itself is insensitive to pain.[10] What was intriguing was that, on occasion, Penfield's stimulation led to the patient's suddenly experiencing a memory. Penfield was tapping into a region of the brain that is associated with memories, yet another region of the cortex, referred to as the *temporal cortex*, which lies on the side of the head by the temples. The reason for mentioning this dramatic observation here is because of the reported quality of the memories, which are often said to be "like a dream" and appear to lack specific time and space frames of reference. I like to interpret these intriguing observations as follows. The electrical current was sufficient to activate enough of the brain for the active experience of a memory, but it was of insufficient intensity to spread to or trigger as normal the participation of the prefrontal cortex, which is somehow necessary for the imposition of space and time constraints. Hence, a semantic memory was generated instead, a memory for an episode, but one that lacked space and time frames of reference, and thus was more generalized. Interestingly, this experience is reported as "dreamlike."

For the dreaming adult, the complex mind is already in place, with its web of prejudices and values stamped into fairly stubborn neuronal circuits. Yet during dreaming those circuits will remain relatively dormant because, compared to normal wakefulness, there is no strong stimulation to recruit them. We are, after all, far less receptive to the lights, noises, textures, and smells of the outside world. I am suggesting, therefore, that the type of consciousness that characterizes dreams, so characteristically devoid of abstract thought, calculations, and future plans, does indeed correspond to a flimsy, mindless consciousness where one is at the mercy of the here and now, a consciousness devoid of continuity, logic, and self-consciousness. In essence, Penfield's patients and dreamers everywhere have temporarily become again like small children.

As it happens, recordings of the brain waves of human fetuses at 11 weeks reveal a fascinating and valuable clue that indicates that dreaming is precisely the dominant type of experience that the brand-new brain might be having. At this point in development the fetus exhibits, for the first time, consistent electrical activity that indicates a cohesive, functioning brain.[11] The dominant electrical activity seen is indicative of a special type of sleep (rapid eye movement, or REM, sleep), which is associated with dreaming. As life progresses, the degree of REM sleep gradually falls.[12] If fetuses, with their potential for only small constellations of neuron connections, have a dreamlike brain state, then perhaps in turn, similar, diminished configurations will underscore the fragmented experience of shifting from beach to kitchen, from darkened wood to sun-flooded desert, that so often characterizes our adult dreaming state.

I am arguing, then, that the active and enlarged prefrontal cortex is a prerequisite for superimposing on a consciousness charged with emotion and accessing only generic memories, a more sophisticated means of categorizing the world in space and time. But the cortex and the logical processes that are usually ascribed to it cannot be divorced from emotion and indeed consciousness. The mind is pressed into the developing brain, but neither uniformly all over nor in any particular brain region. Instead, as I cautioned in Chapter 1, different brain regions to greater or lesser extents all play a part in what is largely still a mysterious final coordination within the holistic brain.

The prefrontal cortex is not the center for anything. All we can say with any conviction is that a dreaming type of consciousness can arise independent of the prefrontal cortex, and moreover, schizophrenics, who also have problems rebuffing the incoming external world with rational inner resources, have problems with the prefrontal cortex as well. Therefore, it might be that the prefrontal cortex contributes to a more robust and continuing reality, the type of reality absent in dreams, drug abuse, any intense physical activity, or childhood. Perhaps when this part of the brain is active in the healthy human adult, it allows the brain as a whole to configure itself in a way that will allow conscious access to the inner resources developed over time through individual experiences. If so, then it is possible that we adult humans might be able to revert temporarily to an alternative type of brain configuration. And if our prefrontal cortex were less active, then we would arguably be temporarily like a child again—or like a schizophrenic or a dreamer, or like someone with source amnesia, where generic semantic memories dominate our consciousness, rather than specific, unique events.

Our dreaming brain, by not accessing the full range of neuronal connections, is perhaps the closest possible state to the waking consciousness of nonhuman animals, where the neuronal networking hardware is just not there. Rather, one is living in the moment, experiencing a constant interaction with the world as one is hunting and hunted. And all the signs are that animals experience some emotions.

Rats appear to be capable of "pleasure" when they engage in the otherwise incomprehensible activity of passing electrical current to parts of their brains by pressing a bar until they drop with exhaustion. If rats can feel some sort of pleasure, it is no great conceptual leap to point to the tail-wagging dog, the purring cat. Because the tail-wagging dog or the purring cat can frequently be observed in the absence of others of the species, it is presumably not meant as a form of communication to conspecifics. Rather, this behavior must have some function for the originator of the behavior themselves. The tail wagging and purring would offer a strong but stable stimulation, as rocking may be for humans who are severely disturbed. This steady but strong stimulation might be akin to the disco beat or the rhythms of sex or dance—a way of freezing a present otherwise fraught with too-rapid changes that are thus characterized, according to the arguments of Chapter 5, more commonly by fear.

It would certainly be rash to assume that pleasure, as fear, is the prerogative of sophisticated brains. But it is not obvious how rodent feelings, presumably evoked during stimulation, might be realized outside the laboratory, in real life. Perhaps the stimulation provided by the electrical current is much stronger than that furnished by the normal rat world, in that it can recruit an abnormally persistent constellation of neurons. In a world constituted of intense and fast interaction with the environment, it is possible to imagine that rats are far more prone to scenarios where one stimulation follows another in startling succession. If rapidly turning-over constellations of neurons are linked to fear, as outlined in Chapter 6, then perhaps stimulation and creation of a prevailing and long-lasting network of cells results in a rodent-type pleasure, or at least some kind of positive experience that offsets rodent fear.

This idea can be carried further. There are other sites in the brain that rats will work to avoid stimulating, the so-called aversive centers. Perhaps these sites are those where, for whatever reason, working networks of neurons are formed more easily and are thus more rapidly displaced such that fear is the consequence. Obviously, we can never climb into the rat's body and peer out from photophobic red eyes stuck on either side of our heads. But if we concede that animals are not unfeeling robots, we need some sort of descriptive terminology. "Pleasure" and "fear" thus could well best be placed in scare quotes but always with the understanding that rodent pleasure or feline fear is obviously beyond our direct access. In any event, the whole point of the self-stimulation experiments is that they are not like real life. Among exploration of garbage, a rat would not normally experience the kind of experience that is generated from the end of an electrode in the brain. I am suggesting that in these experiments, abnormally large (by rat standards) constellations are created in the rodent brain—a brain far better equipped for a fast interaction with the immediate world and hence characterized usually by smaller networks.

For us humans, our problem is the reverse. How do we shut out our highly evolved and nurtured inner world to be receptive again to strong sensory stimulation? Dreams may well be the most common, indeed, the inevitable route for most of us to experience a pure emotional state, but it is hard to see the survival value of losing one's mind nightly. One idea is that dreams are a rehearsal for procedures in which the dreamer will be engaged when subsequently awake.[13] Because we have seen that at one stage the fetus dreams constantly, it is presumably able to spend its entire day-to-day existence rehearsing for life. But how might a fetus know what procedure it will need when it is born? The whole point about the human brain is that although it is the size of a chimpanzee's at birth, unlike our simian cousin, it continues to grow in early life in a way adaptable to its particular environment. There would be no point rehearsing a procedure when it was still not yet revealed to you as a fetus whether you were to be on the savannah of 30,000 years ago or eventually to master a computer game. A related idea is that dreams enable us to rehearse emotions.[14] However, because it is known that we cannot remember most of our dreams, it is hard to envisage how such rehearsal might be beneficial.

Another theory is that dreams might enforce memory. Memory formation probably involves changes in protein synthesis, but protein synthesis in the brain is highest during deep, nondreaming sleep. Dreaming, on the other hand, is identical to wakefulness as regards manufacturing these large molecules.[15]

Finally, there is the idea that dreaming simply enables the replenishment of small molecules,[16] more specifically the amines that are suppressed by an antagonistic system, the chemical cousin acetylcholine. But I personally cannot see why replenishment of such chemicals could not occur in nondreaming sleep where, as we saw, the synthesis of proteins, which are much more complex molecules, is significantly higher than in either dreaming or wakefulness.

Interestingly enough, dreaming and wakefulness are closer to each other than we might think, in subjective terms, too. When stimulation is very strong for some people during wakefulness, for instance when laughing intensely or in midorgasm, they can suddenly fall into dreaming sleep.[17] This amazing phenomenon is accompanied by the muscle paralysis that normally accompanies dreaming. In less extreme examples, usually when very frightened or sexually excited, again, one becomes quasi-paralyzed, literally weak in the knees.[18]

This immobilization could well be an attempt to combat fear by reducing the probability of a high turnover of neuronal constellations, which would have been most likely with excessive movement. In the unusual cases of sudden conversion to a dream state, it could be that the stimulation is so intense that excessive amounts of one of the modulating chemicals suddenly throw the brain into a much smaller constellation mode. As a result, one's mind-set reverts right back to the flimsiest of all—the dreaming state involving paralysis and a bypassing of the sense organs altogether. But if dreams are, as I am suggesting, a cerebral caricature of emotions more generally, then perhaps the question of the function of dreams could be best addressed by asking what is the point of emotions themselves.

If my idea is correct, then the survival value of the emotions, particularly pleasure, would be to anchor us in the here and now. For small-brained animals it could be to slow them down, to maximize pleasure and minimize fear, so that they are kept in a situation where they engage in activities that promoted survival. For us, however, the danger is to stop interacting altogether as we retreat into the fantasy world, the nostalgia of our inner minds. If we do not eat, copulate, or move around, we die. The value of emotion, therefore, would be to make it a sought-after activity to reconnect with the real world. The raver and the skier are in some very basic way thus recapitulating an atavistic past of breastfeeding, a time of pure, unadulterated pleasure.

The idea I have been developing is that emotions, unlike cognitive processes, are present in all animals, and as such are a basic property of the brain. In dealing with the evolution of emotions, we are reaching much further back than we would need had we been simply exploring human cognition—as have Dennett, Deacon, Mithen, and Calvin—all reviewed in Chapter 2. We should look for the evolution of feeling, not merely six million years ago, when we parted company with the chimpanzees, but to the evolution of the animal brain in the first place.[19]

As in our individual development, so with simple brains in evolution. Our brains would be in a dreamlike state reactive to abstracted sensations flooding in. At this time, any strong stimulation—stimulating a rat brain with electrical current, wagging a tail, purring, sucking at the breast, or being rocked—would be pleasurable. Perhaps this is what Freud intended when he spoke of the eroticism of children.[20] The idea was not that children wished to reinvent the Kama Sutra, but rather that they felt intense pleasure and hence indulged in activities that brought strong stimulations—rocking, cuddling, and sucking. In all cases, these activities would be expected to involve contact with others, most usually the parent. The idea of sexuality is apposite, but it is a sexuality in the most general sense of making sensual contact with another person.

If this is the case, then my idea would not be greatly at odds with Freud's in attributing infanthood with maximal degrees of pleasure, which is gradually pruned back in both ontology and phylogeny both as individuals age and as our species evolves. The difference is that Freud saw pleasure as combating the demand of an Id, a subconscious driven to unity with others. Here we can also see that pleasure ensues when one loses one's individuality again, becoming at one with others because one has relinquished one's mind. But the basis of the explanation is different from Freud's. Whereas he interpreted pleasure as drive reduction, the suggestion here is that it is the corollary of a brain configured in a certain primitive way, forming relatively modest constellations of neurons.

Emotions and their most obvious manifestation, dreams, are, above all, intensely subjective; I am suggesting they are caused by fragile, spontaneously active constellations of brain cells that do not need to be driven by the senses. So where does that leave the types of emotional states I listed at the beginning of this chapter, emotional states where, again, there is no trigger from the outside world because it is the inner world has delivered a hammer blow?

Anxiety is a state of mind that is initiated and perpetuated with very little external assistance. Anxiety, one might think, is far closer to fear than is pleasure, but in brain terms, it could be the exact opposite. After all, pure fear, as pleasure, is very much in the here and now. Anxiety, on the other hand, as mentioned in Chapter 6, depends on the ability to forsake the present moment and anticipate an uncomfortable future. It is hard to imagine that the rabbit in his burrow dwells on past times when it managed to escape a fox and is now worrying about whether a fox is going to pass that way once more. Once the fox is there, putting its snout down the hole and exuding all the dreaded fox smells, then the full repertoire of physiological alarm bells, all the wartime reactions of the rabbit's body, will be activated. It will experience "anxiety" by virtue of the associations that the smell reactivates and fear as the here and now starts to change with rapidly cascading scenes. But first, there needs to be the immediate trigger of the smell and sound of the fox.

Nonhuman animal models of anxiety depend on an immediate trigger.[21] A rat, for example, learns to associate the sound of a bell with an electric shock and then develops anxiety when hearing the otherwise neutral sound of the bell. In this sense, anxiety is defined as conditioned fear. These models of anxiety have been invaluable in elucidating the actions of antianxiety drugs, such as Librium and Valium.[22] On the other hand, such an approach is unable to differentiate between a reaction to the outside world and the corrosive sensation that can set us apart from everyday life without any sensory triggers. Fear differs from anxiety, not simply in that one is conditioned whereas the other is not, but in humans, at least, by the fact that anxiety can be internally sustained for very long periods of time. Human adults differ from rabbits, and indeed from very young children, in the ability to construct a personal reality, to turn into their own mind.

In Chapter 3, we traced the idea of burgeoning inner resources that enable us to stem, filter, and annotate the sensory impact of the raw present, as well as to rationalize the current incoming flood of sensory stimulation. As we mature, the inner resources gain even more sway, so that they can minimize the outside world altogether. Apart from daydreams or nostalgic memories, we can also create an internal hell.

If rabbits were somehow lent a human mind, they might start to worry about whether a fox would pass by that night, based on the specific memory of a recent night when they were almost caught by the bushy-tailed predator. The iteration of a painful event in the past or the expectation of an imagined scenario in the future might be one way to describe worry and anxiety that is peculiarly human. Such mental iterations depend on a highly sophisticated brain to conjure up unprompted and nonexistent vistas, and lead to the production of physical body responses appropriate for immediate life-threatening, fearful situations.[23] These inappropriately expressed bodily reactions, when occurring over protracted periods of time, lead to reactions rooted in stress, a sustained activation of the flight or fight response: chronic high blood pressure, headaches, irritability, insomnia.

As with the depressive who featured in Chapter 6, the problem here is one of a persistent state of mind, a persistent and dominant neuronal constellation that is impervious to the outside world. An anxiety state differs from fear in that there is no flooding of the brain with fast, uncontrollable sequences of stimulation. Why should this state of mind be so emotional? If small assemblies of neurons are associated with emotion, and if anxiety is more akin to depression, then surely someone who is anxious would also experience a blanket feeling of numbness. But, as we know, it is quite the opposite: we can feel almost literally sick with worry.

As I see it, the big difference is that whereas depression features a consistent scene, the death of a spouse, say, or a persistent scenario of worthlessness, anxiety is an internal state, too, but one that actually is generating multiple, fast scenes, as though they were occurring in the external world. A worry about the mortgage payments would entail one scenario following another of the imagined consequences of what will happen. No sooner does one scene take place, bankruptcy, let us say, then it is superseded by another—having a trial, going to jail, losing one's partner, and so on.

Perhaps this rapid, internally generated sequence of scenarios is how anxiety can be distinguished from fear on the one hand, where there is a strong sensory input, and depression on the other, where one sluggish internal state merely prevails. If so, then once again we can differentiate one emotion from another using quantity, not quality. In anxiety, the turnover of neuronal constellations would be as high as in fear, and as internalized as in depression. We have seen that drugs can work on these conditions by exploiting the systems for arousal, or the very efficacy of hubs of neurons to communicate with one another. But could the situations be reversed by nondrug treatments? If fear could be combated by being in a situation where there was less rapid change in the inputs bombarding the brain, how might anxiety be tackled?

People find it hard to laugh when they are worried—and the two states are certainly incompatible. Laughter is a marvelous way of coping with stress and another example of a self-generated emotional experience. The process, so commonplace, so desirable, and yet often so elusive, has nonetheless long posed a problem for Darwinists in that its survival value is far from obvious.[24] In fact, such noisy, predator-attracting and energy-consuming activity would, on the face of it, be positively undesirable in terms of benefit to the species. Laughter must have an enormously strong payoff to justify its obvious evolutionary disadvantages. At the sheer physical level of body function, it is now being increasingly acknowledged that laughter has a beneficial effect on health.[25] Respiration is deeper after one laughs, which in turn causes one to be more relaxed. In addition, there is robust evidence that laughter raises the efficiency of the immune system.[26]

Then there is the famous case of Norman Cousins, diagnosed with a spinal disease, ankylosing spondylitis, and given a 0.2 percent chance of survival.[27] Cousins embarked on a self-help regime involving, in part, the watching of comedy videos. Indeed, he found that after a bout of laughter, the sedimentation rate of his red blood cells—a measure directly proportional to the degree of an infection—fell gradually and persistently. Cousins even claimed that laughter could alleviate pain: ten minutes of belly-laughter allowed him two hours of pain-free sleep. This idea has now been tested more formally in a study where subjects who had listened to a laughter-inducing cassette, as opposed to other types of cassettes, had a higher threshold of "pressure-induced" discomfort. Even before these effects could be appreciated, in the seventeenth century, the "English Hypocrite," Thomas Sydenham, remarked that, "The arrival of a happy clown exercises a more beneficial influence upon the health of a town than of twenty asses laden with drugs."[28]

Laughter causes the release of the body's natural morphinelike chemicals, the endorphins, which induce a sense of well-being.[29] This could be the very type of brain mechanism for which I was searching at the beginning of this chapter. It is possible that laughter-induced release of naturally occurring opiates could favor, as does morphine itself, less extensive neuronal connections, which in turn induces a state of mind in the here and now. There is also a simultaneous evolutionary perspective. By laughing and thus placing oneself in the present, one is in a better position to engage in the activities necessary for survival.

When chimpanzees are at play, they frequently vocalize a type of sound that has been referred to as laughter.[30] Perhaps when a cat purrs, it is ensuring it is distracted not so much by a complex, sophisticated inner world it does not have as by a mouse scurrying in a corner. Perhaps this is the equivalent feline strategy to sustain pleasure, albeit one that is less intrusive and thus less likely to attract predators. By the same token, it is only in our own species that the brain has become sufficiently developed to run the substantial risk of straying inwards into a personal reality that would jeopardize eating, copulation, running from danger, or hunting. Interestingly enough, it is only in our own human species that laughter is sufficiently loud and sustained, perhaps because only in our case is the very real risk of attracting predators offset by the dangers to our survival of retreating into our own singularly extensive minds.

In both laughter and the more commonly agreed survival-value-laden means of obtaining pleasure—food and sex—the same ingredients emerge: a powerful sensory stimulus and/or a heightened arousal that both contribute to a sliding scale of increasing focus on the here and now, such that past and future slip away with increasing force. Laughter is one of the most sought after of states. After all, we pay money and set aside time to be in situations that we deem will maximize the chances of laughter occurring. However, as a physiological phenomenon, it is a complete mystery.

As with pleasure itself, it is hard to guarantee absolutely that one will be able to laugh. Yes, tickling will automatically produce laughter, but in a particularly unrewarding, reflex fashion. Tickling elicits laughter, but it does not give pleasure. Hence laughter must be not a cause but a symptom of pleasure, a sign that it is occurring, rather than the reason in the first place. But if laughter is a consequence of pleasure, it is strange that we do not laugh when we are in the very situations that are most pleasurable. Why do we not burst out laughing in midorgasm, while tasting a particularly fine claret, or while bungee jumping? Let's look a little more closely at the situations in which we do laugh.

Most often, we do not laugh in the direct sensual situations where we can be so transported into ecstasy—when we are arrested in a here and now stripped of all meaning, all past or future connotations. Rather, laughter is at rather contrived situations, where we are not so far advanced along the spectrum of strong emotion. For children, the plot is rather simple, but the more we mature, the scenarios that make us laugh become ever more refined, subtle, and above all, culture based.

When I worked in Paris for a year, my French became roadworthy enough to express myself adequately for all but the most philosophical of conversations, and consequently, to follow virtually everything that was said around me. The one problem I found, however, as countless nonnative speakers before me in any country, was that the foreigners laugh for completely incomprehensible reasons. And, of course, it is not just a vocabulary problem. How many Brits have been baffled by the American sense of humor, and vice versa? Laughter, then, is universal to humans and occurs in similar scenarios for the very young, but during development, it becomes increasingly culturally differentiated.

In this respect it differs fundamentally from the sensual means of obtaining pleasure, such as dancing, sport, sex, and food, which transcend all cultures and which do not depend on laughing. I suggest, therefore, that the situations that evoke laughter are not as basic, immediate, and as surefire in delivering the zap of pleasure as the more sensory avenues. It could be that the act of laughter serves somehow to increase the chances of a pleasurable experience that is not as guaranteed as in situations of very strong sensory stimulation. After all, when we are jolted out of personal reality by a taste, an orgasm, or a swift movement, such triggers are strong enough to keep us in the here and now, and to advance us well along in the pleasure spectrum to sheer bliss. However, sitting in front of a TV watching Benny Hill is not in itself a strong sensory stimulus. Our attention is at risk of wandering back to the mortgage worries, the promotion hopes. By laughing we are able to provide our own strong sensory stimulus that prevents other more sophisticated, distracting, personalized associations from creeping in. Our diaphragm is oscillating in a strong gyration, the laughter itself is loud in our ears, and we are breathing in a more exaggerated fashion.

When we say we find a particular TV show or comedian funny, what we are really saying is that the show or the person is giving us a flicker of pleasure that can be fanned into a mental forest fire by laughing. Hence tickling is not pleasurable simply because at the moment of being tickled, there is no preexisting happiness. You cannot fan flames without an initial spark. Instead, we need a feeling of active pleasure nonetheless tied into the context of the here and now. In such situations, rather than in the more extreme shades of emotion, we are primed for laughter. Laughter can itself be graded, from the face-aching, tear-jerking laughter that is strong enough to take us up almost into an ecstatic state, to the sustained giggling of schoolgirls, where the stimulus is like an engine turning over—strong enough to ensure that attention does not wander but mild enough to ensure simply a background, a sustained underlying tone of the here and now. Once the laughter is under way, and we are thus less likely to stray into our inner reality, then it is much easier for the situation to enhance itself still further, hence the common phenomenon that while laughing at one thing, it is so much easier to laugh at something else. Everything becomes funny, produces a gentle wash of pleasure.

But why should a comedian, in the appropriate cultural context, produce amusement in the first place? What ignites the flame? One possible core factor is the unexpected. Consider the year-old child. A simple way of encouraging a child of this age to laugh is to produce one of its toys from surprising locations in the vicinity. Up pops Flopsy Bunny behind the chair, then to the side, and so on. As we become more experienced in the ways of the world, such a game ceases to be funny because it is so predictable.

The dampening effect of predictability leads us into the increasing importance of culture to humor. Increasingly, our views on what is predictable will depend on what we expect and what is surprising. And why in turn should the unexpected in all cases cause amusement? Because it alerts us more than a predictable stimulus would, and then retains us, albeit gently, in the here and now. So, a situation that is surprising will heighten our arousal and focus on this present: precisely the requisites for an emotion, for pleasure. In this case the trigger is cultural and not of intense, abstracted, sensual stimulation. A neuronal constellation is likely to grow, and as it spreads out, using established, experience-forged connections, so pleasure would recede. A new assembly is needed quickly, and then another, so that we do not end up, in phenomenological terms, in a past or a future of our own inner worlds, the adult world of large-neuron connectivity and dampened emotion. We create a new but predictable sensory stimulus for ourselves. Laughter fits the bill perfectly.

Although the mind might be suppressed in the brief moments of sheer pleasure that we all try to snatch throughout each day, there are situations where, sadly, such retrieval is not assured. In Alzheimer's disease,[31] there is a progressive impairment of the higher functions—the ability to place yourself in a meaningful context in what you hear and see around you. Here then is another example where the state of mind will change due to an internal factor, as opposed to any trigger in the environment. The first sign that all is not well is not only loss of memory but confusion. The patient cannot be sure exactly when and where an event occurred, and as the disease advances, even where they are in the present, and finally most tragically of all, who they actually are. Perhaps the nearest we will all come to this experience is on waking up away from home, in a strange room, struggling for just that moment to find our space and time points of reference. Imagine being in that state of confusion all the time.

Alzheimer's disease is caused by widespread loss of certain groups of neurons that nonetheless have a widespread influence throughout the brain, both within and below the cortex.[32] Some of the key areas affected, and apparently the first to be affected, are those that I have dubbed the "fountains" in the brain, from which the amine and acetylcholine chemicals emanate.

As we have already seen, these related yet distinct chemical systems are responsible for energizing, alerting, and modulating the brain in different ways under different conditions of biorhythms and arousal. We have also explored how these chemical fountains could play an important modulatory part in enhancing the effectiveness of neurons in sending signals out in a rippling fashion, so that large numbers were co-opted into a large transient assembly. In any brain where these chemicals are not up to full strength, less effective and thus smaller assemblies will be formed. There will be fewer inner resources contributing to the prevailing mental state. In addition, by a process we have yet to understand in detail,[33] a lack of interaction between these marinating chemicals and their targets in the outer reaches of the brain results not just in a functional impairment but, over time, in the actual dissolution of the physical links between neurons—the "mind" built up through a lifetime, as we saw in Chapter 3.

If the brains of Alzheimer patients can be described in this way, by abnormally small assembly formation, then bizarrely, such individuals might be expected to be abnormally happy or at least abnormally emotional—perhaps even like small children. This is just what happens. The state of mind of the Alzheimer patient is frequently described as infantile,[34] in that they laugh inappropriately and are restless, engaged far more by the sensuality of the environment as the mind slips its moorings.

But as the disease takes its terrible toll, the situation begins to parallel the brain in the very earliest stages of development. As the associations between neurons dissolve, so the world becomes as for the baby, a booming, buzzing confusion where there is no meaning at all in the moment-to-moment sensation. The patient has journeyed back through time, has relinquished the mind altogether.

There is one final extreme scenario, where inner processes alone will, again, determine the state of mind and of feeling. Meditation could be regarded as a situation of a large neuronal constellation. The outside world is precluded in favor of a contrived and meaningless trigger, often a simple sound or word.[35] The idea, however, is not that one becomes, as with small constellations, the passive recipient of whatever the world implodes on to a defenseless and passive brain, but rather the opposite. The meditator is imposing back on the outside world a complete understanding; in Buddhist terminology, *unconditional compassion*.[36]

Note here the importance of the term *unconditional*. The idea runs that usually our selfish self-interest requires feedback from the outside world. In meditation one achieves a state not requiring praise or reassurance, hence the ego, in the narrow selfish sense, ceases to exist (*sunyata*). However, this does not mean that consciousness ceases to exist, nor that it is the unreflective, reactive consciousness that characterizes nonhuman animals, dreamers, or the junkie—the high emotional, small assembly state.

Quite the contrary, the type of consciousness that seems to characterize the supreme state of a Buddhist meditator is one where one's particular consciousness is not bombarded at all as a passive recipient, but where the inner resources are so extensively developed, the significance and meaning to all the things in the outside world so extensive, that any further interaction is completely saturated. In a sense, then, we could view the meditator as displaying the ultimate large neuronal constellation—the ultimate loss of all emotion. There might be no Self in our everyday, selfish sense, but there is an individual, idiosyncratic understanding, a wisdom, and an intelligence, as opposed to a mindless sensuality.

But if this state of unconditional compassion is associated with very large neuronal groupings, the scheme I have been sketching would have predicted that meditation brought depression and even pain. However, just as we saw earlier that manipulation of different factors in the size of a neuronal assembly could determine actual content (e.g., fear from pleasure), so here we see that according to the particular factor that is abnormal in generating an abnormally large neuronal assembly—different types of experience will ensue.

One possibility is that large neuronal assemblies need not only be caused and sustained by a strong stimulus, as in the case of reactive depression or, more excessively, by a painful external stimulus; nor need an abnormal availability of modulating chemicals, as in endogenous depression, be the cause. Alternatively, perhaps manipulation of the third alternative, connectivity, is how a large assembly is achieved in the brain of a meditator. In this case the connections forged between neurons would have been caused by repeated sessions of meditation and would afford the meditator wisdom, in the sense developed in Chapter 3, where we viewed wisdom as arising from a realization of many aspects of an object, person, or event. Perhaps the type of constellation formed not by a persistent central epicenter or by coraling chemicals but by extensive and pervasive neuronal connections will be even larger still than that responsible for the states of depression and pain. A state of no emotion at all, the state of meditation could be viewed, almost literally, as mind over matter, the ultimate and highly unnatural breakdown in interaction of brain and environment characterized by no sensations whatsoever. It is hardly surprising that meditation takes many years to perfect and is a state to which only a tiny minority of humanity has access.

We have seen that emotions, arising in diverse states and conditions, are consistent with the concept of a prevalence of small neuronal constellations, and that various internal factors can trigger the brain into this mode of functioning. Dreams, laughter, and the early stages of Alzheimer's disease are all examples of emotionally charged states, explicable in terms of small neuron constellations, that have been driven not by a vigorous interaction with the outside environment but by an internal trigger.

But what of the frequent type of situation with which we started this chapter? How might an item of news throw our bodies and minds into a turmoil of emotion? Perhaps a physically unobtrusive external stimulus—a small smile from a lover across the room at a party or the news that someone you know has cancer—triggers so many different possible scenarios that no one constellation has time to grow before being superseded by another.

It is often news where we have relatively little information that triggers emotional reactions. For example, it has been said that condemned prisoners will die a thousand times because they do not know what to expect. Different scenarios present themselves, one after the other, in such rapid succession that the state is as emotional as a roller-coaster ride. Every moment of our lives, the inputs from the senses are triggering associations, resulting in a different constellation of active brain cell networks at any one moment. The smaller the networks, even if they are triggered initially by the relaying across internal, idiosyncratic associations, the more emotional one will feel. And the emotion will fluctuate in degree from one moment to the next, as the constellation of neurons mercurially contracts and expands in an ever-changing, never-to-be-repeated configuration. If one scenario persists and a constellation grows abnormally, then, as with the depressive, we become paradoxically free of all emotion—numb. Such is the human condition, an ever-changing symphony of the rational, the abstract, the generalized, the personal with the sensual, the vivid, the new.

The psychologist K. Strongman[37] has listed a series of testing questions for which, he claims, any serious theory of emotions should be able to provide answers. First, one should be able to distinguish between emotion and nonemotion: according to the model I have been developing here, such a distinction could be seen as two ends of a continuum where the more emotional the state, the more the Self is denied. Second, one should be able to state the biological foundation. This foundation has been covered in this chapter and throughout the book in describing emotion or interaction with the outside world in terms of relatively small neuronal constellations. Third, mention should be made of the evolutionary aspects of emotion. As we saw in Chapter 2—and here—I am suggesting that emotion, particularly pleasure, encourages behavior favoring propagation of the species. Fourth, an ideal theory of emotions should give consideration to when emotion goes wrong. This subject was dealt with in Chapters 5 and 6, in our dealings with fear and anguish, as well as in Chapter 4 when we discussed drugs. Fifth, the relationship between cognition and emotion should be made clear. The development of mind and its encroachment on raw emotion was described initially in Chapter 3, and has been developed here again, as an ever-changing, net brain state of changing assembly size of neurons.

But now we come to the biggest question of all, one that does not feature in Strongman's shopping list. If emotions are the most basic form of consciousness, as I am arguing, what is consciousness? As the neurons form and reform in their kaleidoscopic aggregations, what happens in the brain to enable you alone to feel that unique, subjective state?

8

THE ANSWER?

A drug, a dance, or a bungee jump temporarily obliterates your mind. But unalloyed by an idiosyncratic past or future, quicksilver consciousness still streaks through the brain, and it is a subjective sensation: it is your consciousness, which no one else can hack into. Although you may not feel self-conscious, you are, nonetheless, still very much a feeling entity. And feelings, I am arguing, are the most basic form of consciousness. I have tried to show how these feelings increase in intensity as working networks of neurons become transiently smaller. But the ultimate question is this: how do subjective sensations themselves—different states of consciousness—actually occur as a result of these shifting configurations of neurons within the physical brain?

We saw in Chapter 2 that, despite the efforts of many different types of scientists, no single chemical or process in the brain is solely responsible for consciousness. A single brain region or oscillating collection of neurons cannot, if transposed to a dish, autonomously generate a headache or happiness. The only alternative is that garden-variety neurons, not previously committed to any special function, destiny, or cerebral magic bullet could, given the right circumstances, contribute to a moment of consciousness. These circumstances would be above and beyond the normal business of the neurons in question, of sending signals within local circuits or from one brain region to the next. Because there is no single brain region for consciousness, then effectively vast reaches of brain terrain would have to be configured in certain ways from one moment to the next for each fleeting sensation, and it is that dynamic, holistic configuration—those "right circumstances"—that we scientists seek to identify as a realistic and convincing correlate of consciousness.[1]

Such a discovery might well be at last within our grasp if we now take the brain apart and peer into the bustling world of the cellular metropolis. Unlike most of the models surveyed in Chapter 2, real neurons will now form the framework for an as yet uncharted micro landscape of chemicals and as yet hypothetical phenomena.

We can start simply enough, with neurons getting on with their daily life in a way that is already well understood. When I first signed up as a graduate student to study the brain, a sobering quarter of a century ago or more, chemical transmission across synapses within local circuits was the common coinage for describing brain operations. Within my scientific life span, however, there has been a shift away from this simple, unique, on-off signaling. Now grant applications are crammed with aspirations for exploring mechanisms operating within and between brain cells that enable them to adapt in the longer term and hence be involved in undeniable phenomena such as memory, the so-called mechanisms of neuron plasticity. The slowly forming, quasi-permanent connections between the hundred billion neurons in our brains of the type that we explored in Chapter 3 has indeed prompted a neuroscience growth industry.[2]

Such networks of cells, formed after birth and reflecting individual experiences, are, as suggested in Chapter 3, the most plausible physical bases for personalizing the brain into an idiosyncratic conglomeration of experiences, generalizations, prejudices, and propensities: a mind. This mind grows slowly as a life story takes shape and persists throughout nightly ruptures in awareness. Your mind, as it accumulates, will not be your consciousness, but rather it will color the way you feel to varying extents at varying times. As we develop, the contribution of the mind will be to enhance each conscious moment by imbuing each snapshot of the outside world with meaning. Life starts like a lens out of focus with blurred and abstract shapes, but the growth of a mind enables us to home in with increasing precision on specific objects and people.

For example, my mother is of great significance to me, in that the very mention of the word *Mum* will trigger cascades of associations and events. Running as a persistent theme through most of this journey has been the idea that the degree of meaning that we covertly apportion to each person, object, or event as we blunder around in the outside world will, in turn, be matched by a corresponding degree of neuron connections. But whereas individuality might be readily translated into the evolving, personalized microcircuitry of the brain, it remains like an eccentrically furnished, private room left in the dark. Now we have to turn on the neurophysiological light.

So that we can be really clear about what we are going to expect the brain to do, let's look at some features of the feel of consciousness, what philosophers call the *phenomenology*.[3] Once we have a shopping list of possible properties of consciousness, we can then revisit the physical brain and see how well its physical features and processes might cater to them.

The most fundamental item of all is to identify the stage in personal development, or in the evolution of species, when we can expect a brain to be capable of consciousness. This issue is of course highly controversial. The very idea that a fetus might feel pain has only fueled the already heated debate over abortion. Of course, the problem is that no one knows when a baby actually becomes conscious. Perhaps as the midwife dangles it from its ankles and slaps its behind, awareness slams into its brain like the light that struck Paul on his journey from Tarsus. Alternatively, consciousness might dawn sometime in infancy, but if so, when? No new mother would buy into the idea that her baby was merely a vegetable or robot for the first month or so of life. Certainly, no doctor would decline to anesthetize a newborn undergoing surgery on the grounds that it was unlikely to be conscious and therefore unlikely to feel pain. In any event, there is no obvious postnatal turning point when everything would change.

The most plausible explanation is rather that consciousness begins in the womb. If this is true, we bump up against the conundrum of identifying the actual time when consciousness just happens. A newly fertilized egg is but a single cell with no brain, and thus no wherewithal for sentience; but even as generic cells start committing themselves to lives as neurons, there is no obvious brain Rubicon that demarcates consciousness. All number of key events in the growing brain unfold in pregnancy, each occurring at a certain stage of fetal development, but at often very different times, often continuing as a protracted phase—and in each case of arguable degrees of significance.

For example, one of the earliest indications of consciousness might be simple movement of the fetus, which can be detected from eight weeks.[4] On the other hand, a cynic could argue that the nascent nervous system might be merely displaying reflexes, akin to the mindless movements of a headless chicken. Moreover, the appearance of sensory detectors and sensory responses from nine weeks, though possibly of some relevance, have in some cases been mimicked nonetheless on a definitively unconscious computer.[5]

Instead of placing importance on the processing of whatever inputs bombard the brain or emphasizing its output—movements—the deciding factor might be the status of the gray box itself. Take for example the outer layer, the cortex. In mammals, the cortex has been identified by some as the permissive feature for consciousness. However, there are many stages to the development of the cortex, spanning many months.[6] For instance, cortical cells can be present in their correct position in the brain from six weeks after gestation, become insulated with the fatty covering myelin in certain selective regions from about twenty weeks, develop local connections from twenty-five weeks, and generate an electrical wave pattern from about thirty weeks. The development of the cortex thus takes place over a very wide time frame, six months or so. Notice also that all the changes are gradual and merely start to take place at certain times but are by no means complete, sometimes until well after birth.

Another milestone in the development of the brain that could also be critical to the conscious state is the hooking up of the cortex with an important area lying deep below in the center of the brain, the *thalamus*. This region, named after the Greek for room,[7] eventually has extensive connections emanating from deep inside the head to the outer reaches of the brain.[8] However, there is no evidence as yet to believe that the integrity of these connections might be anything more than a necessary rather than sufficient condition for consciousness. In fact, these thalamus-cortex connections—or even the presence of a cortex in the first place—might not even be necessary at all.

Reflect, for example, upon the common octopus. This invertebrate displays sophisticated learning and memory skills,[9] and might thus well be indulging in some molluscan inner life. But the octopus brain is configured very differently from ours, and indeed, from that of mammals in general.[10] Surely the deciding factor for the mere presence of consciousness, however crude or basic or raw, should not be put entirely on the appearance of relatively detailed physical features of the developing fetal mammalian brain, with its characteristic architecture of brain structures and its all-enveloping cortex.

The same riddle of isolating the time or place when consciousness occurs, as I see it, applies to *all* nonhuman animals. Most people would agree that it is highly unlikely that although humans are conscious, chimpanzees—who are only 1 percent different in their DNA from us—are insentient zombies. And moving still further away from our own species in the animal kingdom, most pet owners would make much of the personality and perspicacity of their cats and dogs, if not even of their hamsters. If we carry on in this vein, however, when do we stop? Some scientists—Gerry Edelman, for instance—have come clean and stated explicitly that lower animals are not conscious. He gives as illustration the lobster.[11]

But it is not, at least to me, obvious where exactly we draw the line, and why. After all, evolution within the animal kingdom has been a gradual process, with each species closely related to others. Nature has not demarcated a clear line, on one side of which are biological machines, on the other, sentient creatures. Moreover, most animals, including those with much simpler brains, such as insects, exhibit some kind of circadian sleep-wake cycle.[12] If an animal can have discernibly different global states of something, then surely that "something" cannot be anything other than some kind of crude consciousness!

Clearly, we cannot expect a fetus, locked away in its black, wet, warm world, and hearing distant and meaningless noises via its mother's abdominal wall, to have the same consciousness as we adults. As we saw in Chapter 3, it is during early postnatal life that the individual configurations of neuronal connectivity and hence significance are crafted by the particular environment. Hence if the fetus is conscious, with its newly minted and sparsely networked neurons, its consciousness—as with nonhuman animals—will be something very different from what we adults or even infants experience.

The problem of fetal and nonhuman consciousness is caused, I suggest, by an unnecessary and false assumption that consciousness is either on or off, there or not there. Perhaps a better way to consider consciousness, from octopuses to Van Goghs, could be to view it as a continuum: not as a sudden blinding light but rather as a dimmer switch.[13]

This switch could vary from almost imperceptible light, say, the consciousness of invertebrates, to the floodlit brilliance of adult human consciousness. Quite simply, consciousness could grow in degree as brains do. It seems to make sense, then, that a pivotal property of consciousness is that you can have more or less of it: a continuum. If consciousness is continuously variable as we grow, there is no reason why it should become static once we are mature. If consciousness is variable, then it should also be able to expand not just during childhood, but from one moment to the next. Most of us, after all, will readily talk of "raising" or "deepening" our consciousness by all manner of means, from standing on a mountaintop to listening to Mozart.

Although we all understand the idea of raising or deepening our consciousness, the actual direction does not matter as much as the amplitude of the excursion. It is hard to put into literal terms exactly what one means. A definition of sorts of a "deepening consciousness" might be that you are aware of a greater significance in the world around you, rather than the mere zap of sensation that comes with staring up at the twinkling stars or down at a churning, foaming ocean. The more the stars or the ocean "mean" to you, the more associations they will trigger. Hence a small child or a nonhuman animal would not be able to experience the same depth of consciousness as a human adult.

Although *mind* is far from being a synonym for *consciousness,* the mind, as I have defined it in this book, will influence the degree of consciousness that we experience from one moment to the next. For some, it might be possible to equate this state with the spiritual, as something that goes beyond the mere physical properties of the people and objects that make up their immediate world.[14] The most extreme example would be meditation, where, as we saw in Chapter 7, the associations that are triggered by an initial neutral stimulus such as the sound *om* are so extensive that the sensational aspect of the world, in a literal sense, hardly intrudes at all. For most of us, however, our days are spent with consciousness varying within less dramatic extremes, from a pensive walk in the country to the direct sensual hit of a cold beer on a sweltering day.

The next step is to see how the idea of this continuum of consciousness could in some way be reflected in the physical brain itself. The brain is composed of a hundred billion neurons and ten times as many supporting "glial" cells that ensure a benign and nurturing environment for the neurons themselves to go about their business of sending rapid volleys of signals to one another. At the macro level, there is no consciousness center, and at the micro level there are no committed neurons or genes devoted to consciousness. The only possibility, then, is the middle level—large, uncommitted, and therefore highly transient groupings of brain cells. Such mercurial assemblies of neurons, unlike fixed, macro brain structures, or indeed ephemeral single cells, constitute the only possible level of brain organization left that could vary in size from one moment to the next and thus correlate with—indeed actually accommodate—degrees of subjective, evanescent consciousness.

By now, however, you might be wondering what is new here. After all, I have already made much of the constellations of neurons that riddle the adult brain and turn it into a mind. In themselves, these constellations could not automatically *be* the here-and-now experience of an active feeling. They are too many, too slow to form, too long-lasting, and too local to accommodate a fleeting, holistic brain state. However pervasive and important the mortgage payments, our brains have the capacity for consciousness to be constantly on the move, to make transitions from a worry, to recognition of a blackbird, to a backache, to a telephone call. The adult human brain is most likely seething with myriad operational neuronal networks—constellations that change and evolve, but slowly over long time frames. This mind, as we have seen, is therefore not the same as a unique moment of consciousness itself. There has, obviously, to be something else going on within the brain as well, something that somehow selects certain events, people, or memories to be the transient focus of that unique, brief moment.

Imagine a stone is thrown into a puddle. The stone is, of course, a relatively long-lasting fixture in the world, but when it hits the calm surface of the water, it sends out ripples that last only for an instant, yet far exceed the stony diameter. The bigger the stone or the more forcefully it is thrown, the more extensive the ripples. Let's take the ripples as analogous to a highly evanescent moment of consciousness. The more extensive the ripples, the deeper the consciousness. If so, the right circumstances for consciousness will depend not on the intervention of some magic bullet but simply on the size of the stone. Any quasi-permanent constellation that could suddenly recruit very many more neurons into a working assembly, even for less than a second, would become the focus, the epicenter, of consciousness. And the greater the resulting temporary assembly size, I am suggesting, the deeper the consciousness.

If the adult human brain is already buzzing with local constellations of neuron networks, the second step to work out is what key circumstances might now change in the brain. We need to work out what molecular upheaval might occur so that one alone of the millions of existing constellations is able to act as a stone thrown in a puddle to generate neuronal ripples beyond the boundaries of its hardwired constellation. How might any one of the hubs of hardwired neurons in the brain transiently activate enough other neurons to create a unique and highly unstable assembly—yet one extensive enough to cause a conscious experience?

The answer may be obvious if we simply think more about what it actually means to be conscious. It is impossible to imagine being aware of nothing. We are always conscious of something, although what we mean by "something" can of course vary enormously.[15] If you look at a rose, that rose is the center of your consciousness for that moment, but what if you then start to reflect beyond the rose itself to, say, associations such as the Mona Lisa or Marilyn Monroe? If you were in a really pensive mood, if consciousness was deep, you might pursue these musings in a more general sense still, to consider the abstract concept of beauty itself. And once your thoughts run on more internalized lines such as these, then you as an adult human are capable of locking out altogether not only the outside world but also, so it seems, its icons and images entirely. In the face of a hope for some complex future scenario or rarefied, abstract theory, the immediacy and throb of the raw five senses play little part.

In all cases, the preexisting constellation of brain cells could act like the stone. The size of the stone would be comparable to the complexity of intrinsic connections. A mere photo of my mother, for example, would activate many connections in my brain but not in yours. The force with which the stone is thrown could be analogous to the intensity of physical properties, such as a loud thunderclap, the smell of strong coffee, or the intrusive glare of a spotlight. If the sensory systems are strongly stimulated, relays of neurons will generate more vigorous signals, and an assembly will be more easily recruited. Alternatively, if there is already an extensive hardwired constellation of neurons, its activation will more readily recruit a transient assembly.

So, objects or people or processes that mean a lot to you personally will correspond to an extensive neuron constellation: those that are, literally, sensational will be strongly exciting the senses. In other cases, such stimuli will tend to have the greatest chance of entering, indeed triggering a moment of, your consciousness. As we saw in the preceding chapters, the more we develop, the more the personalized meaning of the world around us tends to dominate over its mere sensuality. Unless you are meditating, you will always be conscious of the pulsating world around you to some extent. The degree to which this raw sensuality intrudes will be buffered by the carefully nurtured inner resources of your own mind. Any latent hardwired constellation will in part be activated by the sense systems directly, and in part by the other ongoing activity of other constellations recruited because of a preexisting association.

If my mother were to enter a room singing loudly and wearing a gold lamé dress while waving a large bunch of fragrant freesias, she would be giving me a different conscious experience than were she to slip quietly through a door wearing a dark coat. In each case, the net consciousness would be composed not only of different sensory elements but of second-order associations, whereby freesias themselves trigger a host of independent, idiosyncratic, and covert associations that nonetheless contribute to that unique moment. Of course, there would also be the comparison of this particular event with previous ones where my mother was, in all probability, not attired in dazzling gold and a little more subdued.

Crude though this example may be, these are the kinds of internal processes that will be set in train for every object and person that you encounter in the world every moment. There will be a mixture, to greater or lesser extents, of personal "significance" and raw sensory stimulation. It is no wonder that each moment of consciousness is unique. The force of the stone (degree of sensory strength) and the size of the stone (degree of connectivity) will combine to determine, for that instance alone, the extent to which the ripples will be generated. The more intense the sensory-stimulated activity of neurons within this expanding constellation, and/or the more extensive the preexisting connections for spreading this activity, the greater the net assembly that will be transiently recruited, the deeper that moment of consciousness. But let's see. By now you are perhaps seriously skeptical that the brain could ever really work like this.

Over the last ten years, working with non-human–animal brains, Amiram Grinvald and his colleagues have shown, by using special fluorescent dyes, that neurons can be made to light up, literally,[16] as they go to work, that is, as they become active by firing electrical signals—action potentials. In the old days of brain research, it was well known that a specified alignment of neurons would become active in response to, say, the presentation of a flash of light, but it was also assumed that the number of neurons and the type of response would always remain the same: that it was a kind of brain knee jerk.[17] But now we know that what happens in the brain is far more sophisticated and versatile. Even with a simple stimulus like a light and a relatively modest brain like that of a frog, neurons will indeed gradually become corralled into a working network, like a stone generating ever-wider ripples.[18] As time goes by, more and more neurons are recruited, rather like more and more people being called in a company as the director instructs the managers, who in turn direct their subordinates, to announce a merger or a pay raise.

Even a simple light shone in the direction of a cat will, as a stone in a puddle, activate an assembly of an estimated 10 million neurons within its outer perimeter within a quarter of a second! What is more, the degree of activity of the neuron assembly decays exponentially as the leading edge spreads out to become ever more remote, just as the ripples from a stone are weaker at the periphery of the disturbance.[19] At the moment, these imaging experiments with fluorescent dyes have not been used to study the process of consciousness as such. The technique requires that the surface of the brain be exposed and potentially toxic dye applied to brain cells. However, this type of study does show that the brain can work on a time scale that is very fast and over a spatial dimension that is far more global than people had realized.

Another type of experiment, this time in humans, suggests that such a transient recruitment of neurons, over about half a second, might indeed underlie consciousness. Neurophysiologist Benjamin Libet has demonstrated that, in human subjects, it is possible to record, almost instantaneously, neurons activated by a pinprick on the skin in the appropriate compartment of the brain.[20] To begin with, the neuronal constellations that show any response to the painful event are a relatively select band in an area of the cortex specifically and primarily linked to the sense of touch.[21] However, only after about half a second—once the electrical signs of a response have visibly spread over much wider areas, beyond the primary somatosensory cortex to nonspecialized areas—will the subject report that he or she is conscious of the tingle elicited by the pin contacting the skin.[22]

My idea is that it is one final, single value—the net size of the resultant transient neuronal assembly—that will determine *directly* the degree of consciousness at any one moment. However, the model deviates from that of a magic bullet because diverse different factors affect just how large an assembly grows. Moreover, and most important, these diverse factors will vary all the time and will be differentially manipulated.

The first factor is the number of neuron connections that actually exist in the first place. Obviously, if there are only relatively modest connections, there will be no extensive lines of communication via which the hardwired constellation can send out its electrical recruiting signals. A very large assembly will simply be unable to occur, and consciousness will be shallow, similar to that of infancy and childhood.

A second factor is chemical. If the normal chemical systems, the amine fountains, are not functioning properly, then cells ripe for recruitment into an assembly will be put on red alert inappropriately or not at all. Consciousness would be either not deep enough, as in schizophrenia, or too deep, as in depression.

A third factor is the degree of stimulation, or the force with which the stone is thrown. Thunderclaps are usually loud enough to break into the most reflective state of mind, as is the smell of blocked drains or the sight of a rainbow. Strong sensory stimulation, with no personal meaning, simply by virtue of its psychophysical intensity, will activate large numbers of neurons. By contrast, if an existing constellation is only weakly stimulated, like a stone placed gently on the surface of the water, there will be insufficient electrical activity to recruit large numbers of brain cells, as, for example, when the senses are understimulated: dreams.

A final factor would be the speed of recruitment of rival assemblies. If the brain is stimulated by a rapid succession of strong sensations, then any resultant assembly will have no time to realize its full potential before, as ripples spreading from an earlier stone, a newer set of ripples from a more recent throw now displaces the previous configuration. Again, consciousness will not be deep. Consider the intense sensual stimulation of food, dance, and sex, or the rapid change of scene that will occur in, say, bungee jumping.

In brief, I am suggesting that not just a necessary but also a *sufficient* condition for consciousness is a large net size of transient assembly of neurons: this phenomenon could be no less than the much sought after neural correlate of consciousness. But although this is both a plausible and potentially testable[23] correlate, the water-to-wine problem remains. It is pointless to sit back and claim, "and then consciousness is generated," because the model does not explain how the subjective feeling might arise from millions of coherent neurons, banding and disbanding in different configurations. If that is truly all that happens, then we are up against the Thing Fallacy. At the same time, there is nowhere else for transient assembly to go, nothing else for it to do, and nothing else for it to become; we are left with the Readout Fallacy. But perhaps something else happens, a route between the cerebral Scylla and Charybdis.

The brain does not function in isolation but is in constant two-way traffic with the rest of the body. Just think about the immune system. The conscious state, more particularly the most basic one—our emotions—is closely linked to our health. One of the many drawbacks of suffering from depression is that it is inevitably associated with physical illness. Similarly, everyone knows that when you are marooned in bed and physically uncomfortable, then you are far from happy, especially if the prospect of being in such a condition is to continue for a long time. Moreover, those who are depressed are more likely to make themselves ill with poor diet, inadequate sleep, drug abuse, and no exercise. Above and beyond these rather indirect factors, however, there could be a more immediate mechanism. For example, in a study conducted over 20 years of 2,000 middle-aged American men, those who showed depressive signs had twice the risk of developing a fatal cancer later on, irrespective of other risk factors such as smoking or family history.[24]

The links between the immune system, which controls the body's defenses against infections, and the central nervous system have been superbly reviewed in a recent book by Paul Martin. Martin describes a definite two-way street whereby changes in immune system function can be linked to states of mind such as depression or stress, via abnormal blood levels of chemicals such as noradrenaline and the stress hormone, cortisol.

Even more astonishing, and far less well-known, is the phenomenon of "immune conditioning," whereby the immune system can be conditioned in just the same way as Pavlov's famous dogs, who learned to salivate at the sound of a bell because the sound had previously been associated with food. In a similar way, a hay fever reaction can be triggered, for example, by simply looking at a photo of a field of midsummer hay. Moreover, in a less anecdotal, more rigorous approach, experiments have been performed in rats whereby a sweet taste came to elicit the same response as an immune suppressant drug, even when administered on its own. Rats ended up with immune systems that were suppressed, not by the drug, but by the mere association of the effects of the drug with the sweet taste. The sweet taste alone had the same effect as the drug and thus finally killed the rats.[25]

It may be easy to accept the idea that a stressful or depressing situation, or one of particular association—the meaning of an otherwise neutral hay field, for example, or a sweet taste—will trigger chemicals that have a simultaneous effect on both the brain and the immune system. In turn, chemicals will be released from each of these systems to affect the other. But we are left with the problem of how this two-way traffic is orchestrated. We speak loudly of "being depressed," for example, or of "stress." Many physiology textbooks will often claim that the brain signals this or that to the rest of the body. In more everyday conversation, we refer to a "state of mind" that might well influence the short- and long-term status of our health and well-being. But this state of mind is never really defined any further. It would be unlikely that anarchy reigns and that local chemical reactions in different circuits unfold with disregard for the status of the organism as a whole because then the body would be receiving mixed messages. And this is where consciousness comes not as a luxury, an "epiphenomenon," but as a physiological necessity.

If even the most rudimentary consciousness—according to my idea, a pure emotion—is associated with fast interactions with the outside world, then all the reactions in all the organs of the entire body must behave in a cohesive fashion and a coordinated manner to be primed for flight or fight, for example. By now I hope you are convinced that there is no little man in the brain who can appreciate the assembly size of neurons. As far as the brain-in-that-head-is concerned, the end result of processing inputs will be a transient neuronal assembly of a certain size. But certainly some sort of readout is nonetheless now needed from the brain to the rest of the body, and vice versa. How does the brain "tell" the multiple organs, as well as the immune system below the neck, of the prevailing state of mind, the degree of consciousness?

Although the spinal cord is essential as a conduit for signals concerned with movement and incoming sensations, it is not essential, as we saw in the tragic case of Christopher Reeve, for feelings. Whereas movements and senses coordinate the individual with the outside world, feelings are more of an internal, private affair, no more and no less than a subjective state — consciousness. And for consciousness, movements and sensations are not essential. Hence the brain and body must have a form of communication that is more related to feelings and not dependent upon the fast zaps of simple electrical signals buzzing up and down the spinal cord. Enter hormones.[26]

The sight of a cake, already associated with the behavior of eating, will elicit pleasure if one is hungry and nausea if one is already sated. Following a broadly similar line of thought, I remember visiting my mother in the hospital after the birth of my brother. To my astonishment, she burst into uncontrollable sobs, and I was quickly hurried away. No one explained postpartum depression to me. Even if a woman has not had a baby, many would recognize only too well that feeling of frustration at realizing that a short-tempered reaction that seemed so justified in the last day or so could in retrospect be written off as premenstrual tension. How cheated one can feel that the emotion, usually of irritation, was not after all "genuine" but merely the enslaving of one's otherwise rational mind with a marinade of hormones. So a further factor, the hormonal status of the brain, also comes into play.

The coordination of hormones governing the basic drives of hunger, thirst, temperature, sex, and sleep takes place in two key brain areas. First, the hypothalamus, situated within the cluster of brain cells that by now should be familiar as the amine fountains modulating the activity of the higher reaches of brain. Second, the final hormone Grand Central Station, the *pituitary gland,* a conspicuous stalk protruding out of the bottom of the brain.[27] The hypothalamus communicates with the pituitary gland swiftly and specifically, by electrical impulses, as though it were the same as any other brain region, but also much more slowly and long-term by using chemicals known as *pro-hormones,* which are released into the bloodstream. However, it is the pituitary gland that is the real bridge linking the brain and bodily needs.

Unlike the rest of the brain, the pituitary gland is not sealed off by the "blood-brain barrier,"[28] which normally ensures a segregation between many large, water-soluble molecules that are released between brain cells or within the body outside of the brain. Hence whereas we saw early on that pleasure, and more generally emotion, cannot be associated exclusively with drive reduction, drives will indisputably play an important part. Hormones influence emotions—somehow making us more emotional directly as, for example, with premenstrual tension. In such scenarios it is easy to envisage that certain hormones could modify the readiness of neurons to be recruited into an assembly by an action within the brain on the local circuit synapses.

Alternatively, it is possible that hormones could transiently strengthen or weaken the recruiting signals from a preexisting constellation, in accordance with the appropriate stage in the cycle of hunger/thirst, diurnal, or menstrual rhythms. In this way hormones would modify indirectly our consciousness by skewing and tilting the more robust associations or by making the target neurons more or less receptive to being included in a large-scale assembly. A further mechanism might be for hormones to modulate the release of the amine fountains, which as we have seen in turn modulate the readiness of cells to communicate and which can vary already with biorhythms.

These same hormones are also intimately connected with the status of the body as a whole, for example, with glucose levels in the blood, the degree of salt in the fluid between body cells, or the levels of epinephrine released into the bloodstream from the adrenal gland during flight or fight. Yet norepinephrine or cortisol will be released only in a *perceived* state of stress or depression. Hence these chemicals are not autonomous, autocratic, molecular triggers. Consciousness is necessary as a means for synchronizing the appropriate readout from brain to body.

Similarly, the hormones and transmitter agents traveling back and forth between the brain and the immune system must have an effect somewhere in the brain to mediate the apparent state of mind. I have tried to convince you that state of mind, the quality of a moment of consciousness, is directly related to the size and turnover rate of neuron assemblies. The next step is to discover how these measures within the brain could be communicated to the rest of the body. In both directions on this two-way street, there needs to be some kind of messenger between the brain and its many operatives throughout the rest of the body.

This go-between messenger would have to be some sort of chemical. After all, how else might the readout of the enhanced activity of ten million neurons be readily distinguished from another set? Surely not in the ubiquitous and uniform electrical coinage of the brain. In any event, were this synchrony of electrical discharge somehow the readout for consciousness, it would simply be informing the body that consciousness was occurring, not even whether the prevailing state was as crude a state as blanket excitement. And as for accounting for the unique mixture of internal mind and external sensuality that, according to my idea, gives a particular moment of consciousness—electrical signals are just not versatile and varied enough in themselves to yield any further information. Moreover, if chemicals are the critical intermediaries that could be transported in the bloodstream, it would account for why those with damage to the spinal cord can still feel emotions.

As it happens, there is a large class of chemicals that exceeds all the other bioactive transmitters in terms of variety. These chemicals have a classic signaling action, yet they can also function as hormones, thereby accessing the endocrine and immune systems as well as the nervous system. The *peptides*[29] thus link all the major control systems of the body. Peptides are larger molecules than the better-known transmitters such as acetylcholine and the amines. As far as brain function goes, they have long proved a puzzle in that they are stored with classic transmitters in the same neurons, yet they have a subtly different role. Like the classic transmitter with which they are stored, they are released in response to the generation of an electrical signal, but only when that electrical signal becomes particularly vigorous.[30]

A further departure from convention is that, unlike the more traditional transmitters, peptides are not always available at the ends of nerve processes (axons) for immediate, classic signaling. Rather, they are made in a distant part of the cell and laboriously transported down to the synapse, ready for use.[31] Therefore, their use is limited. Once peptides are released, the neuron has insufficient reserves to be released until fresh supplies arrive. Hence the use of peptides is somewhat of a luxury, and one that cannot be repeated too often. In view of the fact that these chemicals are released only when the cell is particularly active, it would seem that peptides would optimally be used under the special conditions when the neurons are more active than usual, participating in atypically large enough assemblies for consciousness to prevail. The larger the assembly, the more of a particular type of peptide will be released. The greater the turnover of assemblies, the more variants of small amounts of peptides there will be at any one moment. Peptides, therefore, are the perfect intermediaries between net brain states (net neuron assembly size and turnover rate), the endocrine and immune systems, and the vital organs.

Studies to date attempting to identify neuron correlates of consciousness—conventional recordings from isolated cells in animals,[32] EEG, or imaging electrical fields[33]—have all neglected the fact that the critical issue is how many cells are so firing, and more importantly that different combinations of neurons would release different combinations of peptides. In my view, the electrical activity itself is relatively meaningless (a Thing), a mere means to an end (a Readout), the release of peptide. A neuron will release particular peptides only when it is firing very vigorously, and if the neuron fires vigorously primarily when it is in an assembly, then there is a clear readout for the rest of the body. This readout will signal not only the size of the prevailing assembly, but will also convey information regarding its content, which would be reflected in levels of different combinations of different peptides, released from different brain sites determined in turn by a varying rate of turnover.

A likely scenario is that the peptides can both influence and reflect the size of a momentary assembly, and with it the degree and thus the type of consciousness. In line with this idea, Mark Kramer and his colleagues have recently reported that agents blocking the action of a certain peptide, Substance P, actually have a novel, antidepressant action.[34] Few people have yet recognized how important the peptides may be in emotion. The one conspicuous exception is Candace Pert, who discovered the first receptor for a peptide, the naturally occurring opiate, enkephalin.[35] Over the last two decades, Pert has gone on to show just how pervasive and flexible the peptides can be in orchestrating one's emotions, and indeed health. However, in her recent book she actually claims that peptides are the "molecules of emotion," and even goes on to claim that there may well be a different peptide for each emotion. Of course, this type of deduction leads straight into the same problems we reviewed in Chapters 1 and 2 of reducing a complex phenomenon, a feeling, to a gene or a brain region or a classic transmitter—or in this case, a peptide. In my view the peptides are vitally important, but merely the mechanical intermediaries that operate within the kinds of shifting contexts within the brain that I have tried to sketch in the previous chapters.

The narrative of the current model ends, then, with peptides vying between the brain and the rest of the body, such that a coordination is achieved not only as regards the state of mind of the brain, but of the brain within the body. This internal iteration and orchestration would be impossible without consciousness—if indeed consciousness is an inevitable corollary in the brain of mercurial unique assemblies of neurons temporarily growing so large that they preclude the coexistence of any other.

But I am *not* going to end by simply saying, "and then consciousness happens." Even if you buy into my model, you must recognize that it is still only one of correlation, not cause. The problem with turning water into wine, of explaining how a sequence of objective, neural events translates into a subjective sensation, is frustrating because we have no idea at all as to the nature of the explanation. What would we do or know that we cannot do or know now? If brain, mind, and body are all needed for consciousness, we will never be able to download an isolated moment of simple feeling, say a headache, on to a chip or a computer screen.

If subjective sensation cannot travel outside of the body, the only alternative would be to gain privileged access to the body in question, a scenario that spirals into ever-increasing absurdity because you, the experimenter, would not be able to jettison your own body and brain, or expect your subject to vacate his or her fleshy tenancy.[36] However powerful and aesthetic the windows onto the brain afforded by imaging techniques, we, as scientists, would always be on the outside looking in. It is hard to see how we could have privileged, first-person access to someone else's subjective state, even if we could trace each precise step in the process of generating not only consciousness but a certain type of consciousness, say, pleasure rather than fear. The nearest we may come to sharing someone else's consciousness is via poetry, paintings, and music. An alternative strategy would be to reduce your consciousness to such a degree that only the most generic, nonpersonalized stance dominates, one of abstracted sounds and lights at a rave—since the clear conclusion from this excursion has been that, counterintuitively, the essence of pleasure, and indeed other basic emotions such as fear, is denial of the Self.

Most likely, in the future, I predict that we will be able to correlate the net size of transient neuronal assembly with reported degrees of subjective consciousness. If this idea is taken to its next step, the rather interesting prospect would be that *the degree of emotion at any one time is inversely proportional to the extent of the prevailing neuronal assembly*.

In this way we can proceed scientifically toward an understanding of consciousness rooted in the real brain, but we will only ever "merely" be able to unfold a sequence of objective events with increasing precision. We would be able to manipulate and predict and sympathize with states of consciousness in others, but if "understanding" is being able to manipulate the physical world so that we can actually feel *directly* exactly as someone else feels, then we are against a wall of seeming impossibility.

For some, it might be enough to be so precise in our description of physical brain events that consciousness can be so tractable and malleable that it no longer is secret. Others might shrug and say that theories of consciousness are irrelevant, and if the main thesis of this book is true, all we need is to do is to manipulate our brain chemistry or our immediate environment to cultivate very small assemblies, and hence induce more emotion or cultivate large assemblies to bring about the reverse. How the translation to subjective pleasure occurs might be irrelevant, if after all the main aim in life is to deny the self in order to be part of a collective, mindless consciousness—living for the moment.

We all know, of course, how important it is to let one's hair down, loosen up—literally, it seems—and let oneself go. On the other hand, we are curious animals. It is in our human capacity to exploit our highly plastic brains to work out and work up an individuality, a way of interpreting the world, and to impose back on the world, however slight, our individual retaliatory mark, however slight. This is nothing less than being oneself.

In summary, the key concepts arising from this book are as follows: (1) emotion is the most basic form of consciousness; (2) minds develop as brains do—both as a species and as an individual starts to escape genetic programming in favor of personal experience–based learning;

(3) the more you have of (1) at any moment, then the less you have of (2), and vice versa.

The more the mind predominates over raw emotion, the deeper the consciousness. When I mention this idea, people sometimes think I mean that consciousness is literally deeper: for example, that one would perceive deeper colors, say, a red instead of a pink. That is not what I mean at all. In fact, as I hope I have persuaded you, consciousness characterized by the raw senses is indicative of a consciousness at its most minimal. Instead, I am using *deep* as a metaphor, albeit a very well-worn one. A deeper consciousness is one where the world around you is not so much very bright or very noisy—quite the contrary, it is, instead, a world laden with personal meaning.

In brain terms, the net measure of this depth of consciousness at any one moment will be the extent of the dominant working assembly of neurons at that time. In turn, this single net value is the result of diverse factors that can be expressed bilingually both in brain terms and in terms of everyday life, as shown in Table 8.1.

These multiple factors, which can be expressed bilingually, could in the future be independently manipulated to yield in each case pre-

TABLE 8.1 Net Assembly Size as a Neural Correlate of Consciousness: Different Factors Can Be Manipulated to Yield Predictions of Different Types of Consciousness

Neuronal Connectivity	+ Epicenter	+ Arousal	+Assembly Turnover	→ Assembly Size (Physiology)
Sparse	Strong	High	High	Small—*Childhood*
Extensive	Weak	Low	Low	Small—*Dreaming*
Extensive	Strong	High	High	Small—*Accidents*
Extensive	Strong	High	Low	Large—*Pain*
Extensive	Strong	High	High	Small—*Bungee jumping*
Extensive	Strong	High	High	Small—*Schizophrenia*
Extensive	Strong	Medium	Low	Large—*Abstract thought*
Extensive	Strong	Low	Very Low	Large—*Depression*
Sparse	Strong	Medium	Low	Small—*Alzheimer's disease*
Age/ Species/ Mind	*+ Stimulus/ + Strength/ Significance*	*+ Thrill/ Biorhythms*	*+ Distraction*	→ State (Phenomenology)

dictable changes in assembly size, and hence in depth of consciousness. Children could be compared with adults; successive, bright, abstract stimuli could be compared with drabber, "meaningful" objects or sounds, objects with highly personalized meaning or sentimental value could be compared in an individual with objects that literally mean nothing. Moreover, by giving drugs with known effects on the availability of specific transmitter systems in the brain and consistent effects on subjective mood, we could start to build an ever tighter correlation between what is happening in the brain during certain types of feelings.

At the moment, imaging techniques would be too slow to capture the recruitment of, say, ten million cells or more in less than a quarter of a second, and their equally rapid disbanding. In the future, however, I am confident that imaging techniques will reach a level of sophistication that will permit noninvasive visualization of human brain activity on a time scale of less than a second, and a space scale sufficient to appreciate the fast recruitment and disbanding of many millions of cells, all triggered by relatively modest numbers of neurons operating in quasi-permanent networks. This single, final value of degree of highly transient, dominant assembly by means of brain imaging will, I predict, be backed up with two further measures of degree of consciousness that are completely different, one biochemical and one behavioral.

I have tried to show that consciousness should be viewed as a means for coordination and communication between brain and body, more specifically as a way of unifying the nervous, endocrine, and immune systems. An obvious prediction is that specific types and quantities of hormones in the bloodstream will correlate, in the future, with different sizes of neuronal assemblies, shown by futuristic imaging techniques. In particular, high emotional states will be characterized by a greater combination of different peptides, each in smaller amounts than visibly larger assemblies—where a narrower range of the peptides will be detectable at higher levels for more sustained periods.

In turn, I have suggested that abnormally large assemblies are associated with depression. Because depression is often associated with a deterioration in general health, I would predict that an abnormally large neuron assembly displayed on the imaging screen will be accompanied not only by a sustained plasma level of a narrower range of peptides but that it would also correlate with changes in plasma markers of suppressed immune system function. Perhaps in the distant future we might even be able to track the steps involved in the mysterious process of suppression of pain in acupuncture or in the beneficial effects of an inert placebo drug. Because the peptides act as a two-way street between the body and the brain, it would be fascinating to see how the changes in immune system markers, indicative of a painful disease, might influence plasma peptide levels—and how, in turn, the frequency of larger neuron assemblies than normal in the brain start to grow, and so on.

In addition to these imaging and biochemical indices, there is a third marker. Another type of test could exploit what appears to be a basic feature of the small assembly profile that characterizes high emotional states, that time seems to stand still. A common feature of the mind-set of the junkie, the nightmare, the accident, the child, and the schizophrenic is being trapped in the present. Such an exclusive focus on the here and now would exclude comparison with a past or future, thus there would be no sense of time passing, or at least the passage of time would be markedly slowed down. A sense of time passing is a subjective condition, but one that can be measured objectively. Just as we saw that drugs can offer a bridge between brain events and feelings, so too might simple estimates of how much time has elapsed between one occasion and another. Hence, a further indication of depth of consciousness would be another quantifiable value—subjective estimates of time passing. These estimates could then be compared with the biochemical measurement of peptides and the degree of assembly size, captured in a subsecond of futuristic brain imaging.

Perhaps the type of scheme outlined in this book, testable as it will be once imaging techniques improve and funding bodies become less cautious, will get us far enough along to refute some of the predictions and ideas that the model has prompted—as well as even inspire some radically different alternative. We will be able to see how the different factors that could contribute to assembly size can be manipulated independently to produce certain types of consciousness and, indeed, how those factors vary in conditions such as schizophrenia and depression. We could also go on to examine how this mercurial kaleidoscope in the brain correlates with immune system function and with communication that occurs between the brain and the rest of the body via peptides, and even how it relates to simple tests like estimation of time.

In the end it actually does not matter whether a scheme such as the one I have sketched here is true. It is more important that it should generate falsifiable hypotheses. The contribution that science should surely bring to this erstwhile province of philosophers is some means of *testing* whether ideas suggested are in fact, the case. I am delighted to be able to put forward a potentially testable scheme—no more.

Nonetheless, the model as it stands could be criticized by neuro-scientists because I have not specified the exact brain regions that might be involved in the generation of the final, ever-changing neuron assemblies. Yet surely as soon as you start to delineate a certain area as special, you are on the slippery path to the rigid "brain region for" fallacy that we first faced in Chapter 1. A much more likely scenario is that any one brain region will participate in different ways in the expression of an assembly of a certain size, but that that assembly will not respect traditional anatomical boundaries. Although the association cortex, at least in higher mammals, is the area with the most scope for flexible configurations, there is no reason why a brain region purported to be more primitive should not show a shifting combination of assembly size. In fact, some of the earliest work on transient working assemblies of neurons, as we have seen, was demonstrated in the frog brain. Similarly, even in sophisticated brains, more basic areas below the cortex would be expected to show activity. They would, after all, be making a critical and active contribution to the size of a transient assembly even in the most basic zones, as different fountains of different modulating amines accessed areas like the hippocampus, as well as the outer layer of cortex itself.

Another objection might be that imaging experiments can be performed already, and indeed reveal multiple brain areas lighting up during different tasks in conscious subjects. But interpretation of such data is difficult if there is no preexisting, testable hypothesis that such results will either validate or falsify. If in the future a more precise imaging technique shows different areas and extents of brain activity on different occasions, any information gained concerning the nature of consciousness will not be as insightful as it would be when compared against the predictions of a preexisting theory, such as those that I have gestured at here.

Finally, we come to the basic idea that emotions are an abrogation of the Self. The more I wrote of this book, the more I found it impossible to distinguish *mind* from the concept of *Self.* After all, if *mind* is the personalization of the brain, then what more, or what less, could *Self* actually be? I'll stick my neck out and say that as far as I'm concerned, the two terms might as well be synonymous. For virtually all animals save humans, and for infant humans, the underdeveloped mind would entail a lack of self-consciousness. Consciousness will blossom into self-consciousness only when enough associations are in place to be able to provide a common referent to myriad experiences, like a hub on a wheel. The idea is that the young child is swamped with emotions that are gradually diluted by a growing retaliatory sense of Self and, most important, with a concomitant sense of inner control. Emotions involve relinquishing that control. I think this increasingly interactive and ever-changing dialogue between Self and outside world is important because it highlights the basic issues of how we see ourselves and, indeed, how we chose to live our lives.

We are not fixed entities, certainly not as we grow up, but neither once we live as adults from one year to the next, and even from one day to the next. Even within a day, within an hour, we are different. All the time, experiences leave their mark and in turn determine how we interpret new experiences. As the mind evolves, as we "understand" everything more deeply, we have increasing control over what happens to us: we are self-conscious. But this self-consciousness itself is not fixed. According to the idea developed here, it will ebb and flow in inverse relation to emotions, from one moment to the next. Most important of all, then, we cannot expect, or even want, to be in a state of pleasure all the time. Such is the paradox of adult human existence—the private life of the brain.

Appendix

THE REALITY
OF A NEURAL CORRELATE
OF CONSCIOUSNESS

If highly transient neuron assemblies are indeed a key feature of the brain operations that cause consciousness, a critical issue—for scientists especially—is how they might actually be formed. The idea developed in this book is that because we have only one consciousness at any one moment,[1] then the dominant assembly for that moment would have to be so massive that it precluded the formation of any other sufficiently large rivals—the recruitment of, say, 10^7 neurons in less than 250 milliseconds. However, even this large number is simply the response of a group of neurons to a flash of light and does not necessarily entail consciousness. The requisite size of an appropriate neuron assembly might be far greater still.

Classical synaptic transmission is perfectly adequate for coordinating the firing of a million or so neurons in a fraction of a second. It is important to remember that neuron firing of an action potential is not linear, with one domino causing the fall of its neighbor one at a time. Yet if the firing of one neuron causes N neighbors to fire, then after S steps, N^S neurons will fire in a huge three-dimensional domino effect.

Even if N were as small as 10, only 6 steps would be needed to assemble a million neurons.

But suppose that synaptic transmission is not, after all, doing the job. According to Amiram Grinvald's calculations, the spread of activity from the epicenter activated by the flash of light is some 100 to 250 cm/s. This is much faster than a wave of seizure in epilepsy (1 cm/s), yet it is actually much slower than classic synaptic signaling, where an action potential can be propagated down the neuron axon at speeds of up to 10,000 cm/s. Whereas classic synaptic signaling is useful in local circuits of neurons, perhaps a different process is operational in the more gradual recruitment of very large, global assemblies that will in turn be necessary for consciousness.

A synapse is a highly specialized point of contact, as different from a mere gap as riverboat stations are from featureless banks facing each other across the water.[2] A simpler but less specialized system involves the mere fusion of one dendrite of one cell with that of another, so that electrical current spreads passively, without the need for a participating chemical. These points of fusion are called "gap junctions." Perhaps spread of activation through the agency of gap junctions is what distinguishes the formation of a very large neuronal assembly. In support of this idea, John Jefferys and his colleagues have confirmed that the much-studied oscillations of some 40 Hz are generated as a result of normal synaptic transmission. What is particularly intriguing, however, is that Jefferys has also shown that it is possible for neurons to work collectively at a much faster rate, that there are in addition much faster oscillations of some 200 Hz. This higher-frequency orchestration is mediated not by synapses but by gap junctions.[3]

Perhaps the very extensive type of neuron assembly that mediates consciousness will be composed of synchronous neuron firing at a frequency far higher than the much-studied 40 Hz. However, because this type of activity depends on coherent gap junction signaling—which is less efficient than classic synaptic transmission—the time taken for large numbers of neurons to be recruited into a synchronous, large-scale assembly will be slower—the good half a second observed. These features—relatively slow-to-form but yet high-frequency coherence once established—might be advantageous in first stabilizing a moment of consciousness, and second in optimizing conditions, a very high-frequency firing, for the signature peptide profile to then be released.

Another alternative to the traditional picture involves a very different mechanism that might operate at a much more minuscule level, beyond the cell itself, and beyond the classic physics of Newton,[4] which is successful for describing events in the everyday world, and with it, in principle at least, traditional neuroscience. Just such a vision has captured the imagination of the mathematician Roger Penrose and the anesthetist Stuart Hameroff.[5] Their version of events does not rely on the classic generation of action potentials, but rather on a faster and far more speculative process that is based on quantum theory.[6]

Penrose and Hameroff's speculations about the nature of consciousness begin by noting that in one interpretation of quantum theory, the very act of observation causes a system to be in one type of unpredictable state, a phenomenon they call "subjective reduction."[7] It is subjective because it requires an observer. In the brain, however, there is no outside observer, and hence the appropriate conditions might prevail under which quantum events are not downgraded subjectively, but rather occur spontaneously, without anyone watching. This hypothetical phenomenon has been called "objective reduction" (OR) by Penrose and Hameroff, who believe that the concept of OR could underpin a new type of physics. Because OR would not obey the computable and established rules of either quantum physics or Newtonian physics, they consider that this new physics would be most appropriate for generating consciousness—another incomputable phenomenon.

Already there is a problem with the syllogism that consciousness is not computable, that OR is not computable, and therefore that OR underlies consciousness. We may not operate in a computational manner, as we saw in Chapter 2, and our intuition and common sense do not lend themselves to the plodding algorithms of Turing machines,[8] but that does not mean to say that the underlying brain processes are not individually working in a fashion that, at the mechanistic cellular level, could be modeled on a computer. In any case, just because two processes, consciousness and OR, share a common feature of incomputability, it does not mean to say that the one is caused by—or has any relation to—the other.

Quantum theory offers the appropriate time and space scales for assembling millions of neurons in a fraction of a second into a working assembly. This procedure is known as "quantum coherence." However, we have seen that classical processes can proceed just as well. Yet here, too, in quantum coherence, there might be a good candidate for a neural correlate of consciousness.

Penrose and Hameroff have speculated that the medium of such orchestration could be the tiny, fluid-filled microtubules, which are present in virtually every cell in the body.[9] Coherence would occur, they suggest, by exciting water molecules buried in a protein, *tubulin,*[10] the building block of microtubules. Tubulin can undergo conformational changes in molecular structure. The idea runs that these changes could support wavelike signals propagated in accord with quantum theory.[11] Now comes Penrose and Hameroff's speculation: Once the number of neurons is sufficiently large, then in accord with the as yet nonexistent New Physics, there would be a spontaneous downgrading of the wave, an OR across large numbers of cells. This OR, a sudden commitment to one type of physical state, would somehow correspond to a moment of consciousness in the macro brain.

There are many objections to such a scheme. The most compelling is that there is not one shred of experimental evidence in favor of the inadequacy of more classical neuronal signaling process, be it synaptic transmission or gap junctions, to account for consciousness. More technically, one ought at least to consider the idea that the brain is too hot for it to take place.[12]

Still, if one wants to speculate, one can assert that the brain is a special place. Indeed, the physicist Herbert Frolich has proposed a scheme[13] whereby quantum events could occur across large groups of neurons and last for a more appropriate interval. Unlike quantum events in the outside world, which can achieve coherence only when they are not disturbed by excessive thermal motion, the coherence in the brain might be brought about and sustained by energy provided by chemical reactions occurring within the cell. This, too, is without experimental support and is based on a simplistic vision of the molecular constitution of the brain.

Frolich estimated that the tubulin molecules, and indeed other proteins in the microtubules, could be excited in a coherent fashion for about $10-12$ to $10-9$ s. Over the 500 ms that Libet's studies suggest consciousness dawns, it has been estimated that 10^9 tubulin molecules would be needed, as many as would be found in 100 to 10,000 neurons. But the value of 100 to 10,000 neurons for achieving quantum coherence would still be very few neurons. Remember that even for a flash of light, an estimated 10^7 neurons lit up in the cat brain. In any case, there is as yet no evidence to support Frolich's idea that coherence could be actually be caused, rather than disrupted, by biochemical energy.

From a totally different angle, critics of the scheme have also pointed to the ubiquity of microtubules, not only in neurons, but as present in all kinds of cells. Some further constraining factors are therefore needed to make the scheme realistic. As it stands, the existence of microtubules and the idea of quantum coherence as a basis for consciousness has not so much been shown to be wrong, but on its own, it has simply been unhelpful for biologists—it is too abstract to be usefully applied to the tangible brain, and it is without experimental motivation.

For Penrose and Hameroff's idea to qualify as a successful correlate of consciousness, three basic issues still need to be resolved before biologists can make use of it. First, we need a further feature to the scheme whereby the number of requisite coherent neurons can be increased from the tens and hundred of thousands, to tens and hundreds of millions. Second, a means of catering for the role of chemically diverse transmitter systems is needed. Third, we need a reason for discriminating between certain microtubules, such that only those in certain neurons, and not in just any old cell, are appropriate to mediate consciousness at certain times.

One possible way of overcoming these problems lies in a scheme advanced by the neuroscientist Nancy Woolf.[14] Woolf's model starts off conventionally enough. Neurons in a certain brain region, the *basal forebrain*,[15] are active and release the transmitter acetylcholine, in the accepted fashion, on to neurons in the cortex. Acetylcholine will, again in the traditional way, act via its normal molecular targets, its receptors, on discrete modules of neurons, stretching some 1 to 2 mm^2 in the cortex. But now some of the consequences might be unexpected: in addition to its action within local circuitry, Woolf has suggested a chemical-selective and site-selective means whereby the quantum coherence based on microtubule operations could be set in train.

Before the tubulin in microtubules can reconfigure so that the appropriate signals—quantum waves—can be generated, a special protein called *microtubule associated protein* (MAP2) must be put out of action. Think of MAP2 as a little like glue. It normally keeps the microtubules configured in a certain way, in a local, independent pattern, instead of in the rows of uniform, parallel alignment that are necessary for the requisite flash flood of quantum coherence. Unlike microtubules themselves, MAP2 is not a generic feature of every single neuron in the brain. Rather, in the cortex for example, it is located in only about 15 percent of neurons.[16] There is a further constraint: MAP2 will be activated only under certain conditions,[17] such as when visual stimulation occurs or when specific transmitters activate specific receptors[18]—just the type of macro scenario that neuroscientists need to describe consciousness in terms of different contributions from different brain regions, and different drug-sensitive, selective actions of different brain transmitters.

When acetylcholine, as a typical transmitter, enters into a molecular handshake with its receptor, the result will be to block MAP2 from performing its normal function of freeze-framing microtubules into a small, local configuration.[19] Under the initial direction of acetylcholine, microtubules will be unlocked from the specific, local patterns in which they had been stuck in suspended animation by MAP2. Thus temporarily liberated, the tubules will enter into a process of coherence with the tubules in other neurons. This scenario would circumvent the problem of how to distinguish the key player microtubules needed for consciousness from the microtubules present in all cells, as well as overcoming the problem of needing to incorporate the participation of the specific action of a specific transmitter.

A final problem that we could now overcome is that of accounting for the still larger number of neurons needed—some tens of millions—than those tens of thousands originally estimated using quantum theory. The number of neurons that could be included in an assembly by the enabling action of acetylcholine would be in excess of the number of sites of release of the transmitter—in one module of cortex alone, estimated at around 10^6.[20] This value is now within one order of magnitude of the number of neurons that we have seen can be recruited in response to a flash of light.

Consciousness would occur when a large enough neuronal assembly is made possible. In turn, a large assembly could be possible only when the microtubules are in a period of transition, a little like melted wax on its way to being remolded into another shape. As with melting wax, because such a stage of transition is by definition transient, any permutation of neurons at any one time will only transiently mediate consciousness. Once the effects of the acetylcholine wear off and the MAP2 can return to its normal bonding action, the microtubules will have reconfigured. There will be a change in the brain, and the same moment of consciousness will never return because your brain will never be exactly the same again. The moment of consciousness will have presaged a very large-scale change in one's brain, above and beyond the local micro-circuits that are pushed and prodded by daily experience into progressively shifting alliances that, I have suggested, constitute the subconscious mind.

In my view, quantum theory on its own does not hold the answer to consciousness. However, models such as the one we have just explored, based on Woolf's imaginative exploitation of the known actions of MAP2 and acetylcholine, are at the very least useful in that they cross the traditional disciplines of physics and neuroscience to show how a combination of phenomena, rules, and constraints from each can make a more robust and plausible model.

Note that this hybrid theory is once again dependent on good old-fashioned transmitter signaling. We cannot rule out the possibility that acetylcholine—as a prototype neurochemical—plays an important role in triggering other, nonclassical events as well as at the more macro level of brain function; for example, as a neuromodulator, putting cells on red alert. Physiologist Ole Paulsen and his colleagues have recently discovered that acetylcholine can induce synchrony in a large number of neurons in the hippocampus. All the electrical signals are generated in the same rhythm of oscillations.[21] However, no single cell joins in all the activity all the time, but overall there are sufficient cells to maintain a synchronous activity for very long periods of time. Acetylcholine in this instance has enabled a whole population of cells to become more important than the individual units, a kind of neuroscientific Marxism!

Whatever the eventual mechanisms of attaining a transient coherence in a very large assembly of neurons turn out to be, there is no shortage of candidates even at the moment. The future will no doubt reveal more, along with means for testing which ones really do play a part in formation of assemblies, and hence in the reality of a neural correlate of consciousness that is not just necessary but sufficient.

Notes

Chapter 1: The Idea

1. In 1952, Paul MacLean first coined the term *limbic system* for the brain structures lying between the most primitive core areas (brain stem) and the sensory relay regions (thalamus), and the overlying cortex. Accordingly, he suggested that the limbic system was functionally a middle level between reptilian urges and sophisticated reasoning (see Harrington, 1991). This idea of a tripartite compartmentalization of the brain was popular until the 1970s, and it is still used by some when explaining brain processes. Nonetheless, more recent findings on anatomical and functional discrepancies are now rendering MacLean's theory increasingly unattractive (see LeDoux, 1998).

2. See Gay (1995).

3. MacLean's theory, published as "The Triune Brain" in 1970, sowed the seeds for a one-to-one extrapolation between brain function and complex social behaviors. Once we accept that part of our brain is irrational and held in check by the rational part, the cortex, then it has been all too easy to extrapolate to a neuroscience version of original sin, a fatal flaw in the human mind. The concept of a triune brain has been used as a simplified explanation for social and political problems that in reality are generated by many complex factors beyond brain physiology.

4. See Gay (1995).

5. This syndrome was first described in papers published in 1937 and 1939 by a German psychologist, Heinrich Klüver, and an American neurosurgeon, Paul Bucy. As well as the inappropriate sexual behavior mentioned in the main text, monkeys that had undergone a lesion of the amygdala and overlying temporal cortex displayed an increased placidity, a tendency to place inappropriate objects in the mouth, an inability to recognize objects by visual appearance, and a hyperreactivity to visual stimuli. The full syndrome is rarely seen in humans, presumably because the requisite precision and extent of damage to respective brain tissue is reproduced less reliably in natural brain injuries than under experimental conditions. See several

mentions in Cytowic (1996). See also the entry in *The Blackwell Dictionary of Neuropsychology* (Beaumont, Kenealy, and Rogers, 1996).

6. The amygdala takes its name from the Latin for *almond*. It lies immediately under the part of the cortex related to smell, with which it has direct connections. In addition, other parts of the amygdala are connected to other parts of the limbic system, such as the cingulate cortex and hippocampus. Because it is rich in receptors for the opiate transmitters and because it also has connections with the endocrine and immune functions of the body as well as with autonomic (fight or flight) responses, it is not surprising that the amygdala has been long associated with emotions. More specifically, the signs of Klüver-Bucy syndrome suggest that the amygdala is involved in the linking of emotions to appropriate behaviors.

7. The cingulate cortex is, in evolutionary terms, part of the older region of the cortex, in the middle axis of the brain. In 1937, American anatomist James Papez incorporated it into a circuit that MacLean would later refer to as the limbic system. It links cortical regions involved with sensory processes with areas such as the hippocampus, which is involved in the laying down of memories.

8. The cortex is the outer layer of the brain. More specifically, the term *cerebral cortex* refers to the outer layer covering all of the brain apart from the cerebellum, which has its own cerebellar cortex. The cerebral cortex is between 1.5 and 4.5 mm thick and consists of six layers of different types of cells, organized into vertical modules, or "columns." The total surface area of the cortex is approximately 2,500 cm^2, accommodated in the confines of the human skull by foldings (*sulci*). It is divided into four regions: the frontal cortex, at the front of the brain; the temporal cortex, over the temples; the occipital cortex, at the base of the brain at the back; and the parietal cortex, at the back of the brain at the top. For a concise introduction to the cortex for the general reader, see Greenfield (1998); for a more technical account, see Douglas and Martin (1990); for a comprehensive review of the cortex, see the series edited by Jones and Peters (1991).

9. An alternative term for leukotomy, preferred by Americans, is *lobotomy*. The number of these operations performed worldwide until the late 1970s has been estimated at 100,000. For a general review of psychosurgery, see Valenstein (1986).

10. The three main systems in the brain concerned with movement are:

1. The basal ganglia, the collective term given to a group of diverse structures below the cortex that span virtually the entire length of the brain. Damage to key components of the basal ganglia will result in movement disorders such as Parkinson's disease and Huntington's chorea.
2. The cerebellum, the "autopilot" of the brain, is easily recognized as the distinct cauliflower-shaped structure at the very back of the brain, just above where the spinal cord merges with the core of the brain, the brain

stem. Damage to the cerebellum results in poor coordination and clumsiness, or *ataxia*.

3. The motor cortex is the region of cortex that sits over the brain like a hairband. It sends the final signals down the spinal cord to cause contraction of muscles. Just in front of the primary motor cortex are supplementary regions that play a more sophisticated part in readiness before the movement itself. Although these three systems can be described separately, it is important to remember that they do not function in isolation but are highly interactive with one another. A crude generalization would be that the cerebellum and basal ganglia free us up from conscious control of each movement: the cerebellum is involved in movements that are under constant sensory control and feedback, whereas the basal ganglia are linked to internally generated movements that occur without any particular external sensory cue or trigger.

In both cases, these complementary systems function in the planning of movements that are then executed under the control of the primary motor cortex. For a more detailed description of movement systems, see Greenfield (1998).

See Squire (1998) for an overview of areas used in memory and Posner and Raichle (1994) for a brain scan showing multiple regions involved in language.

11. The action potential is the ubiquitous and final expression of the degree of activity of a neuron. The more action potentials a neuron generates in a given time, the more "excited" that neuron is said to be. An action potential occurs when microscopic channels in the wall of the cell open and allow sodium ions to enter. Because sodium carries a positive charge, the inside of the cell becomes more positive and thus the potential difference, the voltage, decreases (i.e., it becomes depolarized). This depolarization causes another set of channels to open. These second channels are permeable to another ion, potassium. Normally, potassium is inside the neuron: because it is also positively charged, its exit from the cell will leave the interior negative again (i.e., hyperpolarized). For more details for the general reader, see Greenfield (1998); for a more technical and rigorous description, see Levitan and Kaczmarek (1996).

12. Once it is generated in the main body of the neuron, the action potential is conducted on to the next cell via an *axon*. The diameter of the axon, as well as its degree of insulation with a fatty sheath of myelin, will determine how fast the signal will reach the end of the axon. The bigger the diameter and the greater the insulation, the faster the action potential will travel. For more details, see Greenfield (1998); for a more technical and rigorous description, see Levitan and Kaczmarek (1996).

13. Although an action potential can be rapidly conducted to the extremity of a neuron, it cannot cross the gap (i.e., the synapse) that separates one neuron from

another. Nonetheless, the change in voltage at the end of the axon causes the chemical transmitter to be released. The transmitter can readily flood across the synapse to act on the target neuron. There are many different types of transmitter in the brain, and they are classified into groups according to chemical structure. They can range in size from the large peptides of some twenty or so amino acids to the newly discovered bioactive gasses, which consist of merely two atoms. For a simple description, see Greenfield (1998); for a more detailed and technically rigorous description, see Cooper, Bloom, and Roth (1991).

14. *Receptor* is the general term used to describe the molecular complex expressed on the outside of the target cell, into which the transmitter will lock in order to instigate a change in the electrical signaling of the receiving neuron. Each transmitter has its own specific receptor that usually exists as further different subtypes. The subtypes can be differentiated according to the amount of transmitter that is needed to activate them and their sensitivity to different drugs. When a transmitter, or drug, locks on to a receptor, the molecular handshake causes channels to open or close in the wall of the neuron. Because different channels will let certain ions into or out of the cell and because some ions, such as sodium, carry a positive charge, whereas others, such as chloride, carry a negative charge, each receptor will be linked to a different type of change in the voltage of the neuron. Some receptors can cause such a change directly, whereas others work by triggering a cascade of chemical reactions inside the cell that finally leads to a channel opening or closing. For a more detailed description, see Greenfield (1998); for a more technical and rigorous exposition, see Levitan and Kaczmarek (1996) and Nicholls et al. (1992).

15. Although synaptic transmission has long been established as a building block of brain operations, more recent evidence is challenging the idea that it is the only process by which neurons communicate with each other. See Kaczmarek and Levitan (1987), Greenfield (1998), and Agnati et al. (1995).

16. The neuronal wall consists of a phospholipid bilayer, two layers of molecules about 75 nm thick, with a charge on each of the outer surface and an oily fluid phase in the middle. It is this oily fluid phase that prevents the passage of sugars or any substance carrying a charge that would thus be soluble in water. However, any agent that is soluble in fat will have no problem gaining access to neurons. Hence substances such as anesthetics, which must gain ready access to the brain, are highly hydrophobic (water-aversive). On the other hand, ionic substances like sodium chloride, which are present in water as ions, will never penetrate the wall. However, under certain conditions and with the exception of the intracellular, negatively charged proteins, the sodium, potassium, calcium, and chlorine ions can, after all, cross through this barrier. Particular proteins in the neuronal membrane act as pores by which ions can pass into or out of the cell, protected from the lipid interface. These pores, or channels, are particularly useful because they can be selective for each of the three ions and because they are open only under certain conditions.

When the cell is at rest, the channels for sodium and calcium are mainly closed. However, the channels for potassium and chlorine tend to be open.

17. How does the particular distribution of ions on either side of the membrane come about? In all cases, the ions will flow one way or the other as a spontaneous process stemming from two forces: the tendency to equalize concentrations (a chemical, or "diffusional" force) and to be attracted to an opposite, negative charge inside the neuron (an electrical force). Because there are a finite number of ions, this movement will not continue indefinitely: there is a stage when the concentration and charge of each particular ion is balanced on either side of the membrane, and as a result, no net flux of ions occurs. There would be a state of dynamic equilibrium, like two individuals of equal weight on a seesaw that was perfectly motionless. The potential difference corresponding to this equal distribution of ions is given by the Nernst equation:

$$E = (RT/nF) \ln C_o C_i$$

The critical parameters in determining this value are: the concentrations of the ion both inside C_i and outside C_o the neuron; and the absolute temperature T. In addition, three further, non-changeable factors have to be taken into account: the charge on the ion in question, n; the Faraday constant, F; the magnitude of the charge per mole of electrons; and the universal gas constant, R.

At room temperature (20°C), RT/nF is approximately 25 mV, whereas at body temperature (37°C), it is 26.5 mV. Given this scenario, we might imagine that the resting potential could be maintained due to the chlorine and potassium ions, for which the membrane is permeable, being in equilibrium. However, the situation is not quite so simple. In the neuron at rest, sodium-ion channels are mainly closed. Nonetheless, there is still a gradual leakage of sodium ions into the neuron (at a rate of 1 percent to 10 percent that of potassium ions) through nonspecific channels for cations (i.e., ions carrying a positive charge). If this process were allowed to continue, the inside of the neuron would gradually become more positive, and hence drive even more potassium ions outside the neuron. In this way we would end up with a reduced potential difference and a more equal concentration of both potassium and sodium ions inside and outside of the cell: the resting potential would be effectively abolished. To forestall this eventuality, the neuronal membrane has a very important feature. The ions are distributed as they are by means of an energy-consuming "pump." This pump is actually a protein. This is the third example we have now encountered (ion channels were the first, receptors the second) where proteins are incorporated into the membrane. The separation of sodium and potassium ions is an active process that is continued throughout the life of the neuron: the death of the neuron will amount to the end of this imbalance of ions. In the case of an ion pump, the ion in question is going to be passed across the membrane, so it is obvious that the protein should be in contact with both sides. In the case of the sodium-potassium pump, the molecule acts a little like a revolving door, pushing one ion into the interior as slightly more are expelled to the outside. This pump can exchange up to 200 sodium ions for 130 potassium ions every second for each square millimeter of membrane surface. However, the sodium/potassium pump is an energy-consuming entity. In fact, a staggering 80 percent of the energy of the neuron is devoted to maintaining this pump. Hence if the asymmetry of potassium and sodium distribution is to be sustained in the neuron, there must be a constant input of energy. This energy is obtained from the glucose and oxygen, which we as individuals provide for our brains.

18. In *The Selfish Gene,* Dawkins (1976) has argued for the importance of the gene over the expendable individual. The contentious issue, however, is not that genes are important in the expression and continuation of certain traits, but that human personality can be reduced to traits that have a one-to-one relationship with a single gene.

19. Steven Pinker has also argued recently in *How the Mind Works* that genes determine brain function (Pinker, 1998). He points out that the processes that make up brain function are not themselves conscious and that each subroutine could be reduced ultimately to servo-mechanisms that could realistically be attributable directly to a mindless genetic tyranny, functioning by means of robotic-type algorithms.

20. In his book *Lifelines,* Steven Rose has produced a robust and eloquent defense against the idea that we are simply a conglomerate of "genes for" a cocktail of specific and independent traits. His work has been viewed by some as a clear critique of Dawkins. All too often the debate between protagonists such as Dawkins and Rose is seen as simply one of nature (genes) versus nurture (environment). However, the real argument arises over the extent to which gene expression translates in a linear fashion into brain functions. Rose does not deny the power and influence of the genes, but he asserts that such power is so indirect that in some cases it is virtually impossible to trace.

21. See Keverne et al. (1996).

22. The striatum is part of the basal ganglia (see Note 11). It is a large structure lying in the front part of the brain, below the cortex. In more sophisticated species, it is divided into two subregions, the caudate nucleus and the putamen. The organization of the striatum has not proved as easy to understand as, say, the cerebellum (see Note 11) or cortex (see Note 8). The striatum is now believed to be composed of different functional modules, all making separate contributions to the control of movement: see Alexander et al. (1986). A further complication is that, unlike regions such as the cortex and cerebellum, the striatum is very rich in many different bioactive chemicals. It is possible that a further subtlety in the operations of this brain region could be related to a poorly understood chemical system of organiza-

tion, as opposed to mere anatomical configurations of circuits of neurons. The striatum is best known as the structure that normally acts as the target of the connections from the substantia nigra, the area primarily lost in Parkinson's disease. Huntington's chorea, a disorder characterized by wild, involuntary movements, is also attributable to damage to the striatum, more specifically, the caudate nucleus.

23. Angelmann Syndrome is characterized by mental retardation, absence of speech, seizures, and motor dysfunction. It has a genetic basis that has now been identified; see Fang et al. (1999).

24. Prader-Willi Syndrome is another genetically based disorder, often compared to Angelmann Syndrome. It manifests as highly maladaptive behavior (e.g., skin picking, nail biting, hoarding, overeating, sulking, and withdrawal). See Dykens et al. (1999).

25. One way of circumventing Cytowic's calculations would be to say that each complete synapse was the result of expression of a single gene, or that nutritional and biochemical factors could still play an influential role, independent of the larger-scale environment. Even so, the factors would then be reduced only by some 1,000 to 100,000. Cytowic thus concludes that there are internal organizing principles at work in each individual brain and that such forces are strongly influenced by experience, that is, the environment (Cytowic, 1996).

26. Darwin's groundbreaking work *The Expression of the Emotions in Man and Animals,* first published in 1872 by John Murray, has recently been published in a "definitive" edition with an introduction, afterword, and commentaries by Paul Ekman (Darwin, 1998).

27. Of all the ancient Greek playwrights, Euripides is surely the most "modern." Whereas Aeschylus and Sophocles still deferred to the gods and to external Fates, Euripides was the first to internalize conflicting emotions within each individual. For me, *The Bacchae,* written in 407 B.C., stands as an eloquent description of the conflicting urges within us all.

28. See Bettelheim (1959).

29. See Olds and Milner (1954).

30. In 1974, the philosopher Thomas Nagel published a paper titled "What is it like to be a bat?" The crucial point was that material accounts of the brain omit the crucial issue of actual subjective experience.

31. As its name suggests, an *aversive stimulus* is a stimulus or treatment that an animal will make an effort to avoid, such as a mild electric shock. For a fuller description and examples of "active avoidance" studies, see Gray (1991).

32. *Passive avoidance* is the term given to a supression of behavior in order to avoid an aversive stimulus (see Note 31). In contrast to active avoidance, where an animal will take measures to avoid the unpleasant scenario, passive avoidance entails doing nothing.

33. See LeDoux (1998).

34. The hippocampus is another brain region classified as part of the limbic system. Lying beneath the cortex, it curls round the central core of brain, rather like a ram's horns. Nonetheless, it is named after the Greek for *sea horse* because of its purported similarity in shape. Although the hippocampus has been classed with a system associated closely with emotion, it itself has been closely linked to memory processes. For more detailed but nonspecialized accounts see Rose (1992), Greenfield (1998), and Squire (1998). For more detailed and technical accounts, see Squire (1987, 1991), Squire and Knowlton (1994), and Squire and Zola-Morgan (1991).

35. The hypothalamus is a very small brain region, lying deep in the brain. It is divided into different compartments, each with a specific role in the regulation of hunger, thirst, temperature, and sex. The hypothalamus relays signals to the pituitary gland in the base of the brain, which in turn regulates the levels of hormones that will circulate in the body. For an overview of the hypothalamus, see Greenfield (1996); for more detailed information, see Kandel, Schwartz, and Jessell (1991).

36. This dissociation between subjective states and external, objective behavior is critical. Even in behavioral terms alone, Kalin shows how limited in usefulness a term such as *fear* might be—if there are, as he shows, distinct sets of fear-related behaviors. See Kalin (1997).

Chapter 2: The Story So Far

1. Baars not only acknowledges that the image of theater stretches back into ancient history but that it might be rooted in evolution itself. Just as darting insects could be said to have anticipated jet fighters and the construction of the animal rib the Roman arch, so the concept of the theater might have been prompted by biology itself. In my view, however, such conversions of metaphor into reality only muddle the whole point of developing a metaphor in the first place.

2. For a detailed and beautifully illustrated exposition of how the idea of a theater of memory was developed in the sixteenth century, see the chapter by Lina Bolzoni in *The Enchanted Loom* (Corsi, 1991).

3. Francis Crick originally developed this idea some fifteen years ago (Crick, 1984). Since then, he has modified his views away from the idea of a single beam, a projection from thalamus and cortex, to multiple reverberating thalamo-cortical "projection units" (Crick, 1994). For a more detailed critique of this idea, see Greenfield (1995). As a metaphor, the searchlight image is a striking one for application to consciousness: yet once multiple systems are introduced, along with the idea that the thalamus not only projects to the cortex but receives a looplike projection back, then the original image loses much of its impact.

4. For a nontechnical account of the teletransporter thought experiment, see Parfit's chapter in *Mindwaves* (Blakemore and Greenfield, 1989). The general issue of

identity in the continuity of an individual life is dealt with in depth in his book *Reasons and Persons* (Parfit, 1984).

5. This metaphor was developed by Dennett in *Consciousness Explained* (1991). Although it is successful in portraying the idea that we have changing views of the same event, person, or object, the concept of a draft implies there will be an eventual, final version.

6. The idea that brain and mind are effectively synonymous is not only a basic premise in *Consciousness Explained* but is expounded explicitly in Dennett's compilation of essays, *Brainchildren* (1998).

7. For a general account of working memory, see Goldman-Rakic (1993). More technical accounts can be found in *The Prefrontal Cortex* (Roberts, Robbins, and Weiskrantz, 1998).

8. As its name suggests, the prefrontal cortex lies at the very front of the brain. It is the area that is separated from the rest of the brain in the lobotomy procedure, which was commonly practiced some forty years ago. The ensuing syndrome of frontal damage has thus provided many clues as well as paradoxes as to the function of this brain area. For a recent overview of the debate, see Roberts et al. (1998). For a more concise exposition, see pp. 247–251 in Cytowic (1996) or the "frontal lobes" entry in *The Blackwell Dictionary of Neuropsychology* (Beaumont, Kenealy, and Rogers, 1996).

9. Weiskrantz's book *Consciousness Lost and Found* (1997) is written from the stance of the clinical psychologist. Though intended for the general reader, the narrative can become quite technical in places. On the other hand, the more detailed passages can be skimmed without the central points of the work being lost.

10. Since the formal identification of blindsight in the early decades of the twentieth century, the phenomenon has understandably aroused the interest of philosophers and psychologists. An extensive body of work has been published on the subject. The interested reader should see Weiskrantz (1996), Cowey and Stoerig (1991), Stoerig and Cowey (1997), and Zeki (1993).

11. See Dennett (1991).

12. In *The Chemistry of Conscious States,* psychiatrist Alan Hobson gives his own theory of consciousness based on his clinical experiences and on his experiments on sleep (Hobson, 1994). The book is easy for the general reader to follow, and it is one of the few of its type that actually includes the underlying chemical signaling systems in the brain. Most other neuroscientific accounts of consciousness focus on the electrical blips (action potentials) generated by neurons and ignore the essential subsequent process of conversion of that blip into the release of a chemical that will in turn act as a transmitter. However, Hobson's book contains some dangerous assumptions, such as those discussed in the main text. See also Searle (1998).

13. See Searle (1992).

14. See p. 46 in Penrose (1994).

15. See Edelman (1992).

16. See Sporns and Tononi (1994).

17. Edelman is at pains to point out in his books that "reentry" should not be confused with feedback. With feedback, a certain state results from an existing repertoire of possibilities, whereas reentry is more of a bootstrapping process whereby new states are reached as a result of an iterative relationship between brain inputs and networks of neurons (Edelman, 1978, 1992).

18. The idea that artificial systems of the future could be, in a sense, our children is a theme common to both Dennett (1998), who sees them as "Brain Children," and Marvin Minsky (1994), for whom they are "Mind Children." In both cases the implication is that in the future our mental abilities will be invested in artificial systems. The respective terminologies demonstrate well that for those adopting the nonbiological approach, the terms *mind* and *brain* can indeed be interchangeable.

19. *Cognition* is a term widely used in neuroscience, but it has no obvious counterpart in everyday language. Derived from the Latin *cogito,* "I think," it is an umbrella term for brain functions that are not directly related to brain inputs (i.e., sensory processing) or brain outputs (i.e., the generation of movement). In addition, the term is often implicitly contrasted with the emotions and generally is reserved for activities such as learning, memory, and language. However, because the term is so vague and because we are realizing increasingly that our perceptions (e.g., see Zeki, 1993) and our feelings (e.g., see Whybrow, 1997) are strongly influenced by the prevailing inner state of the individual brain, any dichotomies where cognition is contrasted with other functions should be approached with caution.

20. See Minsky (1994).

21. See Aleksander (1996).

22. The doctrine of pan-psychism arose out of the apparent frustrating paradox that mental phenomena could arise from nonmental, material entities such as brains. If brains are physical entities attributed with minds, then surely other physical objects also have some kind of inner aspect. Although this inner aspect would never be seriously equated with minds, it is unclear what it might actually be: See Nagel (1979). Although pan-psychism might seem hard to countenance, given the current trend for equating brain and mind, a form of pan-psychism has recently been proposed by David Chalmers (1996) and is discussed in the main text.

23. Among the brain chemicals contributing to different states of arousal and sleep are the amines: serotonin, dopamine, noradrenaline, and histamine, as well as a related molecule, the ester acetylcholine. All these substances can act as transmitters, and have a pervasive distribution in the brain. See Cooper, Bloom, and Roth (1991). For the relation of these transmitters to arousal levels and sleep, see Hobson (1994), and for more detail on the phenomenon of arousal itself, see Steriade (1991).

24. Skilled movements such as when driving are often described as unconscious, though the driver is certainly conscious! The idea, however, is that the skilled motorist is freed from the painstaking sequence of events required, which are all too familiar to the novice. The cerebellum, situated at the back of the brain, has been dubbed the autopilot of the brain, because it appears to free up conscious processes for other thoughts. For a simple account of the cerebellum for the general reader, see Greenfield (1997); for a more detailed, technical account see Kandel, Schwartz, and Jessell (1991).

25. For a detailed description of pain processing, see Melzack and Wall (1996) and Wall and Melzack (1994). For a more concise but still technical description, see Kandel, Schwartz, and Jessell (1991). See also Wall (1999).

26. The issue of the value of robots with complex thought processes that nonetheless are still not conscious has been addressed recently by Kevin Warwick in *In the Mind of the Machine* (1998).

27. See Jackson (1984).

28. The theory of functionalism was developed by philosophers such as David Armstrong (1981). For more examples of functionalism at work, see different contributions by Chalmers, Dennett, and Birnbacher in Metzinger (1995). See also "Troubles with Functionalism" by Ned Block (1980).

29. The term *qualia* is the plural of the Latin singular *quale* and is used to signify the direct feel of a sensation as its seems to the individual. Qualia could therefore be regarded as the building blocks of subjective consciousness. For those who try to adopt a scientific approach to consciousness, qualia seem to prove an unnecessary impediment; see for example Dennett in *Consciousness Explained* (1991). My own view is that the problem with many scientific approaches is that they ignore the subjectivity of consciousness and concentrate instead simply on unusual, novel properties of the objective physical brain. Perhaps the distaste for the term lies in the implication that qualia are in some way things that exist in some mystical way, independent of the everyday objects that engender them. I personally do not share this anxiety. One should bear in mind that, in effect, qualia is simply a shorthand term for subjective sensations.

30. See Teasdale and Jennett (1974).

31. In anesthesia there are recognized stages: analgesia, excitation, reflex abolition, and finally, depression of the medulla, which is the part of the brain that controls respiration. When it is depressed, the patient will have to be artificially ventilated. See Rang and Dale (1991). Similarly, sleep can be classified into four different stages, each giving a characteristic electroencephalogram (EEG) pattern; see Pinel (1993).

32. Dopamine is a transmitter in the brain (see Note 23). It is best known as the transmitter that is deficient in Parkinson's disease, where there is selective loss of a

key group of dopamine cells in the substantia nigra, an area (see England and Wakely, 1991) in the core (midbrain) of the brain. Dopamine has also been associated with schizophrenia, where in an adjacent (mesocortical) pathway it seems to be in functional excess (see Strange, 1992). Hence, drugs that treat Parkinson's disease by increasing dopamine availability can produce schizophrenia-like hallucinations, whereas drugs that treat schizophrenia by blocking dopamine can cause Parkinson's-like problems with movement: see also Cooper, Bloom, and Roth (1991) and Rang and Dale (1991). For a less technical introduction to drug action in the brain, see *Drugs and the Brain* (Snyder, 1996).

33. In Homer's *Odyssey,* the two dangers Scylla and Charybdis lurked on either side of narrow waters, later localized as the Straits of Messina, and it was impossible for sailors to avoid both. Scylla had twelve feet and six heads, and she devoured anyone who came within reach of her lair. Meanwhile, Charybdis was personified as a deadly whirlpool that swallowed ships and belched forth waters three times a day. Odysseus himself actually survived by clinging to a tree until Charybdis belched back his raft.

34. The idea of mental processes existing as a kind of by-product is reminiscent of the famous statement by Julien Offroy de la Mettrie, in 1747, that "the brain secretes thoughts like the liver secretes bile." The Thing Fallacy is discussed, though not by that name, by Karl Popper in *The Self and Its Brain* (1977).

35. See Chalmers's *The Conscious Mind* (1996).

36. For a nontechnical overview of imaging techniques, see *The Human Brain: A Guided Tour* (Greenfield, 1998). For a much more detailed and technical treatment, see Toga and Mazziotta (1996) or the more readable *Mapping the Mind* (Carter, 1998).

37. The thalamus, derived from the Greek word for *room,* is a large structure in the central part of the brain. Each of its subdivisions performs a distinct role in the processing of the senses. Some of these subdivisions, such as the lateral geniculate nucleus, relay information about a single sense, in this case vision, whereas other parts, such as the reticular nucleus, are less specific in terms of sensory modality. For a cursory overview see Greenfield (1998). For more detail on the anatomy of the thalamus, see England and Wakely (1991), and for a more technical account of the physiology of the thalamus, see Kandel, Schwartz, and Jessell (1991).

38. Francis Crick and Christof Koch seem to have more recently shifted emphasis from the relations between the thalamus and cortex, in favor of certain neurons within the cortex that could be directly correlated with, or symbolize, visual awareness. See Crick and Koch (1997). Yet surely this way of thinking is an example of the Readout Fallacy. What are the neurons actually doing when they discharge as a result of consciousness alone, and nothing else? If the neurons in question report to other systems, then we are faced with the prospect of the target region, whatever and wherever it is, acting as a mini-brain in its own right. My own view is that con-

sciousness cannot be reduced to a small population of cells, but must involve the whole brain, or a large part of it. If only a small population of cells controlled consciousness, we would see abolition of consciousness in an all-or-none way following damage to a specified area. This does not occur.

39. See Chapter 1 by Llinas and Paré in *The Mind-Brain Continuum*, Llinas and Churchland (1996).

40. The thalamocortical oscillations that are so attractive a feature for Llinas have been recorded in all animals tested so far (see Llinas and Paré, 1991). On the other hand, no one would contest that consciousness within the animal kingdom was similar from one species to another (see Nagel, 1974, and Dennett, 1996).

41. See Gahwiler (1997).

42. For a nontechnical critique of how the phenomenology of arousal translates into actual neuronal mechanisms, see *Journey to the Centers of the Mind* (Greenfield, 1995). For a more comprehensive and technical account, see Steriade (1991).

43. See Plum (1991) and Young, Ropper, and Bolton (1998).

44. The earliest examples of sensory processing without consciousness were reported when Nobel laureates David Hubel and Torsten Weisel showed the responses of individual brain cells to different kinds of visual stimuli in the anesthetized animal. See original paper by Hubel and Weisel, published in 1965. For a more general overview of their work, see *A Vision of the Brain* (Zeki, 1993).

45. See Hameroff, Kaszniak, and Scott (1998).

46. See *How Brains Think* (Calvin, 1996).

47. See *Kinds of Minds* (Dennett, 1996).

48. The sloppiness of neuroscientists in their use of language is discussed by the philosopher Peter Hacker in "Languages, Minds and Brain" (1985).

49. The psychologist Donald Hebb developed the concept of an "assembly" of neurons, where the connections between component neurons were strengthened by experience: see *The Organization of Behavior* (Hebb, 1949). More recently "correlational assemblies" have been used to describe brain processes operating in parallel, where groups of neurons are active in the same way, to the same extent, at the same time (see Gerstein, 1989).

50. See Pinker (1998).

51. See Darwin (1859).

52. See *The Language Instinct* (Pinker, 1994).

53. See a recent edition of Darwin's great work, *The Expression of the Emotions in Animals and Man,* edited by Paul Ekman (1998).

Chapter 3: The Child

1. See *The Principles of Psychology* (James, 1890).

2. The initial stage in concept formation is the recognition of an object that can move as a connected whole; see Spelke, Vishton, and von Hofsten (1995). The sec-

ond step is to view an object not as all or none, but as composed of a number of different variables (Baillargeon, 1996). However, the abstraction of the overriding property that distinguishes, say, a cat from a dog, irrespective of variables such as size, remains largely a debate for philosophers and is referred to as the question of "universals." For an overview, see the entry on universals in *The Oxford Companion to Philosophy* (Ted Honderich, Ed.), and for a more detailed treatment, see Lowe (1989).

3. The neuronal mechanisms underlying the formation of new associations are still a subject of intense investigation. However, the best-known process is that of *long-term potentiation,* whereby a priming stimulation of a neuronal connection makes that connection more sensitive to subsequent, incoming signals; see Bliss and Collingridge (1993). A further important process is the modification to sticky sugars (cell adhesion molecules) that will help determine the configuration of neuronal connections: see Rose (1995) and Bailey and Kandel (1995).

4. Descartes's original dichotomy, that mind and physical matter are two separate entities, is known as "substance dualism." The problem with this distinction is that the concept of the nonphysical as it stands can conflate mind, a mortal property of an individual, from soul, an entity that is allegedly immortal. This blurring has been circumvented by double aspect, or property, dualism, which acknowledges that the nonphysical aspect of a person, his or her mind, is an implicit feature of his or her physical body, yet one not reducible to the physical components; see Kripke (1980) and McGinn (1982). The problem now, however, is that there will be a different blurring of terms, this time between mind and consciousness, as discussed in the main text in this chapter. Not surprisingly, most scientists reject dualism, with the notable exception of John Eccles (Eccles, 1989). Then again, much of Eccles's argument was based on quantum theory, which has now been used by Roger Penrose (see Chapter 8) to give an account of consciousness that does not invite a dualist stance.

5. The implications of Skinner's ideas were that humans possessed no inner life, will, or intentions at all—that we possess no mind; see Skinner (1971).

6. See Dennett (1998).

7. The distinction between neurology and psychiatry is really a distinction in the type of diagnosis and treatment available for any particular brain disorder. Neurological conditions are traditionally ones where there is a clear impairment in the structure or function of discrete parts of the brain, whereas a psychiatric condition is not initially based on overt physical signs. This distinction can be traced back to the time of Freud, who himself abandoned neurology for a new, nonphysical approach to seemingly intangible problems of the mind. Nowadays, however, more modern techniques, such as neuropharmacology and imaging, are helping to show that erstwhile mental conditions do, after all, have chemical and brain region selective correlates.

8. Philosophy of mind is recognized as a distinct field of philosophy; see, for example, Ryle's *The Concept of Mind* (1984). On the other hand, the questions raised by philosophers within this specialty are increasingly attracting the attention of scientists. In some cases, the emphasis is different. For example, philsophers will debate the issue of the epicenter of one's awareness ("intentionality"), whereas scientists may be concerned with the physical mechanisms of perception. Philosophers are concerned with the nature of persons, whereas scientists turn more to the physical basis of memory in a more generic sense. The biggest difference, in my view, is that philosophers of mind are most interested in the subjective aspects of the human condition, whereas scientists are concerned only with what they can see and measure—the physical brain. This difference in approach, expectation, and type of question asked is nowhere more apparent than in the common ground of the study of consciousness. Despite attempts to bridge the impasse, such as Pat Churchland's *Neurophilosophy* (1986), Blakemore and Greenfield's *Mindwaves* (1989), and the now-flourishing *Journal of Consciousness Studies,* the scientific and philosophical stances remain clearly identifiable as such.

9. See Lacoutere (1995).

10. See Devlin, Daniels, and Roeder (1997).

11. The phrase *Brave New World eugenics* refers, of course, to Aldous Huxley's *Brave New World,* where society was stratified into genetically determined levels of ability and power, from the high-status alphas to the epsilons, who were fit only for jobs such as operating elevators.

12. For a technical account of brain development in utero, see Chapter 4 in Kolb (1995). For a more concise account for the general reader, see Greenfield (1997).

13. See Purves (1994).

14. See Kolb (1995).

15. See Levitan and Kaczmarek (1996).

16. See Parnavelas (1998). This article, written in a style that is only a little technical, is also a useful overview of the early development of the brain.

17. See Purves (1994).

18. See Kandel, Schwartz, and Jessell (1991).

19. Plasticity has long been recognized in the CNS. The observation that the young brain will adapt more readily than the mature one was first proposed by Margaret Kennard in 1938. She reported a degree of recovery of function after damage to the motor system of young subhuman primates than was greater than would have been expected in their mature counterparts. Another important factor in determining degree of plasticity is the sophistication of the brain. In 1961, Roger Sperry reported that rotation of the newt eyeball resulted in permanent impairment. However, similar visual distortions produced in humans by wearing inverting prisms over the eyes resulted in an adaptation within 15 minutes. See Sperry (1961).

20. See Spinelli et al. (1980).

21. See Buonomano and Merzenich (1998) and Xerri et al. (1998).

22. See Kolb (1995).

23. See Ricklefs and Finch (1995).

24. See Harth (1993).

25. See Zeki (1993).

26. The most familiar accounts of brain pathways related to vision emphasize those that transmit signals from the retina and are relayed into the brain via the thalamus (see Chapter 2, Note 38) and on to different regions of cortex. However, Zeki (1993), for example, argues that in itself the multiple pathways, subserving different aspects of vision—movement, color, and form—do not account for the integration of the visual world. Instead, even the early relays of the visual process will be intercepted by the later and more specialized visual areas, which project back. Zeki dubbs these returning pathways "reentrant" connections, after Edelman (1978). Both Zeki and Edelman prefer this term, perhaps because they are anxious to distinguish the reciprocal connections between neurons, such as those in the visual system, from mere thermsostat-like feedback.

27. Donald Hebb was a pioneer in psychology. As far back as the 1940s he was already suggesting that synapses could be strengthened by experience (Hebb, 1949), a phenomenon shown experimentally some thirty years later (see Note 28).

28. For the original paper reporting the phenomenon of long-term potentiation, see Bliss and Lomo (1973). For a detailed, if somewhat technical, overview, see Churchland and Sejnowski (1992). For a shorter, less technical version, see Bliss and Collingridge (1993). For an overview for the more general reader, see Bliss (1998).

29. See Rose (1995) and Martin et al. (1996, 1997).

30. See Livingstone and Hubel (1987). For a more general and concise account see Van Essen, Anderson, and Felleman (1992). For a brief overview for the general reader, see Greenfield (1997).

31. See Neville, Mills, and Lawson (1992).

32. See Rose (1992) and Squire and Knowlton (1994) for a general account of parallel processing in memory. For a simplified overview for the general reader, see Greenfield (1997). For more emphasis on procedural memory, see Ito (1998).

33. See Chapter 1, Note 11.

34. See the chapter on *Sensorimotor Integration* in Churchland and Sejnowski (1992, pp. 331–411).

35. See Squire (1998).

36. See Chapter 1, Note 34.

37. For the original account of H. M.'s case, see Scoville and Milner (1957). Although H. M. is the only case in which both sides of the medial temporal lobe were removed, other comparable cases have arisen after a unilateral excision, when the

reamining side turned out, in retrospect, to have a preexisting pathology; see Penfield and Milner (1958); Warrington and Duchen (1992).

38. For recordings from slices of cerebellum, see Llinas and Sugimori (1980). For recordings from slices of hippocampus, see Bliss and Lomo (1973) and Bliss and Collingridge (1993).

39. For an account of "Orwellian" and "Stalinist" brain processes, see Dennett (1992).

40. See Howe (1990).

41. See Steven Mithen's *The Prehistory of the Mind* (1996), a highly readable account for the general reader of "the search for the origins of art, religion, and science." This book is ambitious in scope but clearly illustrated with provocative ideas.

42. See Lucretius (1994).

43. See Lieberman (1991).

44. In his book *The Symbolic Species* (1997), Deacon attempts to explain the question posed by his small son, "Why don't animals speak a simpler language?" The book is on the whole comprehensible to the general reader but becomes rather drawn out as it progresses. Perhaps too many unnecessary excursions into, for example, the nature of consciousness distract the reader from the original question, but on the whole, it is a good and facinating read.

45. See Herb Terrace's chapter in *Mindwaves* (Blakemore and Greenfield, 1987).

46. See Calvin (1996).

47. See Falk (1990).

48. See Seyfarth and Cheney (1992).

49. See Mithen (1996).

50. See Frith (1992).

51. For a concise and highly readable account of autism for the general reader, see the article by Uta Frith in the special edition of *Scientific American* "Mysteries of the Mind" (1997). For a fuller account of autism, see Simon Baron-Cohen's 1995 book, *Mindblindness*.

CHAPTER 4: THE JUNKIE

1. The first deliberate distillation has been dated at around 800 A.D. and attributed to one Jabir Iban Hayyan. The distillation process, *alkuhl,* and the word *alcohol* itself are both of Arab derivation. Although very potent beverages would have been evident only as a result of this vital step, accidental fermentation of honey, grain, or fruit juices would have led to the production of, respectively, mead, beer, and wine for thousands of years previously. Such alcoholic beverages are thought to have been produced since prehistoric times. See Winger, Hofmann, and Woods (1992); Goldstein (1994); and Hanson and Venturelli (1995).

2. A *drink* is defined as one measure of spirits, one small glass of wine, or half a pint of beer or lager.

3. For a review of the history of inhalational drugs, see Hanson and Venturelli (1995).

4. Amyl nitrite was first synthesized in 1857. Ten years later it was found by the physician Lauder Brunton to relieve the effects of angina. Amyl nitrite was itself given as a vapor but has been replaced by longer-acting drugs such as pentaerythritol tetranitrate and isosorbide dinitrate. The mechanism of action is to dilate the blood vessels so that more blood can be delivered to the heart. See Rang and Dale (1991).

5. See Chapter 1, Note 17. For a more comprehensive description of neuronal membranes, see Levitan and Kaczmarek (1996).

6. Alcohol has a fluidizing effect on the fat (lipid) phase of cell membranes. Because a variety of important proteins for ion traffic (ion channels) and transmitter action (receptors) are embedded in the cell membrane, it is clear that such an action would disturb their operations and hence disturb the whole process of neuron signaling. There is a strong correlation, with a variety of alcohols, between the disturbance to the cell membrane and the degree of psychoactive intoxication. On the other hand, small increases in body temperature can result in similar changes at the level of the cells, without being accompanied by a concomitant drunken state. The alternative mechanism would be for alcohol to work at a specific custom-made receptor. On the other hand, many different molecules, from the large isopropyl alcohol to the single atom xenon, all have similar effects. It would be hard to attribute such effects to a specific target site because the agents that would be acting on it are so variable in size and shape. Moreover, the concentration of alcohol needed for even the mildest effects is millions of times higher than the typical concentrations of other psychoactive agents acting at specific receptors. One possible compromise between the scenario of nonspecific action on membranes and action at a specific receptor could be a differential action on membranes in the vicinity of key receptors for other transmitter substances; see Goldstein (1994).

7. The principal active ingredient of cannabis, tetrahydrocannabinol (THC), is contained in the leaves of the hemp plant. The leaf concentration of THC is highly variable: wild cannabis plants, grown for hemp fiber, contain less than 1 percent THC. However, the concentrated hemp resin hashish is much stronger, containing 7 to 14 percent THC. The naturally occurring THC receptor seems to bind a naturally occurring compound similar to the hormones of the prostaglandin family. For an easy-to-read and informative review of all aspects of cannabis, from the biochemical to the social, see Chapter 12 in Goldstein (1994).

8. Time perception, as we all know, can vary enormously, from when time "flies" to the protracted present of an accident. In this case, drugs, not external events, can cause time to slow down. In some way, then, drugs such as cannabis re-

configure the brain into a form more like that of the child. The issue of time perception may be vital to understanding the physical correlate of certain subjective states. See Colarusso (1991), Zakay (1992), and Levin et al. (1984).

9. For a comprehensive review on all aspects of the opiate drugs, see *Opium* (Booth, 1996).

10. See Hanson and Venturelli (1995).

11. See *Confessions of an English Opium Eater* (De Quincey, 1930).

12. See Booth (1996).

13. See Hayter (1968).

14. The use of an extract of the opium poppy has been dated as far back as 4000 B.C. However, it was not until the end of the nineteenth century that it was found that adding two acetyl groups to morphine made it far easier to dissolve in fats (lipids) and hence gain far easier access to the brain. The resultant substance, heroin, was first marketed by Bayer as a nonaddictive treatment for coughs. For a concise and readable overview of the neuroscientific aspects of the opiates, see Snyder (1996).

15. For an engrossing account of the discovery of the enkephalins and their receptors, see Pert (1997). Aimed at the general reader, Candace Pert's account not only covers the science behind one of the biggest breakthroughs in neuroscience but will also be of interest to those concerned about the problems facing women in scientific research.

16. The question of possible analgesia caused by natural opiates during dental surgery has now been challenged. See Olausson et al. (1986).

17. See Rang and Dale (1991) for a brief description of the actions of naloxone. For a more comprehensive exploration of the relation between naturally occurring opiates and pain, see Woolf and Wall (1983).

18. See Wildmann et al. (1986).

19. The uncontrolled use of opioid drugs in large quantities to an otherwise healthy brain results in addiction; see Goldstein (1994). On the other hand, opioid medication has not been associated with long-term dependence (see Taub, 1982, and Portenoy and Foley, 1986). One factor might be that if medication is given to someone already in pain, that there might be a rebalancing of chemical seesaws in the brain, as opposed to an *unbalancing* of a previously healthy chemical scenario by the potent opiate drugs. Alternatively, but not exclusively, other factors could be critical, such as the context in which the drug was taken. The addiction or otherwise of Vietnam veterans depended strongly on environment and personality (Robins et al., 1974). For a comprehensive if technical review on the medicinal aspects of opioids, see Twycross (1994).

20. When a drug, given repeatedly at a certain dose, has a decreasing effect on each occasion, *desensitization* is said to have occurred. Desensitization can be the result of several nonmutually exclusive factors: change in conformation of the recep-

tor molecule itself; frank loss in the number of receptors; exhaustion of mediating chemicals; an increase in the speed of naturally occurring metabolic processes for removal of the drug; or a more general change in body systems to restore a form of homeostasis. See Rang and Dale (1991).

21. See Bowman and Rand (1984).

22. See Arntz et al. (1991) and Gross (1992).

23. See Snyder (1996); Pert (1997).

24. These are the same chemicals mentioned in Chapter 2, Note 23.

25. For a fuller account of Hofman's experiences and subsequent experiments, see Goldstein (1994). For firsthand accounts of LSD, see a concise report in Snyder (1996) and a much fuller description in Huxley (1954).

26. The figures quoted in the text are from Hanson and Venturelli (1995). Psychotic episodes lasting for more than 48 hours have been reported to occur at a rate of 0.8 to 1.8 per 1,000 administrations of LSD (Smart and Bateman, 1967).

27. The neuron groups using serotonin are all situated in the core part of the brain, the brain stem. There are several groups (nuclei) of such cells, which cluster one in front of the other along the central axis. Because they are situated in the midline of the brain, these serotonin-containing nuclei are called "raphe" nuclei, after the Greek for *seam*. The projections from the tightly localized raphe system are very diffuse, accessing the outer layer of the brain (the cortex), the cerebellum (see Chapter 2, Note 24), and the spinal cord. For a detailed description, see Cooper, Bloom, and Roth (1991). Somewhat confusingly, serotonin is also known as 5-hydroxytryptamine (5-HT).

28. For an account for the general reader of the actions of serotonin in the brain, see Hobson (1994); for a slightly more technical account, see Strange (1992).

29. See Hobson (1989) for a general review of sleep. For a more technical treatment, see Ashton (1992).

30. See Nedergaard et al. (1987).

31. See Green et al. (1995).

32. Neuromodulation is said to have occurred when neurons do not respond consistently in the same way to the same signal at a subsequent time. A formal way of defining this phenomenon might therefore be that *neuromodulation is a variant response to an invariant stimulus*. Neuromodulation can thus be a shorthand way of referring to a host of processes that sometimes involve different numbers of neurons and substances. Although it is usually undefined, neuromodulation has become a term that has crept into medical textbooks, usually altered and incorporated into a phrase such as "neurotransmitters and neuromodulators." It is important to note that what has happened here is that the *process* of neuromodulation has by a sleight of hand become a *molecule* (a "neuromodulator"). However, transmitters and modulators, as molecules, are *interchangeable*. The crucial difference is that instead of simply causing or preventing the generation of an action potential, a range

of transmitters can also interact with other ionic conductances. For further, somewhat technical reading, see Kaczmarek and Levitan (1987). For a general overview, see Greenfield (1998).

33. See O'Shea et al. (1998).

34. In modest amounts, serotonin will hyperpolarize neurons, so that the new potential difference across the cell membrane is within a critical range. This range of voltage is critical because if a stimulation occurs while the cell is hyperpolarized to this extent, the conditions will be fulfilled for a certain type of calcium channel to open and for calcium to enter the cell for some 100 to 200 ms. For a simplified account see Greenfield (1998); for a more rigorous yet technical account, see Ashcroft (1999). However, if the amounts of serotonin are large, and the resulting hyperpolarization extensive, then the critical voltage range will have been surpassed. In this case, not only will the calcium influx not take place, but the extreme hyperpolarization will make it more difficult even for normal action potentials to be generated, because they are more readily generated the more the cell is depolarized. Hence high doses of serotonin, such as might be expected to be elicited by Ecstasy, could have the net effect of shutting down all electrical signaling.

35. Amphetamine was first synthesized in 1927, when it was marketed as a nasal decongestant under the trade name Benzedrine. Its general action is to increase the availability of the transmitter dopamine (see Note 36) in the brain, which in turn has a stimulatory effect. In the rest of the body, however, noradrenaline and adrenaline will also be released and will trigger all the responses of the peripheral systems to fight and flight, including increased heart rate and increased blood pressure, the so-called "pressor effects." For a fuller account, see Rang and Dale (1991).

36. For highly readable accounts of all aspects of cocaine, from biochemistry to sociology, see Winger, Hofmann and Woods (1991) and Goldstein (1994).

37. Like dopamine (Chapter 2, Note 32) and serotonin (Chapter 4, Note 27), norepinephrine is used by a very discrete population of neurons in the brainstem: the locus coeruleus. Some estimates of the numbers of neurons in this region have been as low as 20,000 and yet the system sends diffuse projections to all areas of the cortex, as well as to the cerebellum. As with serotonin and dopamine, norepinephrine plays an important part in the sleep-wake cycle and in arousal in general; see Ashton (1992), Hobson (1994), and Cirelli et al. (1996).

38. See Kandel, Schwartz, and Jessell (1991) and Rang and Dale (1991).

39. When the oxygen we breathe is combined with glucose derived from the carbohydrates in our diet, the ensuing energy would normally be given off as heat and light. However, because only a portion of this energy is needed to keep us warm, it is essential that cells have a means for storing energy for more controlled use in all the chemical and mechanical work that is needed. Energy is stored by using the chemical adenosine triphosphate (ATP), which has three phosphate groups joined in a row (*tri* is from Latin for *three*). When one of the phosphate groups is

broken off, only two remain, and the molecule is thus adenosine diphosphate (ADP—*di* comes from the Latin for *two*). The liberation of the third phosphate releases an enormous amount of energy, leaving the ADP molecule available for storing up new energy by aquiring a third phosphate group again, thus becoming ATP once more. ATP can be remade in two ways, with (aerobic) or without (anaerobic) oxygen. In both cases the process starts with glycolysis, the gradual dismantling of glucose molecules. Glycolysis results in the transfer of energy from the chemical bonds in the glucose molecule to a net gain of two ATP molecules. Further products of this process are pyruvate and hydrogen. When no oxygen is present, these two combine to form lactic acid. In this case, the energy used to carry the hydrogen is wasted. From one glucose molecule, there is a net gain of only two ATP molecules. However, when oxgygen is present, it can serve as the receiver for hydrogen, eventually forming water. Before this happens, however, the energy stored by carrying hydrogen can be used to create many more ATP molecules. The hydrogen enters a chain of reactions, called the respiratory chain, in the *mitochondria* (specialized structures within the cell) whereby the charge it carries is transferred from one chemical to the next such that there is a high concentration of protons within the mitochondria. These protons enable newly made ATP to be released from the mitochondria. Anaerobic synthesis yields two molecules of ATP, whereas aerobic synthesis gives a net gain of thirty-eight molecules of ATP from one molecule of glucose.

40. Theobromine is a constituent of cocoa and belongs to a group of drugs known as methylxanthines: other methylxanthines are caffeine and theophylline, found in tea and coffee.

41. In a 1987 UK questionnaire supervised by Research Director Dr. Neil Ward, HAGSG database, Department of Chemistry, University of Surrey, of 357 children diagnosed as hyperactive, 60 percent reacted to chocolate.

42. In a survey in which people were asked, "Which of the following, if any, would you say were the typical pleasures of everyday life?", an average of 78 percent replied positively to "Drinking tea or coffee." When broken down into different European countries, the British were the most enthusiastic (87 percent) and the Spanish the least (67 percent). The survey was in a MORI poll conducted for ARISE (Associates for Research in Substance Enjoyment), and was published on page 6 of the *British Public Opinion Newsletter,* November 1993.

43. Of the many articles on pleasure, addiction and nicotine, see for example: Pontieri et al. (1996), Pich et al. (1997), Joseph et al. (1996), Stolerman and Jarvis (1995), and Robinson and Pritchard (1995).

44. The specific molecular target sites for nicotine are a particular subset of receptors normally activated by the transmitter acetylcholine. These nicotinic acetylcholine receptors are distributed throughout the brain and the rest of the body. Hence the intense stimulation of these receptors that will occur following nicotine

intake will have a spectrum of effects. For a full account of the effects of nicotine in the body, see Rang and Dale (1991).

45. See Yerkes and Dodson (1980).

CHAPTER 5: THE NIGHTMARE

1. The autonomic nervous system is so called because it seems to operate independent of conscious intervention, that is, autonomously. It is the control system of the body whereby the vital organs are coordinated for changes in how the body will interact with the environment. Crudely, the two patterns of response fit an animal for immediate action—fight or flight—or enable it to invest in longer-term activities, such as the digestion of food, that can take place when there is no immediate danger or other urgent imperative, such as copulation. These two broad patterns of response are effected by different chemical systems acting on the vital organs. The fight-or-flight response is triggered and maintained by the "sympathetic" division of the autonomic nervous system, whereas the "parasympathetic" component prevails most of the time, when the body is in a more relaxed mode. For a nontechnical expansion of this description, see Greenfield (1997). For a much more detailed and technical account, see Kandel, Schwartz, and Jessell (1991).

2. For a lengthier critique of this hypothesis, see Gray (1991).

3. The brain communicates rapidly with the rest of the body via nerves coursing to and from it via the spinal cord. The obvious exceptions are the senses that are processed in the region of the head: hearing, sight, smell, and taste, which are already above the spinal cord and are relayed to the brain by specific cranial nerves. The senses of touch, pain, and temperature, however, relate to all parts of the body. Special sensors in the skin transduce these physical influences into electrical signals that are then transmitted up the spinal cord to the brain via two systems of ascending pathways of nerves. One system is more primitive and relays the signals relating to pain. The other is, in evolutionary terms, newer, and it is related more to fine touch. Just as these ascending sensory pathways are the major inputs to the brain, so movement is the main output. Five descending pathways control the contracting of muscle, and hence movement. Each pathway is responsible for a different part of the body and different types of movement, although some adaptations can be seen following injury. For a nontechnical account, see Greenfield (1997). For a more detailed, technical account see Kandel, Schwartz, and Jessell (1991).

4. See Zakay (1992).

5. See Colarusso (1991) and Levin et al. (1984).

6. See Valentine (1930).

7. An explanation (see Gray, 1991) for innate fears is that because certain situations, phenomena, or animals have been repeatedly responsible for the death of large numbers of a species, appropriate avoidance responses triggered by fear have evolved accordingly. On the other hand, the actual physical basis within the brain of

this innate fear has yet to be elucidated. The idea is discussed in the main text that the basis for innate fear is connections between certain groups of neurons. However, even though these connections are genetically directed, their growth occurs over time. Hence the *delayed* appearance of innate fears in the young child.

8. "Human nature" is a phrase frequently used to excuse bad behavior, but it is a term rarely defined. It subsumes a strong element of inheritance, hence its citation as an excuse, but at the same time, the prefix "human" suggests something a little more complex. Pinker (1998) attempted an exploration of human nature, but failed to find a way to blend our genes with our learned behaviors. Instead, he ended up with unhelpful explanations for his decision not to reproduce, for example, with unhelpful statements such as "if my genes don't like it, they can jump in the lake!" Such a dichotomy is as unrealistic as are genes, a few strands of DNA, with complex personal preferences.

9. Schizophrenia is traditionally divided into two basic types; see Crow (1980). Type I consists of florid disorders of thought and perception, whereas Type II presents with more negative symptoms, where the patient seems oblivious to all around them. It is still a matter for debate as to whether these two extremes are in fact two separate disorders or whether they represent different stages in one disorder (such that Type II follows on from Type I), or whether the different symptoms can alternate. For an explanation of schizophrenia using a psychology model, see Frith (1992); for an explanation based on genes, see Crow (1998). For edited collections of general reviews, see Hirsch (1986), Sedvall and Farde (1995), Andreasen (1995), and Crow (1998).

10. See Rokeach (1964).

11. See Bleuler, translated by Zinkin (1987).

12. There are two basic reasons why an individual might be unable to sustain a train of thought. If there are no internal associations with a stimulus, that stimulus will have only a flimsy significance and will readily be supplanted. Similarly, if the outside world implodes with strong, sensory impact, then one stimulus will readily oust another, especially if it has no personal significance. Immature brains, I have argued, have less connectivity, whereas in schizophrenia, an imbalance of chemicals may render such connectivity less extensive than normal. The net effect, however, might be similar in that the outside world, particularly its raw sensory qualities, would hold more sway.

13. See Rosenfield (1992).

14. For an account of the inability of schizophrenics to interpret proverbs or attach a significance to objects beyond the literal, see Rosenfield (1992).

15. Latent inhibition was first reported by Lubow and Moore (1959) in animals and is reviewed in man by Lubow (1989). For a general discussion of the use of the model, see Joseph et al. (1996).

16. See Joseph et al. (1996).

17. See Chapter 13 in Strange (1992).

18. See Strange (1992).

19. See Strange (1992).

20. See Strange (1992).

21. See Strange (1992).

22. See Reynolds (1989).

23. See Dunn et al. (1993).

24. For a highly readable description of the history and mechanisms of the action of these drugs, see Snyder (1996).

25. For an illustration of dopamine pathways in the brain, see Appendix C of Nicholls, Martin, and Wallace (1992) and Chapter 10 of Cooper, Bloom, and Roth (1991). The dopamine-containing mesocortical pathway, originating in the ventral tegmental area and projecting to a specific part of the cortex, the prefrontal region, has long been implicated in schizophrenia (Glowinski, Tassin, and Thierry, 1985).

26. See Roberts, Robbins, and Weiskrantz (1998).

27. See Parkin (1997).

28. See Goldman-Rakic (1993).

29. See Weinberger and Berman (1998).

30. See Frith (1992).

31. See Cloninger (1996).

32. See Gray (1991).

33. See Reid (1989).

34. See Menks (1979) and Hoorwitz (1995).

35. Frustrative nonreward, as its name suggests, occurs when an individual (rat or human) does not obtain an expected reward. For details of the experimental protocols used to test this phenomenon in animals, see Gray (1991).

36. See Brown and Wagner (1964).

37. When dopamine locks into its receptor, it can trigger the opening of channels for the potassium (Lacey et al., 1986, 1989) to leave the interior of the neuron. Because potassium carries a positive charge, the inside of the cell will thus become more negative, or hyperpolarized.

38. As with the hyperpolarizing actions of serotonin (see Chapter 4, Note 34), the degree to which dopamine hyperpolarizes the neuron is also critical. In modest amounts, the hyperpolarization will be just enough to fulfil the first requisite for opening of calcium channels, and hence ultimately the discharge of more action potentials. In high amounts, the degree of hyperpolarization will be such that the appropriate voltage window is exceeded.

39. See Note 38.

40. See Michel and Moore (1995).

Chapter 6: The Depressive

1. See Willner (1997).

2. See Whybrow (1997).

3. See Whybrow (1997) and Strange (1992).

4. The distinction between reactive and endogenous depression mentioned in the text is the most common classification for unipolar depression, a state that, unlike bipolar depression, does not alternate with mania. Although the reactive/endogenous distinction is commonly used, it is unlikely that the underlying causes can be so clearly and unambiguously differentiated; see Bebbington et al. (1988). The terms *neurotic* and *psychotic* have also been used to distinguish mild from severe depression and are often conflated with the reactive/endogenous dichotomy, where endogenous depression is contrasted with neurotic depression. A further distinction is sometimes made between primary and secondary depression, where the latter accompanies an illness such as glandular fever. For further, general reading on types of depression, see Whybrow (1997). For a more technical discussion on different types of depression, see Andrews et al. (1990) or Duggan, Lee, and Murray (1990).

5. The term *minor tranquilizer* covers medication used to combat anxiety disorders, as opposed to psychotic conditions such as schizophrenia, which are treated with *major tranquilizers,* such as chlorpromazine. First introduced in the 1960s, prescriptions for Librium and Valium are less frequent than in their heyday, due to side effects of drowsiness and impaired concentration, and an unforeseen tolerance/dependency; see Ashton (1989). For a technical review of the action and effects of the minor tranquilizers, see Rang and Dale (1991).

6. The precise number of GABA synapses is difficult to estimate. See Beaulieu et al. (1992).

7. For a concise discussion of the evidence for an inherited vulnerability to depression, see Gilbert (1992, pp. 54–56). For a lengthier, more technical review, see McGuffin and Katz (1989).

8. For a fuller and highly readable account of the development of the monoamine oxidase inhibitors, see Healy (1997).

9. Monoamine oxidase is an enzyme that breaks down the amine transmitters serotonin, dopamine, and norepinephrine (see also Chapter 2, Note 23) if they are not stored in protecting compartments (vesicles) inside neurons. So when an amine is released in the course of synaptic transmission (see Chapter 1, Notes 14–16,) it is subsequently inactivated by monoamine oxidase. Any drug that blocks this action (i.e., a monoamine oxidase inhibitor) will therefore have the effect of prolonging the action of the amine transmitter.

10. One of the problems with medication based on monoamine oxidase inhibition is the "cheese reaction." When the actions of the enzyme are inhibited, other

substances, as well as the amine transmitters, increase in the body. These other substances, in particular another amine, tyramine, can compete with norepinephrine from its storage in vesicles (see Note 9) within the neuron. As more norepinephrine is released into the body, the greater its effects on the fight-or-flight response (see Chapter 5, Note 1), that is, an increase in heart rate and blood pressure. This pressor response can sometimes lead to a hypertensive crisis, resulting in heart attacks or stroke. Because tyramine is derived from diet, more specifically from certain foods such as cheese, red wine, yeast extract, and herring, it follows that restriction of consumption of such foods while under medication on monoamine oxidase inhibitors will reduce the risk of hypertensive crisis.

11. Imipramine and amitriptyline are examples of tricyclic antidepressants, so called because of their three-ringed molecular structure. These drugs do not work by inhibiting monoamine oxidase. Instead, they prevent the process of the amine transmitter being recycled back up into the cell in the first place. Hence the transmitter is present longer in the synapse and thus has a more sustained action. For a general account see Healy (1997); for a more detailed, technical account, see Rang and Dale (1991).

12. Many reviews have been written recently on Prozac. For a general discussion, see Healy (1997) or Whybrow (1997). For more specific and personal accounts see Wolpert (1999).

13. See Snyder (1996).

14. See Chapter 1, Note 15, and Chapter 4, Note 20.

15. For more technical and detailed accounts of how little is known of the underlying mechanisms, see Fink (1989); for the efficacy of ECT in depression, see Hay and Hay (1990).

16. For a general account of how ECT can fit into the spectrum of antidepressant treatments, see Whybrow (1997).

17. For a graphic account of mania, see Whybrow (1997). For a more analytical yet nontechnical account, see Rosenfield (1992).

18. For concise accounts for the general reader, see Snyder (1996) and Healy (1997); for a more in-depth, technical account, see Rang and Dale (1991).

19. We still need to know why lithium works only in the manic phase. Certainly, its action in blocking electrical signaling would explain how it might retard the high turnover of assemblies, which I have suggested is the basis for mania. But why does it not also have an effect on abnormally large assemblies, which I suggest underlie depression? Perhaps the clue lies in the fact that if given as a preventive measure, lithium can combat the depressive phase of manic depression, too. It might well have an action on internal events within the neuron that prevent the stabilization of long-lasting connections. However, the inefficacy of lithium for depression once manifest would suggest that once these connections were established, the action of lithium would not be very marked.

20. See Affleck et al. (1987). For a general though technical discussion of the contribution of emotion to pain perception, see Craig (1994). For a more specific review of raised pain perception in depression, see Diener et al. (1995).

21. See Rosenfield (1992).

22. For a concise account of the actions of histamine following injury, see Rang and Dale (1991). It should also be noted that histamine is also an amine and is distributed in a similar fountain-like arrangement (see Chapter 1, Note 15) as the more familiar transmitters, noradrenaline, dopamine, and serotonin. Its functions in the CNS as a bioactive substance have, surprisingly, received relatively little attention.

23. For a general overview of pain fibers (C-fibers), see Kandel, Schwartz, and Jessel (1991). For a more specific account, see Wall (1999).

24. The phenomenon of double pain is due to the fact that C-fibers (see Note 23) have such a slower conduction velocity compared with the Ad-fibers, which transmit in a more specific and short-lasting fashion information on more mechanical touch. The effect is most noticeable in the toe, as that is the most remote part of the body from the brain, and hence from where the differences in nerve impulse speed will be most exaggerated.

25. For example, see Bates, Edwards, and Anderson (1993).

26. Beecher (1946) reported that 65 percent of soldiers severely injured in battle felt little or no pain.

27. For a highly readable account of patients' descriptions of pain, see Frank Vertosick's (1997) moving account of the life and times of a neurosugeon.

28. See Hall and Stride (1954).

29. See Melzack (1994) for a comprehensive survey of how stimulation of the senses can modify pain. This phenomenon prompted Melzack and Wall to develop the *Gate Theory of Pain,* some thirty years ago. Although the idea initially met with opposition, the basic idea is now accepted that nerve pathways entering the spinal cord that are activated by ordinary mechanical stimulation of the skin can trump the signals—and hence the ultimate sensation—relating to pain. For a more comprehensive review of the Gate Theory, see Melzack and Wall (1996).

30. For a full and fascinating read, see V. S. Ramachandran (1998). For a more technical account, see Jensen and Rasmussen (1995).

31. See Wall (1999).

32. For a concise review of body maps in the brain, see Greenfield (1998). For a more detailed, technical account, see Kandel, Schwartz, and Jessell (1991).

33. See Note 32.

34. For a general but technical introduction to anesthetics, see Rang and Dale (1991).

35. The basic stages of anesthesia are (1) analgesia, where the patient is conscious, but pain sensitivity is reduced; (2) excitement, where the patient is unconscious but may appear delirious; (3) surgical anesthesia, where reflexes are abolished

and the patient is deemed ready for surgery; (4) medullary depression, where the neurons in the medulla, a basic part of the brain that controls respiration, are silenced: the patient now needs a respirator.

36. See Rang and Dale (1991).

37. Ketamine and phencyclidine (PCP) are structurally similar molecules that block the NMDA receptor. The n-methyl-d-aspartate (NMDA) receptor is activated by the transmitter glutamate. Once activated, the NMDA receptor is the most powerful way known for calcium to enter the neuron. However, such activation depends on the contingent occurrence of two independent events, a prior depolarization, as well as the presence of the glutamate transmitter (a *ligand*). Hence the NMDA receptor differs from most other receptors that are activated by either ligand or voltage: this receptor requires both. Because its activation represents the co-occurrence of two events, and because calcium can trigger neuronal adaptations, it is easy to see why the NMDA receptor has become the darling of learning theorists searching for appropriate brain mechanisms. For a review of PCP as a drug of abuse, see Winger, Hofmann, and Woods (1992).

38. See Winfree (1987).

39. See Chapter 1, Note 15.

40. As stated in the main text, the analgesic effect of morphine has been reported to be somewhat more subtle than the mere suppression of pain. Instead, the patient might say that they are still aware of the pain but that it no longer matters. See Rang and Dale (1991) for mention of this "affective" or "psychological" aspect to the experience of pain. On the other hand, the subjective attitude to pain is not necessarily emphasized by some clinicians. The problem is that subjective reports of this type inevitably prevent any clear-cut, simple conclusion as to the precise effects of morphine on someone in pain. It is also important to note that prescribed use of morphine is very different from abuse of comparable opiates such as heroin. In the clinical situation, the drug is titrated against the degree of pain, and addiction is not regarded as the same hazard as on the streets.

41. See Lautenbacher and Krug (1994) and Guieu et al. (1994).

42. See Faneslow and Baackes (1982).

43. See LeDoux (1998).

CHAPTER 7: THE HUMAN CONDITION

1. Many studies of the emotions are from a psychiatric stance, where emphasis is on the abnormality of the actual expression of emotions. Another approach is the psychological, where attention is paid to responses to a situation, as opposed to the neurological mechanisms of causation, or indeed to the subjective sensation itself (see LeDoux, 1997). In approaches such as that adopted by Gray (1991), the cause of the emotion is usually an external and uncontestable source of, say, fear or pain, or a conditioned stimulus paired to it. To the best of my knowledge, little has

been explored in realtion to how a purely cognitive stimulus might give rise to an emotion.

2. See Hobson (1994).

3. See Chapter 1, Note 15.

4. Hobson (1994) claims that dreaming and schizophrenia differ in that in schizophrenia the emotions are *inappropriate* to cognitive experiences, whereas in dreaming the emotions and cognitive experiences, thought processes, match perfectly. My own view is that such a distinction is not really valid. In dreaming, the cognitive experiences are themselves so unconstrained by any external influences that any comparison with the strong and steady intrusion of the external world that occurs in the schizophrenic's waking hours cannot hold. The thoughts and emotions of a dreamer match so well because the thoughts themselves are so transient and flimsy. For the schizophrenic, however, the superficial interpretations placed on events, people and objects in the real world are compared with the normal types of reactions of others. In dreams there are no such comparisons, and it is easier for the dreamer to seem normal as regards the compatibility of their thoughts and emotions. In all other regards, where comparisons are not contaminated by differences in the actual situations, dreaming and schizophrenia are very similar: strong emotional tone, lack of logic, ruptures in continuity of thought, passive recipient of the senses, and a raw phenomenological consciousness.

5. See Hobson (1994).

6. See Whybrow (1997). For a graphic illustration of increased activity on the prefrontal cortex, see Posner and Raichle (1994, p. 219).

7. See Deacon (1997).

8. See Squire (1987) for a definition of source amnesia. See also Parkin (1997).

9. See Penfield and Perot (1963).

10. Pain is normally sensed when free nerve endings within the skin are stimulated by chemicals released locally as a result of tissue damage, or by other forms of deformation of the skin or tissue in the viscera. No such endings are present in the brain, and hence direct chemical stimulation will not result in the sensation of pain. On the other hand, pain can be reproduced if key pathways are stimulated, that is, if the normal sequence of events in the relaying of pain signals via certain key pathways is mimicked.

11. See Hobson (1989).

12. See Hobson (1989).

13. See Hobson (1994).

14. See Hobson (1994).

15. See Ramm and Frost (1986).

16. See Hobson (1994).

17. See Morrison (1990).

18. See Morrison (1990).

19. See Bradshaw (1997).

20. See "The Classic Theory: Three Essays on the Theory of Sexuality" (Gay, 1995, pp. 239–292).

21. See Gray (1996).

22. Librium and Valium are commonly known as the "minor" tranquilizers, in contrast to the "major" tranquilizers like the phenothiazines, used to treat psychoses. These major tranquilizers work by blocking the dopamine system; but the minor tranquilizers work in a completely different way—to enhance the action of GABA. Librium and Valium actually act on an auxiliary (*allosteric*) part of the receptor, so that they are not serving as impostors for GABA directly, but enhancing its action once it comes into operation. Because there is this special site on the GABA receptor, upon which Librium and Valium work so effectively, it has been suggested that the brain must have its own naturally occurring equivalents. For further details, see Strange (1992).

23. See Chapter 5, Note 1.

24. Darwin himself, in *The Expression of the Emotions in Man and Animals,* wrote that the causes of laughter were "extremely complex." He conceded that the process was far more than a mere response to being tickled and that the mind had already to be in a "pleasurable state."

25. For a highly readable and intriguing account of the therapeutic effects of laughter, see Holden (1993).

26. Paul Martin has written a truly excellent book (1997) that presents a convincing and clearly argued case for close interactions between the CNS and the immune system. It is a highly engaging read for the nonspecialist.

27. For a moving, autobiographical account of Cousins's experience, see Cousins (1979).

28. See Holden (1993).

29. See Holden (1993).

30. See Heltne and Marquardt (1989).

31. Books, reviews and articles on Alzheimer's disease are being published almost daily. Here is a small selection. For the general reader: Ricklefs and Finch (1995). For more technical, specialized accounts: Gauthier (1996) and Dawbarn and Allen (1995).

32. The most conspicuous areas affected postmortem in the Alzheimer brain are certain regions of the cortex and hippocampus, which show massive degeneration as well as the pathological markers, *plaques* and *tangles*. On the other hand, other brain regions, such as the amine fountains (see Chapter 2, Note 23), are also lost. One theory actually asserts that it is this more primitive region that might be the primary site lost in neurodegenerative disorders such as Alzheimer's disease, and indeed Parkinson's disease; see Rossor (1981).

33. There are many theories for cell death in Alzheimer's disease. See, for example, Smith (1998); Rothwell, Loddick, and Lawrence (1995); and Sapolsky (1992).

Clearly, many different factors can trigger cell death. However, the big question is why only certain populations of neurons are so vulnerable. One possibility is that these key neurons retain the ability to regenerate (Woolf, 1996), but that the mechanisms of regeneration are toxic if aberrantly activated in maturity (Woolf and Butcher, 1991). This idea can actually be applied to specific neurochemical events in Alzheimer's disease (Greenfield, 1996, 1998).

34. See Reisberg et al. (1999).

35. See Russell (1990) and Allan (1980).

36. See Varela, Thompson, and Rosch (1991).

37. See Strongman (1996).

CHAPTER 8: THE ANSWER?

1. The issue of neural correlates of consciousness was actually the subject of a complete session at the 1996 Conference on Consciousness, held in Tucson, Arizona. Some objections have been raised, however, that establishing physical correlations of conscious states is merely resorting to a dualist stance of various mind states with, in this case, respective matching brain states. Moreover, it could be argued that by studying neural correlates of consciousness, the subjective state itself can be reduced to a mere epiphenomon. Both critiques are concisely and clearly refuted by a recent review by Searle (1998), which is for the most part comprehensible to the general reader.

2. See Chapter 3, Notes 4, 20, 29, and 30.

3. A central problem in philosophy of mind is the phenomenon of the first person, the direct feel of conscious experience. This subjectivity is captured in the concept of qualia (see Chapter 2, Note 29). For a more detailed discussion of progress in understanding the feel or phenomenology of consciousness, see the chapters by Joseph Levine, Dianna Raffman, and David Chalmers in Metzinger (1995). For a concise refutation of the idea that consciousness might be studied scientifically without recourse to phenomenology, see Searle (1998).

4. See Lou (1982).

5. See Note 4.

6. See Spreen, Risser, and Edgell (1995).

7. See Chapter 2, Note 39.

8. For the anatomy of the physical connections between the specific sensory subdivisions (nuclei) of the thalamus and respective areas of primary cortex, see Kandel, Schwartz, and Jessell (1991). Harth (1993) has related consciousness to connections between the lateral geniculate nucleus of the thalamus, and the corresponding visual cortex. However, most work basing explanations of consciousness on the connections between thalamus and cortex has focused on the connections with areas of the thalamus (reticular nucleus, intralaminar nucleus, and posterior nu-

cleus) not linked to one or another sensory modality; see, for example, Crick (1994) and Llinas and Paré (1996).

9. See Young (1978).

10. See Wells (1968) and Miklos (1993).

11. "An amusing speculation is that cold-blooded animals with primitive cortices would face severe restrictions on primary consciousness because their value systems and value-category memory lack a stable enough biochemical milieu in which to make appropriate linkages to a system that could sustain such consciousness. So snakes are in (dubiously, depending on the temperature), but lobsters are out." See Edelman (1992).

12. See Kaiser and Steiner-Kaiser (1983).

13. The idea of a continuum of consciousness was first raised in Greenfield (1995). Subsequently, there has been some discussion on the linearity of such a continuum. My original suggestion was, and still is, to provide an alternative to the common perception of consciousness as an all-or-none phenomenon. Beyond this fundamental concept it is of no immediate relevance to the current model presented in this chapter whether the gradient of consciousness remains constant or changes in its slope. In any event, until we have an objective, net measure of degree of consciousness, such as extent of a transient neuron assembly, it will not be possible to describe the more precise features of the continuum of consciousness.

14. By *spiritual* here, I mean simply an experience that is derived in great part from one's own inner cerebral resources, rather than from the pure sensory quality of the external person/object. I have not intended to include any theological considerations of soul. The principle feature of the soul is that it is immortal. Because we are concerned exclusively with the physical and very mortal brain, religious convictions or otherwise as to the existence of a soul should not feature here.

15. A frequently debated issue in philosophy of mind is the question of the subject of one's consciousness, referred to, rather confusingly for the layman, as *intentionality*. The term, introduced by Franz Brentano in 1874, is incorporated in the hypothesis that one cannot have beliefs, desires and so on without having those beliefs and desires *be* about something. According to the property of consciousness I have proposed in the main text, that we are always conscious of something, it would follow that all conscious states are intentional states. For a fuller discussion of intentionality, see Tye (1995), where the author presents a view that preserves the personal, subjective quality of consciousness, while embracing its objective, physical basis (as Note 1 indicates is needed). However, if brain states and phenomenal perspectival experiences are indeed two sides of the same coin, this "perspectival physicalist" stance throws no light on the nature of the coin.

16. Voltage-sensitive dyes, as their name suggests, exploit the fact that the functional state of neurons is reflected in changes in the voltage across the cell wall (see

Chapter 1, Note 18). See, for example, Grinvald, Manker, and Segal (1982), Grinvald et al. (1984, 1988), and Grinvald et al. (1994).

17. Standard recording techniques, where the activity of a single neuron is monitored, have a precision (the single cell) and a time resolution (one-thousandth of a second) that have been tempting to relate directly to mental events. Since Hubel and Weisel (1965) first showed selectivity of a stimulus object in activating different cells in the visual system, it has been assumed that the relation of outside object to brain processes was fixed—that an object would activate a predetermined cell, or more likely, group of cells. However, in the light of studies such as those of Arieli et al. (1995), it is clear that brain processing is highly dynamic and will probably vary from one moment to the next, even if the stimulus object is constant.

18. See Frostig et al. (1991). In this study, groups of neurons in the frog brain are excited by a flash of light within 152 ms. This response then inhibits the response of a second group of cells at 465 ms.

19. Grinvald et al. (1994), Figure 17, actually shows two concentric ellipses of exponentially decaying activity from a highly activated epicenter. It is calculated that 10 million neurons are contained within the outer ellipse, and activated over 230 ms.

20. See Libet et al. (1979).

21. The somatosensory cortex straddles the brain like a hairband, toward the center of the head, and just behind the corresponding area of motor cortex. Signals relating to touch, pain, and temperature arrive first in this area of cortex, having been relayed from sensors in the skin, up the spinal cord, via either of two ascending pathways and subsequently via the thalamus (see Chapter 2, Note 39). For a general introduction to the sense of touch, see Greenfield (1997); for a more detailed and technical account, see Kandel, Schwartz, and Jessell (1991).

22. One of Libet's experiments was to ask subjects to report when they felt a tingle in their hand, following stimulation either of the hand itself or of the relevant strip of cortex (somatosensory cortex). Even though the impulse would have to travel longer from hand to brain, subjects claimed they felt the effects of stimulation of the hand earlier than stimulation of the cortex, where the distance for the signal to travel would be far greater that following stimulation within the brain itself. Dennett (1991) dismisses the cop-out reply that subjective reports cannot be trusted. Instead he emphasizes the importance in distinguishing the actual timing of representations from the representation of timing. Although such a distinction might address some of Libet's critics as to the plausibility or otherwise of what he reports, Dennett himself does not produce a convincing model for what might be happening. On the other hand, the model I have been developing in this book might well accommodate the apparent anomaly. If consciousness depends on a sufficiently large assembly of neurons, it will take time, about 500 milliseconds, to grow. However, the efficiency with which it forms will depend, as we have seen, on the strength of the epicenter. It could be the case that relatively few neurons would

be recruited, or they would be recruited more slowly, with the artificial external stimulation during surgery, compared with the tried and tested physiological route that is activated once the hand is pricked.

23. One day it might be possible to measure degrees of consciousness (i.e., size of neuron assemblies): different factors could be manipulated (e.g., arousal levels, presentation of significant stimuli, drug-induced changes in amine availability, and different ages/psychiatric conditions) to predict net assemblies of different sizes, with different accompanying phenomenological states, as detailed in Table 8.1.

24. See Martin (1997).

25. See Ader and Cohen (1982).

26. See Richard Brown (1994).

27. For a general and concise account of the pituitary gland and hypothalamus, see Greenfield (1996). For a more detailed, technical account, see Brown (1994).

28. The blood-brain barrier consists of tightly packed glial cells that line the walls of blood vessels in the brain, thus preventing the easy traffic of substances from blood to brain, and vice versa. The only molecules that can usually access the brain from the bloodstream are relatively small, and highly soluble in fat (lipid).

29. For a fascinating read and easy introduction to the peptides, see Pert (1997).

30. See Hokfelt (1991).

31. See Hokfelt (1991); for a less technical account, see Pert (1997).

32. See, for example, how the theories of Crick and Koch (1994, 1997) are based on single neuron activity.

33. See Llinas and Paré (1996).

34. See Kramer et al. (1998).

35. See Pert and Snyder (1973).

36. The only possible scenario might be as in a movie I saw once on late-night TV. In *The Thing with Two Heads,* a dying professor had his head (along with his valuable brain) grafted onto the body of a death-row criminal. The technicalities were such that the original criminal head had to stay in place for a convalescent period of time. During this crucial period, the body was at the command of the two heads, and thus the two consciousnesses. Even here, the idea has not been realized of hacking into another consciousness. Although the feedback from the body will be authentic, the dialogue with the brain will be different due, of course, to a different brain.

APPENDIX: THE REALITY OF A NEURAL CORRELATE OF CONSCIOUSNESS

1. See Arieli et al. (1995).

2. For a slightly technical but clear and concise account of the actual structure of a synapse, see Levitan and Kaczmarek (1996).

3. See Draguhn et al. (1998).

4. In the seventeenth century, Sir Isaac Newton formulated three laws that enabled the prediction of the behavior of particles of matter according to the forces acting upon them. In the first few decades of the twentieth century, however, the development of quantum theory (see Note 6) challenged the unconditional application of these laws. For a highly readable account of Newton and his work, see Michael White's recent book, *The Last Sorcerer* (1997). For a more technical account, see Penrose (1987).

5. For a detailed account of the application of quantum theory to consciousness, see Penrose's two books, *The Emperor's New Mind* (1989) and *Shadows of the Mind* (1994). For a more concise account of the theory developed by Penrose and Hameroff, see the series of articles, critique by Grush and Churchland, and replies between 1994 and 1995 in *The Journal of Consciousness Studies* as well as the Web entry by Hameroff and Penrose (1998).

6. Quantum theory recognizes the wave-particle duality of matter. As such, it eliminates the concept of trajectory that is central to classical mechanics and replaces it with the prediction only of possibilities of outcomes of observations. For a general overview of quantum theory for the general reader see Gribbin (1999). For more technical accounts, see Penrose (1987).

7. The *Copenhagen interpretation* is that the very act of measuring a quantum event, inevitably entailing entanglement with the environment, distorts the phenomenon under study. Two mutually exclusive states are reduced to a single state that corresponds to the single outcome of an observation: this process is described as "collapse" of the wave function.

8. A Turing machine is in Penrose's (1994) words "a mathematically idealized computer." The term derives from Alan Turing, the mathematician who developed the first modern computer in the 1940s. The concept of a Turing machine is valuable because it circumvents any practical constraints of storage space, running time, and indeed the constituent material of a real computer. Like a real computer, however, it functions algorithmically.

9. Microtubules are important in a vital cellular process, the fast transport of material within the cell. It is important to have such an active system for transport of materials within a cell: if an average protein were left to diffuse passively, it would take about fifty years to travel one meter! The active process of axonal transport can be "slow" (1 to 2 mm per day) or "fast" (up to 400 mm per day). It involves the carriage of proteins necessary for the maintenance of neuronal structure, usually by slow transport, whereas fast transport is "particulate," carrying substances destined for specific organelles. Microtubules are hollow tubes manufactured from the protein tubulin and are found in both axons and dendrites. They are relatively large, about 23 nm in diameter. These microtubules act like railway tracks for the rapid transport of material away from (anterograde transport) and back toward (retrograde transport) the cell body. The material in question is packaged in large

membrane-bound organelles, which are carried along the external surface of the microtubule in a stop-go saltatory fashion, by means of a special protein, kinesin. One end of the kinesin molecule straddles the microtubule as the other cradles the organelle. At the center of the molecule is a kind of hinge that enables the kinesin molecule to slide along the microtubule while retaining contact with the organelle. However, an obvious puzzle regarding microtubules is how the appropriate material is transported either to dendrites or axons. Given that these two neuronal processes have very different functions, presumably they will require different materials to be sent to each of them. Indeed, we know that at least one major difference between dendritic and axonal transport is that dendrites alone, never axons, transport RNA. It turns out that different microtubules have different accessory proteins associated with them, microtubule-associated proteins (MAPs). It is possible that these MAPs confer greater specificity on the microtubules, thus helping in the routing of specific material destined either for dendrites or axons. For an introduction to the role of microtubules in quantum events, see Hameroff and Watt (1982) and Hameroff et al. (1992).

10. See Andreu (1986) and Amos and Klug (1974).

11. See Vassilev, Kanazirska, and Tien (1985).

12. When first discovered, superconductivity was observed only for temperatures a few degrees above absolute zero ($-273°C$), where no molecules are in motion. In 1987, a major advance took viable temperatures close to 100 K ($-173°C$).

13. See Frolich (1968, 1970, 1975).

14. See Woolf (1997).

15. The basal forebrain consists of several clumps of neuron populations that use the transmitter acetylcholine and send diffuse projections to the cortex. In this regard, they are analogous to the fountains of amine transmitters, described in Chapter 2, Note 23. For a more detailed account of this and other acetylcholine-using systems in the brain, see Steriade and Biesold (1990). For evidence that the basal forebrain contributes to arousal and even to consciousness, see Jones and Cuello (1989) and Semba et al. (1988).

16. For a general review of MAP2, see Johnson and Jope (1992). For evidence that it is found selectively only in 15 percent of cortical neurons, see Woolf (1993).

17. For MAP 2 changes with visual stimulation, see Aoki and Siekevitz (1985), and following auditory stimulation, see Woolf et al. (1994).

18. See Halpain and Greengaard (1990).

19. See Woolf (1997).

20. See Oh, Butcher, and Woolf (1991).

21. See Fisahn et al. (1998).

BIBLIOGRAPHY

Ader, R., and Cohen, N. (1982). Behaviorally conditioned immunosuppression and murine systemic lupus erythematosus. *Science, 215,* 1534–1536.

Affleck, G., Tennen, H., Pfeiffer, C., and Fifield, J. (1987). Appraisals of control and predictability in adapting to a chronic disease. *J. Personality and Social Psychology, 53,* 273–279.

Agnati, L. F., Zoli, M., Grombny, I., and Fusu, K. (1995). Intracellular communication in the brain: wiring versus volume transmission. *Neuro., 69,* 711–726.

Aleksander, I. (1996). *Impossible Minds: My Neurons, My Consciousness.* London: Imperial College Press.

Alexander, G. E., De Long, M. R., and Gwick, P. L. (1986). Parallel organization of functionally segregated circuits link basal ganglia and cortex. *Ann. Rev. Nurosci., 9,* 357–381.

Allan, J. (1980). *TM: A Cosmic Confidence Trick: Transcendental Meditation Analysed.* Leicester, UK: Inter-Varsity Press.

Amos, L. A., and Klug, A. (1974). Arrangements of subunits in flagellar microtubules. *J. Cell Sci., 14,* 523–550.

Andreasen, N. C. (1995). Symptoms, signs and diagnosis of schizophrenia. *The Lancet, 346,* 477–481.

Andreu, J. M. (1986). Hydrophobic interaction of tubulin. *Ann. NY Acad. Sci., 466,* 626–630.

Andrews, G., Neilson, M., Hunt, C., Stewart, G., and Kiloh, L. G. (1990). Diagnosis, personality and the long-term outcome of depression. *Brit. J. Psychiat., 157,* 13–18.

Aoki, C., and Siekevitz, P. (1985). Ontogenetic changes in the cyclicadenosine 31,51 monophosphate-stimulatable phosphorylation of cat visual cortex proteins, particularly of microtubule-associate protein 2 (MAP2): effects of normal and dark rearing and of the exposure to light. *J. Neurosci., 5,* 2465–2483.

Arieli, A., Shoham, D., Hildesheim, R., and Grinvald, A. (1995). Coherent spatiotemporal patterns of ongoing activity revealed by real-time optical imaging coupled with single-unit recording in the cat visual cortex. *J. Neurophys., 73,* 2072–2093.

Armstrong, D. M. (1981). What is consciousness? In *The Nature of Consciousness,* N. Black, O. Flanagan, and G. Guzeldere (Eds.). Cambridge, Mass.: MIT Press.

Arntz, D., Dressen, L., and Merckelbach, H. (1991). Attention, not anxiety, influences pain. *Behav. Res. Ther., 29,* 41–50.

Ashcroft, F. (1999). *Ion Channels and Disease.* San Diego: Academic Press.

Ashton, H. (1989). Anything for a quiet life. *New Scientist, 122,* 52–55.

———. (1992). *Brain Function and Psychotropic Drugs.* New York: Oxford University Press.

Atkins, P. W. (1998). *Physical Chemistry,* 6th ed. New York: W. H. Freeman and Co.

Baars, B. J. (1997). *In the Theater of Consciousness: The Workspace of the Mind.* New York: Oxford University Press.

Bailey, C. H., and Kandel, E. R. (1995). Molecular and structural mechanisms underlying long-term memory. In *The Cognitive Neurosciences,* M. S. Gazzaniga (Ed.). Cambridge, Mass.: MIT Press, 19–36.

Baillargeon, R. (1996). Physical reasoning in infancy. In *The Cognitive Neurosciences,* M. S. Gazzaniga (Ed.). Cambridge, Mass.: MIT Press, 181–204.

Baron-Cohen, S. (1995). *Mindblindness: An Essay on Autism and Theory of Mind.* Cambridge, Mass.: MIT Press.

Bates, M. S., Edwards, W. T., and Anderson, K. O. (1993). Ethnocultural influences on variation in chronic pain perception. *Pain, 52,* 101–112.

Beaulieu, C., Kipvarday, Z., Somogyi, P., Cynader, M., and Lowes, A. (1992). Quantitative distribution of GABA-immunopositive and immunonegative neurons and synapses in the monkey striate cortex (area 9). *Cerebella Cortex, 2,* 295–309.

Beaumont, J. G., Kenealy, P. M., and Rogers, M.J.C. (1996). *The Blackwell Dictionary of Neuropsychology.* Oxford: Blackwell Scientific Publishers.

Bebbington, P. E., Brugha, T., MacCarthy, B., Potter, J., Sturt, E., Wykes, T., Katz, R., and McGuffin, P. (1988). The Camberwell collaborative depression study I, Depressed probands: adversity and the form of depression. *Brit. J. Psychiatr., 152,* 754–765.

Beecher, H. K. (1946). Pain in wounded men in battle. *Annals of Surgery, 123,* 96–105.

Bettelheim, B. (1959). Joey: A Mechanical Boy. *Sci. Am. March.* Reprinted in *Contemporary Psychology,* R.C. Atkinson (Ed.). (1971). New York: W. H. Freeman and Co.

Birnbacher, D. (1995). Artificial consciousness. In *Conscious Experience,* T. Metzinger (Ed.). Thorverton, UK: Imprint Academic, 489–506.

Blakemore, C. B., and Greenfield, S. A. (Eds.). (1989). *Mindwaves.* Oxford: Basil Blackwell.

Bleuler, E. (1987). Dementia praecox or the group of schizophrenias, J. Zinkin (Trans.) In *The Clinical Routes of the Schizophrenia Concept,* J. Cutting and M. Shepeherd (Eds.). New York: Cambridge University Press.

Bliss, T. V. P. (1998). The physiological basis of memory. In *From Brains to Consciousness?* S. Rose (Ed.). Princeton, N.J.: Princeton University Press, 73–93.

Bliss, T. V. P., and Collingridge, G. L. (1993). A synaptic model of memory: long-term potentiation in the hippocampus. *Nature, 361,* 31–39.

Bliss, T. V. P., and Lomo, T. (1973). Long-lasting potentiation of synaptic transmission in the dentate area of the anaesthetized rabbit following stimulation of the perforant path. *J. Physiol, 232,* 331–356.

Block, N. (1980). Troubles with functionalism. In *Readings in Philosophical Psychology,* N. Block (Ed.). Cambridge, Mass.: Harvard University Press.

——. (1997). *The Nature of Consciousness.* N. Block, O. Flanagan, and G. Guzeldere (Eds.). Cambridge, Mass.: MIT Press.

Booth, M. (1996). *Opium: A History.* New York: Simon & Schuster.

Bowman, W. C., and Rand, M. J. (1984). *Textbook of Pharmacology,* 2nd ed. Oxford: Blackwell Scientific, 16.

Bradshaw, J. L. (1997). *Human Evolution: A Neuropsychological Perspective.* Hove, UK: Psychology Press.

Brown, R. E. (1994). *An Introduction to Neuroendocrinology.* New York: Cambridge University Press.

Brown, R. T., and Wagner, A. R. (1964). Resistance to punishment and extinction following training with shock or non-reinforcement. *J. Exptl. Psych., 68,* 503–507.

Buonomano, D. V., and Merzenich, M. M. (1998). Cortical plasticity: from synapses to maps. *Ann. Rev. Neurosci., 21,* 149–186.

Calvin, W. H. (1996). *How Brains Think: Evolving Intelligence, Then and Now.* London: Weidenfeld & Nicolson.

Carter, R. (1998). *Mapping the Mind.* London: Weidenfeld & Nicolson.

Chalmers, D. J. (1995). Absent qualia, fading qualia, dancing qualia. In *Conscious Experience,* T. Metzinger (Ed.). Thorverton, UK: Imprint Academic, 309–330.

——. (1996). *The Conscious Mind: In Search of a Fundamental Theory.* New York: Oxford University Press.

Churchland, P. (1986). *Neurophilosophy.* Cambridge, Mass.: MIT Press.

Churchland, P., and Sejnowski, T. J. (1992). *The Computational Brain.* Cambridge, Mass.: MIT Press.

Cirelli, C., Pompeiano, M., and Tononi, G. (1996). Neuronal gene expression in the waking state: a role for the locus couruleus. *Science, 274,* 1211–1215.

Claridge, G. (1994). LSD: a missed opportunity? *Human Psychopharm., 9,* 343–351.

Cloninger, S. C. (1996). *Personality: Description, Dynamics and Development.* New York: W. H. Freeman and Co.

Colarusso, C. A. (1991). The development of time sense in young adulthood. *Psychoanal. Study. Child., 46,* 125–144.

Cooper, J. R., Bloom, C. E., and Roth, R. H. (1991). *The Biochemical Basis of Neuropharmacology,* 6th ed. New York: Oxford University Press.

Corsi, P. (Ed.) (1991). *The Enchanted Loom: Chapters in the History of Neuroscience.* New York: Oxford University Press.

Cousins, N. (1979). *Anatomy of an Illness: As Perceived by the Patient.* New York: W. W. Norton & Co.

Cowan, M. (1990). The development of the brain. In *The Workings of the Brain,* R. Llinas (Ed.). New York: W. H. Freeman and Co., 39–57.

Cowey, A., and Stoerig, P. (1991). The neurobiology of blindsight. *Trends Neurosci., 29,* 65–80.

Craig, K. D. (1994). Emotional aspects of pain. In *Textbook of Pain,* 3rd ed., P. D. Wall and R. Melzack (Eds.). Edinburgh: Churchill Livingstone, 261–274.

Crick, F. (1984). The function of the thlamic reticular complex: the searchlight hypothesis. *Proc. Natl. Acad. Sci. USA, 81,* 4586–4590.

——. (1994). *The Astonishing Hypothesis: The Scientific Search for the Soul.* New York: Macmillan.

Crick, F., and Koch, C. (1997). The problem of consciousness. In *Mysteries of the Mind., Sci. Am. Special Ed.,* 18–29.

Crow, T. (1980). Molecular pathology of schizophrenia: more than one disease process? *Brit. Med. J., 280,* 66–68.

——. (1998). Nuclear schizophrenic symptoms as the key to evolution of modern homo sapiens. In *From Brains to Consciousness?* S. Rose (Ed.). Princeton, N.J.: Princeton University Press, 137–153.

Cytowic, R. E. (1996). *The Neurological Side of Neuropsychology.* Cambridge, Mass.: MIT Press.

Darwin, C. (1859). *The Origin of Species.* London: John Murray.

——. *The Expression of the Emotions in Man and Animals,* 3rd ed. New York: HarperCollins.

Dawbarn, D., and Allen, S. J. (Eds.). (1995). *Neurobiology of Alzheimer's Disease.* Oxford: Bios Scientific.

Dawkins R. (1976). *The Selfish Gene.* Oxford: Oxford University Press.

De Quincey, T. (1930). *Confessions of an English Opium Eater.* London: Bodley Head.

Deacon, T. (1997). *The Symbolic Species: The Co-evolution of Language and the Human Brain.* New York: W.W. Norton & Co.

Dennett, D. (1991). *Consciousness Explained.* Boston: Little, Brown & Co.

——. (1992). Temporal anomalies of conciousness: implications of the uncentered brain. In *Neurophilosophy and Alzheimer's Disease,* Y. Christen and P. Churchland (Eds.). New York: Springer-Verlag, 5–17.

——. (1995). Cog: steps towards consciousness in robots. *In Conscious Experience*, T. Metzinger (Ed.). Thorverton, UK: Imprint Academic, 471–488.

——. (1996). *Kinds of Minds: Towards an Understanding of Consciousness*. London: Weidenfeld & Nicolson.

——. (1998). *Brainchildren: Essays on Designing Minds*. New York: Penguin.

Devlin, B., Daniels, M., and Roeder, K. (1997). The heritability of IQ. *Nature, 388,* 468–471.

Diener, H. C., van Schayck, R., and Kastrup, O. (1995). Pain and depression. In *Pain and the Brain from Nociception to Cognition,* B. Bromm and J. E. Desmedt (Eds.). New York: Raven Press, 345–355.

Douglas, R., and Martin, K. (1990). Neocortex. In *The Synaptic Organization of the Brain,* 3rd ed., G.M. Shepherd (Ed.). New York: Oxford University Press, 389–438.

Draguhn, A., Traub, R.D., Schmitz, D., and Jefferys, J.G. (1998). Electrical coupling underlies high-frequency oscillations in the hippocampus in vitro. *Nature, 394,* 189–192.

Duggan, C.F., Lee, A.S., and Murray, R.M. (1990). Does personality predict long-term outcome in depression? *Brit. J. Psychiat., 157,* 19–24.

Dunn, L.A., Atwater, G.E., and Kilts, C.D. (1993). Effects of antipsychotic drugs on latent inhibition: sensitivity and specificity of an animal behavioral model of clinical drug action. *Psychopharm., 112,* 315–323.

Dustin, P. (1984). *Microtubules,* 2nd revised ed. New York: Springer.

Dykens, E.M., Cassidy, S.B., and King, B.H. (1999). Maladaptive behavior differences in Prader-Willi Syndrome due to paternal deletion versus maternal uniparental disomy. *Am. J. Ment. Retard., 104,* 64–77.

Eccles, J. (1989). *Mind and Brain: Two or One in Mindwaves,* C. Blakemore and S.A. Greenfield (Eds.). Oxford: Basil Blackwell, 293–306.

Edelman, G. (1978). *The Mindful Brain.* Cambridge, Mass.: MIT Press, 51–100.

——. (1992). *Bright Air, Brilliant Fire: On the Matter of the Mind.* New York: Allen Lane, Penguin.

England, M.A., and Wakely, J. (1991). *A Colour Atlas of the Brain and Spinal Cord.* London: Wolfe Publishing Ltd.

Euripides (1973). *The Bacchae.* P. Vellacott (Trans.). New York: Penguin.

Falk, D. (1990). Brain evolution in Homo sapiens: The "radiator" theory. *Behav. Brain Sci., 13,* 333–381.

Faneslow, M.S., and Baackes, M.P. (1982). Conditioned fear-induced opiate analgesia on the formalin test: evidence for two aversive motivational systems. *Learning and Motivation, 13,* 200–221.

Fang, P., Lev-Lehman, E., Tsai, T.F., Matsuura, T., Benton, C.S., Sutcliffe, J.S., Christian, S.L., Kubota, T., Halley, D.J., Megers-Hegboer, H., Langlois, S., Graham, J.K. Jr., Beuten, J., Willems, P.J., Leadbetter, D.H. (1999). The spectrum of mutations in UBE3A causing Angelmann Syndrome. *Human Molecular Genetics, 8(1),* 19–35.

Fink, M. (1989). Convulsive therapy: A reappraisal. In *Modern Perspectives in the Psychiatry of the Affective Disorders: Modern Perspectives in Psychiatry,* Vol. 13, J.G. Howells (Ed.). New York: Brunner/Mazel.

Fisahn, A., Pike, F.G., Buhl, E.H., and Paulsen, O. (1998). Cholinergic induction of network oscillations at 40Hz in the hippocampus in vitro. *Nature, 394,* 186–189.

Frith, C.D. (1992). *The Cognitive Neuropsychology of Schizophrenia.* Mahwah, N.J.: Lawrence Erlbaum Associates.

Frith, U. (1989). *Autism: Explaining the Enigma.* Oxford: Blackwell.

——. (1997). Autism. In *Mysteries of the Mind Sci. Am. Special Ed.,* 92–101.

Frolich, H. (1968). Long range coherence and energy storage in biological systems. *Int. J. Quanum Chem., 2,* 641–649.

——. (1970). Long range coherence and the actions of enzymes. *Nature, 228,* 1093.

——. (1975). The extraordinary dielectric properties of biological materials and the action of enzymes. *Proc. Nat. Acad. Sci. USA, 72,* 4211–4215.

Frostig, R.D., Lieke, E.E., Arieli, A., T'so, Y., Hildesheim, R., and Grinvald, A. (1991). Optical imaging of neuronal activity in the living brain. In *Neuronal Cooperativity,* J. Kruger (Ed.). New York: Springer-Verlag, 52–67.

Gahwhiler, B.H., Capagna, M., Debanne, D., McKinney, R.A., and Thompson, S.M. (1997). Organotypic slice cultures: a technique has come to age. *TINS, 20,* 471–473.

Gauthier, S. (1996). *Clinical Diagnosis and Management of Alzheimer's Disease.* London: Dunitz.

Gay, P. (Ed.). (1995). *The Freud Reader.* New York: Vintage.

Genberg, L., Richard, L., McLendon, G., and Dwayne-Miller, R.J. (1991). Direct observation of global protein motion in hemoglobin and myoglobin on picosecond time scales. *Science, 251,* 1051–1054.

Gerstein, G.L., Bedenbaugh, P., and Aertsen, A. (1989). Neuronal assemblies. *IEEE Transactions on Biomedical Engineering, 36,* 4–14.

Gilbert, P. (1992). *Depression: The Evolution of Powerlessness.* Mahwah, N.J.: Lawrence Erlbaum Associates.

Glowinski, J., Tassin, J.P., and Thierry, A.M. (1985). *Neurotransmitters in Action,* D. Bousfield (Ed.). New York: Elsevier.

Goldman-Rakic, P. (1993). Working memory and the mind. In *Mind and Brain: Readings from Scientific American.* New York: W.H. Freeman and Co., 66–77.

Goldstein, A. (1994). *Addiction: From Biology to Drug Policy.* New York: W.H.Freeman and Co.

Gray, J.A. (1991). *The Psychology of Fear and Stress.* New York: Cambridge University Press.

——. (1996). A model of the limbic system and basal ganglia: applications to anxiety and schizophrenia. In *The Cognitive Neurosciences,* M. S. Gazzaniga (Ed.). Cambridge, Mass.: MIT Press, 1165–1180.

Green, A. R., Cross, A. J., and Goodwin, G. M. (1995). Review of the pharmacology and clinical pharmacology of 3,4-methylenedioxes methamphetamine (MDMA or Ecstasy). *Psychopharm., 119,* 247–260.

Greenfield, S. A. (1995). *Journey to the Centers of the Mind.* New York: W. H. Freeman and Co.

——. (1996). Non-classical actions of cholinesterases: Role of cellular differentiation, tumorigenesis, and Alzheimer's disease, a critique. *Neurochemistry International, 28,* 485–490.

——. (1997). *The Human Brain: A Guided Tour.* London: Weidenfeld & Nicolson.

——. (1998). Molecular biology of the brain: future prospects. In *Essays in Biochemistry 33,* S. J. Heggian (Ed.). London: Portland Press, 179–191.

——. (Ed.). (1996). *The Human Mind Explained.* Pleasantville, N.Y.: Cassell/Reader's Digest.

Greenough, W.T., Black, J.E., and Wallan, C.S. (1987). Experience and brain development. *Child Development, 58,* 539–559.

Greenough, W. T., Juraska, J. M., and Vollemer, R. E. (1979). Maze training effects on dendritic branching in occipital cortex of adult rats. *Behavioral and neural biology, 26,* 287–297.

Gribbin, J. (1999). *The Birth of Time.* London: Weidenfeld & Nicolson.

Grinvald, A., Anglister, J. A., Freeman, R., Hildesheim, A., and Manker, A. (1984). Real-time optical imaging of naturally eveoked electrical activity in intact frog brain. *Nature, 308,* 848–850.

Grinvald, A., Frostig, R. D., Lieke, E., and Hildeshiem, R. (1988). Optical imaging of neuronal activity. *Physiol. Rev., 68,* 1285–1366.

Grinvald, A., Lieke, E. E., Frostig, R. D. and Hildesheim, R. (1994). Cortical point-spread function and long-range lateral interactions revealed by real-time optical imaging of Macaque monkey primary visual cortex. *J. Neurosci., 14,* 2545–2568.

Grinvald, A., Manker, A., and Segal, M. (1982). Visualization of the spread of electrical activity in rat hippocampal slices by voltage sensitive optical probes. *J. Physiol., 333,* 269–279.

Gross, P. R. (1992). Is pain sensitivity associated with dental avoidance? *Behav. Res. Ther., 30,* 7–13.

Grush, R., and Churchland, P. S. (1995). Gaps in Penrose's toiling. *J. Consc. Studies, 2,* 10–29.

Guieu, R., Samuelian, J.C., and Coulouvat, H. (1996). Objective evaluation of pain perception in patients with schizophrenia. *British Journal of Psychiatry, 164,* 253–255.

Hacker, P. (1985). Languages, minds and brain. In *Mindwaves*, C. Blakemore and S. A. Greenfield (Eds.). Oxford: Basil Blackwell, 485–506.

Hall, K. R. L., and Stride, E. (1954). The varying response to pain in psychiatric disorders: a study in abnormal psychology. *Brit. J. Med. Psychol., 27*, 48–60.

Halpain, S., and Greengaard, P. (1990). Activation of NMDA receptors induces rapid dephosphorylation of the cytoskeletal protein MAP2. *Neuron, 5*, 237–246.

Hameroff, S. (1994). Quantum coherence in microtubules: a neural basis for emergent consciousness? *J. Consc. Studies, 1*, 91–118.

Hameroff, S., Dayhoff, J. E., Lahoz-Beltra, R., Samsonovich, A., and Rasmussen, S. (1992). Conformational automata in the cytoskeleton: models for molecular computation. *IEEE Computer* (October special issue in Molecular Computing), 30–39.

Hameroff, S., Kaszniak, A. W., and Scott, A. C. (Eds.). (1998). *Toward a Science of Consciousness II*. Cambridge, Mass.: MIT Press.

Hameroff, S., and Penrose, R. (1998). Orchestrated objective reduction of quantum coherence in brain microtubules: the "Orch OR" model for consciousness. http://www.u.arizona.edu.

Hameroff, S., and Watt, R. C. (1982). Information processing in microtubules. *J. Theor. Biol., 98*, 549–561.

Hanson, G., and Venturelli, P. J. (1995). *Drugs and Society*, 4th ed. Boston: Jones and Bartlett.

Harrington, A. (1991). Beyond phrenology: localization theory in the modern era. In *The Enchanted Loom: Chapters in the History of Neuroscience*, Pietro Corsi (Ed.). New York: Oxford University Press, 207–239.

Harth, E. (1993). *The Creative Loop: How the Brain Makes a Mind*. Reading, Mass.: Addison-Wesley.

Hay, D. P., and Hay, L. K. (1990). The role of ECT in the treatment of depression. In *Depression: New Directions in Theory, Research and Practice*, C.D. McCann and N.S. Endler (Eds.). Toronto: Wall and Emersen.

Hayter, A. (1968). *Opium and the Romantic Imagination*. London: Faber and Faber.

Healy, D. (1997). *The Antidepressant Era*. Cambridge, Mass.: Harvard University Press.

Hebb, D. O. (1949). *The Organization of Behavior*. New York: John Wiley & Sons.

Heltne, P. G., and Marquardt, L. A. (Eds.). (1989). *Understanding Chimpanzees*. Cambridge, Mass.: Harvard University Press.

Hirsch, S. R. (Ed.) (1986). *The Psychopharmacology and Treatment of Schizophrenia*. New York: Oxford University Press.

Hobson, J. A. (1989). *Sleep*. New York: Scientific American Library.

——. (1994). *The Chemistry of Conscious States: How the Brain Changes Its Mind*. New York: Little, Brown and Co.

——. (1999). *Consciousness*. New York: Scientific American Library.

Hokfelt, T. (1991). Neuropeptides in perspective in the last ten years. *Neuron, 7,* 867–879.

Holden, R. (1993). *Laughter: The Best Medicine.* New York: Thorsons/Harper-Collins.

Homer. *The Odyssey.* (1998). R. Fitzgerald (Trans.) New York: Farrar, Straus & Giroux.

Honderich, T. (Ed.). (1995). *The Oxford Companion to Philosophy.* New York: Oxford University Press.

Hoorwitz, L. G. (1985). Progressive relaxation and implosion therapy for dental phobias. *Clinical Preventative Dentistry, 7,* 11–17.

Howe, M. J. A. (1990). *Sense and Nonsense About Hothouse Children: A Practical Guide for Parents and Teachers.* Leicester, UK: BPS Books.

Hubel, D. H., and Weisel, T. N. (1965). Receptive fields and functional architecture in the two non striate visual areas (18 and 19) of the cat. *J. Neurophysiol., 28,* 289–299.

Huxley, A. (1932). *Brave New World.* New York: Harper and Row.

——. (1954). *The Doors of Perception.* New York: Harper and Row.

Ito, M. (1998). Cerebellar learning in VOR. *Trends Cog. Sci., 2,* 313–321.

Jackson, F. (1984). Epiphenomenal qualia. *Phil. Quarterly, 34,* 127–136.

——. (1986). What Mary didn't know. *J. Philos., 83,* 291–295.

James, W. (1890). *The Principles of Psychology,* Vol I., Reprinted 1981. New York: Cambridge University Press.

Jensen, T. S., and Rasmussen, P. (1995). Phantom pain and other phenomena after amputation. In *Textbook of Pain,* 3rd ed., P. D. Wall and R. Melzack (Eds.). Edinburgh: Churchill Livingstone, 651–666.

Johnson, G. V. W., and Jope, R. S. (1992). A role of microtubule-associated protein 2 (MAP-2) in neuronal growth, plasticity, and degeneration. *J. Neurosci. Res., 33,* 195–209.

Johnson, M. H. (Ed.). (1993). *Brain Development and Cognition: A Reader.* Oxford: Blackwell Scientific Publishers.

Jones, B. E., and Cuello, A. C. (1989). Afferents to the basal forebrain cholinergic cell are from pontomesencephalic-catecholamine, serotonin, and acetylcholine-neurons. *Neurosci., 31,* 37–61.

Jones, E. G., and Peters, A. (Eds.). (1991). *Cerebral Cortex* (9 vols.). New York: Plenum Press.

Joseph, M. H., Young, A. M. J., and Gray, J. A. (1996). Are neurochemistry and re-inforcement enough—Can the abuse potential of drugs be explaind by common actions on a dopamine reward system in the brain? *Human Psychopharm., 11,* s55–s63.

Kaczmarek, L. K., and Levitan, I. B. (Eds.). (1987). *Neuromodulation.* New York: Oxford University Press.

Kaiser, W., and Steiner-Kaiser, J. (1983). Neuronal correlates of sleep, wakefulness and arousal in a diurnal insect. *Nature, 301,* 707–709.

Kalil, R. E. (1989). Synapse formation in the developing brain. *Sci. Am., 261,* 76–79, 92–95.

Kalin, N. H. (1997). The neurobiology of fear. In *Mysteries of the Mind, Sci. Am. Special Ed.* 76–83.

Kandel, E. R., Schwartz, J. H., and Jessell, T. M. (Eds.). (1991). *Principles of Neural Science,* 3rd ed. New York: Elsevier.

Keverne E. B., Eundale, R., Narsimha, M., Barton S. C., and Surani, M. A. (1996). Genomic imprinting and the differential roles of parental genomes in brain development. *Developmental Brain Research, 29,* 91–100.

Kolb, B. (1995). *Brain Plasticity and Behavior.* Mahwah, N.J.: Lawrence Erlbaum Associates.

Kramer, M. S., Cutler, N., Feighner, J., et al. (1998). Distinct mechanism for antidepressant action by blockade of central substance P receptors. *Science, 281,* 1640–1645.

Kripke, S. (1980). *Naming and Necessity.* Cambridge, Mass.: Harvard University Press.

Kruger, J. (Ed.). (1991). *Neuronal Cooperativity.* New York: Springer-Verlag.

Lacey, M. G., Marcuri, N. B., and North, R. A. (1986). Dopamine hyperpolarizes neurons in the rat substantia nigra pars compacta in vitro by increasing a potassium conductance. *J. Physiol (Cond), 381,* 157.

———. (1989). Two cell types in rat substantia nigra zona campacta distinguished by membrane properties and the action of dopamine and opioids. *J. Neurosci., 9,* 1233–1241.

Lacoutere, J. (1995). *Results: A Multibiography.* Washington, D.C.: Counterpoint.

Lautenbacher, S., and Krug, J. C. (1994). Pain perception in psychiatric disorders: a review of the literature. *J. Psychiat. Reg., 28,* 109–122.

LeDoux, J. (1998). *The Emotional Brain.* New York: Simon & Schuster.

Levin, I., Goldstein, R., and Zolniken, T. (1984). The role of memory and integration in early time concepts. *J. Exp. Child Psychol., 37,* 262–70.

Levitan, I. B., and Kaczmarek, L. K. (1996). *The Neuron: Cell and Molecular Biology,* 2nd ed. New York: Oxford University Press.

Libet, B., Wright, E. W., Jr., Feinstein, B., and Pearl, D. K. (1979). Subjective referral of the timing for a conscious experience. *Brain, 102,* 193–224.

Lieberman, P. (1991). *Uniquely Human: The Evolution of Speech, Thought and Selfless Behavior.* Cambridge, Mass.: Harvard University Press.

Livingstone, M. S., and Hubel, D. H. (1987). Psychophysical evidence for separate channels for perception of form, color, movement, and depth. *J. Neurosci., 7,* 3416–3468.

Llinas, R., and Paré, D. (1991). Of dreaming and wakefulness. *Neuroscience, 44,* 521–535.

———. (1996). The brain as a closed system modulated by the senses. In *The Mind-Brain Continuum,* R. Llinas and P. S. Churchland (Eds.). Cambridge, Mass.: MIT Press, 1–18.

Llinas, R., and Sugimori, M. (1980). Electrophysiological properties of in vitro Purkinje cell dendrites in mammalian cerebellar slices. *J. Physiol., 305,* 197–213.

Lou, H. C. (1982). *Developmental neurology.* New York: Raven Press.

Lowe, E. J. (1989). *Kinds of Being.* New York: Oxford University Press.

Lubow, R. E. (1989). *Latent Inhibition and Conditioned Attention Theory.* New York: Cambridge University Press.

Lubow, R. E., and Moore, A. U. (1959). Latent inhibition: the effect of nonrein-forced preexposure to the conditioned stimulus. *J. Comp. Phys. Psych., 52,* 416–419.

Lucretius. (1994). *On the Nature of the Universe.* R. E. Latham (Trans.). Revised and annotated by J. Godwin. New York: Penguin.

MacLean, P. (1970). The triune brain, emotion and scientific bias. In *The Neuro-sciences: Second study program,* F. O. Schmitt (Ed.). New York: Rockefeller University Press, 336–349.

Martin, K. C., and Kandel, E. R. (1996). Cell adhesion molecules, CREB, and the formation of new synaptic connections during development and learning. *Neuron, 17,* 567–570.

Martin, K. C., Michael, D., Rose, J. C., et al. (1997). MAP kinase translocates into the nucleus of the presynaptic cell and is required for long term facilitation in Aplysia. *Neuron, 18,* 899–912.

Martin, P. (1997). *The Sickening Mind: Brain, Behavior, Immunity and Disease.* New York: HarperCollins.

McGinn, C. (1982). *The Character of Mind.* New York: Oxford University Press.

McGuffin, P. and Katz, R. (1989) The genetics of depression and manic depressive disorder. *Brit. J. Psych., 129,* 294–304.

Melzack, R. (1994). Folk medicine and the sensory modulation of pain. In *Textbook of Pain,* 3rd ed., P. D. Wall and R. Melzack (Eds.). Edinburgh: Churchill Livingstone, 1209–1217.

Melzack, R., and Wall, P. D. (1996). *The Challenge of Pain.* New York: Penguin.

Menks, F. (1979). Behavioural techniques in the treatment of a writing phobia. *Am. J. Occup. Ther., 33,* 102–107.

Metzinger, T. (Ed.) (1995). *Conscious Experience.* Thorverton, UK: Imprint Academic.

Michel, G. F., and Moore, C. L. (1995). *Developmental Psychobiolgy: An Interdisciplinary Science.* Cambridge, Mass.: MIT Press.

Miklos, G. L. (1993) Molecules and cognition: the latterday lesson of levels, language, and lactose. Evolutionary overview of brain structure and function in some vertebrates and invertebrates. *J. Neurobiol., 24,* 847–890.

Minsky, M. (1994). Will robots inherit the Earth? *Sci. Am., 271,* 86–91.

Mithen, S. (1996). *The Prehistory of the Mind: A Search for the Origins of Art, Religion and Science.* London: Thames and Hudson.

Morrison, A. R. (1990). A window on the sleeping brain. In *The Workings of the Brain: Development, Memory, and Perception,* R. R. Llinas (Ed.). New York: W. H. Freeman and Co., 133–148.

Nagel, T. (1976). What is it like to be a bat? *Phil. Rev., 83,* 435–450.

——. (1979). *Mortal Questions.* New York: Cambridge University Press.

——. (1986). *The View from Nowhere.* New York: Oxford University Press.

Nedergaard, S. Engberg, I, and Flatman, T. A. (1987). The modulation of excitatory amino acid responses by serotonin in the cat neocortex in vitro. *Cell Mol. Neurobiol., 7,* 367–379.

Neville, H., Mills, D., and Lawson, D. (1992). Fractionating language: different neural subsystems with different sensitive periods. *Cerebral Cortex, 2,* 244–258.

Nicholl, R. A. (1988). The coupling of neurotransmitter receptors to ion channels in the brain. *Science, 261,* 545–550.

Nicholls, J., Martin, A. R., and Wallace, B. G. (1992). *From Neuron to Brain,* 3rd ed. Sunderland, Mass.: Sinauer.

Nowakowski, R. S. (1993). Basic concepts of CNS development. In *Brain Development and Cognition,* M. Johnson (Ed.). Oxford: Blackwell Scientific Publishers, 54–92.

Oh, J. D., Butcher, L. L., and Woolf, N. J. (1991). Thyroid hormone modulates the development of cholinergic terminal fields in the rat forebrain: relation to nerve growth factor receptor. *Dev. Brain Res., 59,* 133–142.

Olausson, B., Erikson, E., Ellmarker, C., Rydenhag, B., Shyu, B. C., and Andersson, S. A. (1986) Effects of naloxone on dental pain threshold following muscle exercise and low frequency transcutaneous nerve stimulation: a comparative study in man. *Acta. Physiol. Scand., 126,* 299–305.

Olds, J., and Milner, P. M. (1954). Positive reinforcement produced by electrical stimulation of septal area and other regions of rat brain. *J. Comp. Phys. Psych., 47,* 419–427.

O'Shea, E., Ceranado, R., Esteban, B., Colado, M., and Wein, A. R. (1998). The relationship between the degree and neurodegeneration of rat brain $5=HT$ nerve terminals and the dose and frequency of administration of MDMA (Ecstasy). *Neuropharmacology, 37,* 914–926.

Parfit, D. (1984). *Reasons and Persons.* New York: Oxford University Press.

Parkin, A. J. (1997). The neuropsychology of false memory. *Learning and Individual Differences, 9,* 341–357.

Parnavelas, J. (1998). The human brain: 100 billion connected cells. In *From Brains to Consciousness?* S. Rose (Ed.). Princeton, N.J.: Princeton University Press, 18–32.

Penfield, W., and Milner, B. (1958). Memory deficits produced by bilateral lesions in the hippocampal zone. *Arch. Neurol. Psychiatr., 79,* 475–497.

Penfield, W., and Perot, P. (1963). The brain's record of auditory and visual experience. *Brain, 86,* 595–697.

Penrose, R. (1987). Newton, quantum theory and reality. In *300 Years of Gravity,* S. W. Hawking and W. Israel (Eds.). New York: Cambridge University Press, 17–19.

——. (1989). *The Emperor's New Mind.* New York: Oxford University Press.

——. (1994). *Shadows of the Mind: A Search for the Missing Science of Consciousness.* New York: Oxford University Press.

Penrose, R., and Hameroff, S. (1995). What gaps? Reply to Grush and Churchland. *J. Consc. Studies, 2,* 98–111.

Pert, C. B. (1997). *Molecules of Emotion: Why You Feel the Way You Feel.* New York: Scribner.

Pert, C., and Snyder, S. (1973). Opiate receptor: demonstration in nervous tissue. *Science, 179,* 1011–1014.

Pich, E. M., Pagliusi, S. R., Tessari, M., Talabot-Ayer, D., Hooft van Huijsduijnen, R., and Chiamulera, C. (1997). Common neural substrates for the addictive properties of nicotine and cocaine. *Science, 275,* 83–86.

Pinel, J. (1993). *Biopsychology.* Boston: Allyn and Bacon.

Pinker, S. (1994). *The Language Instinct.* New York: HarperCollins.

——. (1998). *How the Mind Works.* New York: Penguin.

Plum, F. (1991). Coma and related disturbances of the human conscious state. In *Cerebral Cortex Vol. 9, Normal and Altered States and Functions,* A. Peters and E. G. Jones (Eds.). New York: Plenum Press, 359–426.

Pontieri, F.E., Tanda, G., Orzi, F., and DiChiara, G. (1996). Effects of nicotine on the nucleus accumbens and similarity to those of addictive drugs. *Nature, 382,* 255–257.

Popper, K. R., and Eccles, J. C. (1977). *The Self and Its Brain.* New York: Springer-Verlag.

Portenoy, R. K., and Foley, K. M. (1986). Chronic use of opioid analgesics in non-malignant pain: report of 38 cases. *Pain, 25,* 171–186.

Posner, M. I., and Raichle, M. E. (1994). *Images of Mind.* New York: Scientific American Library.

Purves, D. (1994). *Neural Activity and the Growth of the Brain.* New York: Cambridge University Press.

Putnam, H. (1988). *Representation and Reality.* Cambridge, Mass.: MIT Press.

Ramachandran, V. S., and Blakeslee, S. (1998). *Phantoms in the Brain*. London: Fourth Estate.

Ramm, P., and Frost, B. J. (1986). Cerebral and local cerebral metabolism in the cat during slow wave and REM sleep. *Brain Res., 365,* 112–126.

Rang, H. P., and Dale, M. M. (1991). *Pharmacology,* 2nd ed. Edinburgh: Churchill Livingstone.

Reid, W. H. (1989). *The Treatment of Psychiatric Disorders: Revised for the DSM-III-R.* New York: Brunner/Mazel.

Reisberg, B., Kenowsky, S., Franssen, E. H., Auer, S. R., and Souren, L. E. (1999). Towards a science of Alzheimer's disease management: a model based upon current knowledge of retrogenesis. *Int. Psychogeriatr., 11(1):* 7–23.

Reynolds, G. P. (1989). Beyond the dopamine hypothesis. The neurochemical pathology of schizophrenia. *Brit. J. Psychiat., 155,* 305–316.

Ricklefs, R. E., and Finch, C. E. (1995). *Aging: A Natural History.* New York: Scientific American Library.

Roberts, A. C., Robbins, T. W., and Weiskrantz, L. (Eds.). (1998). *The Prefrontal Cortex: Executive and Cognitive Functions.* New York: Oxford University Press.

Robins, L. N., Davis, D. H., and Nurco, D. N. (1974). How permanent was Vietnam drug addiction? *Am. J. Public Health, 64,* 38–43.

Robinson, J. H., and Pritchard, W. S. (1995). Reply to Stolerman and Jarvis. *Psychopharm., 117,* 16–17.

Robinson, S. R., and Smotherman, W. P. (1992). Fundamental motor patterns of the mammalian fetus. *J. Neurobiol., 23,* 1574–1600.

Rokeach, M. (1964). *The Three Christs of Ypsilanti: A Psychological Study.* London: Arthur Barker Limited.

Rose, S. (1992). *The Making of Memory.* New York: Bantam Books.

——. (1995). Cell adhesion molecules, glucocorticoids and long-term memory formation. *Trends Neurosci., 18,* 502–506.

——. (1997). *Lifelines: Biology, Freedom, Determinism.* New York: Allen Lane, Penguin.

——. (Ed.) (1998). *From Brains to Consciousness?* Princeton, N.J.: Princeton University Press.

Rosenfield, I. (1992). *The Strange, Familiar and Forgotten: An Anatomy of Consciousness.* New York: Alfred A. Knopf.

Rossor, M. (1981). Parkinson's disease and Alzheimer's disease as disorders of the isodendritic core. *Biomed. J. Clin. Rd. Ed., 283,* 1588–1590.

Rothwell, N. J., Loddick, S., and Lawrence, C. (1995). Cytokines and neurodegeneration. In *Immune Responses in the Nervous System,* N. J. Rothwell (Ed.). Oxford: Bios Scientific, 77–100.

Russell, P. (1990). *The TM Technique: An Introduction to Transcendental Meditation and the Teachings of Maharishi Mahesh Yogi.* 3rd Ed. London: Arkana.

Ryle, G. (1984). *The Concept of Mind*. Chicago: Chicago University Press.

Sapolsky, R. M. (1992). *Stress, the Aging Brain, and the Mechanisms of Neuron Death*. Cambridge, Mass.: MIT Press.

Scoville, W. B., and Milner, B. (1957). Loss of recent memory after bilateral hippocampal lesions. *J. Neurol. Neurosurg. Psychiat., 20,* 11–21.

Searle, J. (1992). *The Rediscovery of the Mind*. Cambridge, Mass.: MIT Press.

——. (1998). How to study consciousness scientifically. *Brain Res. Rev., 26,* 379–387.

Sedvall, G., and Farde, L. (1995). Chemical brain anatomy in schizophrenia. *Lancet, 346,* 743–749.

Seebach, B. S., Intrator, N., Lieberman, P., and Cooper, L. N. (1994). A model of prenatal acquisition of speech parameters. *Proc. Natl. Acad. Sci. USA, 91,* 7473–7476.

Semba, K., Reiner, P. B., McGeer, E. G., and Fibiger, H. C. (1988). Brain stem afferents to the magnocellular basal forebrain studied by axonal transport, immunohistochemistry, and ectrophysiology in the rat. *J. Comp. Neurol., 267,* 433–453.

Seyfarth, R. M., and Cheney, D. L. (1992). Meaning and mind in monkeys. *Sci. Am., 267,* 122–128.

Skinner, B. F. (1971). *Beyond Freedom and Dignity*. New York: Knopf.

Smart, R. G., and Bateman, K. (1967). Unfavourable reactions to LSD: a review and analysis of the available case reports. *Canad. Med. Assoc., 97,* 1214.

Smith, A. D. (1998). Ageing of the brain: is mental decline inevitable? In *From Brains to Consciousness?* S. Rose (Ed.). Princeton, N.J.: Princeton University Press, 94–108.

Snyder, S. (1996). *Drugs and the Brain*. New York: W. H. Freeman and Co.

Spelke, E. S., Vishton, P., and von Hofsten, C. (1995). Object direction, object direction action and physical knowledge in infancy. In *The Cognitive Neurosciences*, M. S. Gazzaniga (Ed.). Cambridge, Mass.: MIT Press.

Sperry, R. (1961). Cerebral organization and behaviour. *Science, 133,* 1749–1757.

Spinelli, D. H., and Jensen, F. E. (1979). Plasticity: the mirror of experience. *Science, 203,* 75–78.

Spinelli, D. H., Jensen, F. E., and DiPrisco, G. V. (1980). Early experience effect on dendritic branching in normally reared kittens. *Exp. Neurol., 62,* 1–11.

Sporns, O., and Tononi, G. (Eds.). (1994). *Selectionism and the Brain*. New York: Academic Press.

Spreen, O., Risser, A. T., and Edgell, D. (1995). *Developmental Psychology*. New York: Oxford University Press.

Squire, L. R. (1987). *Memory and Brain*. New York: Oxford University Press.

——. (1998). Memory and brain systems. In *From Brain to Consciousness?* S. Rose (Ed.). Princeton, N.J.: Princeton University Press, 53–72.

Squire, L. R., and Knowlton, B. (1994). Memory, hippocampus and brain. In *The Cognitive Neurosciences*, M. Gazzaniga (Ed.). Cambridge, Mass.: MIT Press, 825–838.

Squire, L. R., and Zola-Morgan, S. (1991). Memory and brain systems. *Science, 253,* 1380–1386.

Steriade, M. (1991). Alertness, quiet sleep and dreaming. In *The Cerebral Cortex, Vol. 9: Normal and Altered States of Function,* A. Peters and E. G. Jones (Eds.). New York: Plenum Press, 279–358.

Steriade, M., and Biesold, D. (Eds.). (1990). *Brain Cholinergic Systems.* Oxford: Oxford Scientific Publications.

Stoerig, V., and Cowey, A. (1997). Blindsight in man and monkey. *Brain, 120,* 535–559.

Stolerman, L. P., and Jarvis, M. J. (1995). The scientific case that nicotine is addictive. *Psychopharm., 118,* 2–10.

Strange, P. G. (1992). *Brain Biochemistry and Brain Disorders.* New York: Oxford University Press.

Strongman, K. T. (1996). *The Psychology of Emotion,* 4th ed. New York: John Wiley & Sons.

Taub, A. (1982). Opioid analgesics in the treatment of chronic intractable pain of non-neoplastic origin. In *Narcotic Analgesics in Anaesthesiology,* L. M. Kitahata and J. D. Collins (Eds.). Baltimore: Williams and Wilkins, 199–208.

Teasdale, G., and Jennett B. (1974). Assessment of coma and impaired consciousness. *Lancet ii,* 81–84.

Terrace, H. (1989). Thoughts without words. In *Mindwaves,* C. Blakemore and S. A. Greenfield (Eds.). Oxford: Basil Blackwell, 123–138.

Thach, W. T., Goodkin, H. G., and Keating, J. G. (1992). Cerebellum and the adaptive coordination of movement. *Ann. Rev. Neurosci., 15,* 403–442.

Toga, A. W., and Mazziotta, J. C. (1996). *Brain Mapping: The Methods.* New York: Academic Press.

Twycross, R. G. (1994). Opioids. In *Textbook of Pain,* 3rd ed., P. D. Wall and R. Melzack (Eds.). Edinburgh: Churchill Livingstone, 943–962.

Tye, M. (1995). *Ten Problems of Consciousness: A Representational Theory of the Phenomenal Mind.* Cambridge, Mass.: MIT Press.

Valenstein, E. S. (1986). *Unkind Cuts: The Rise and Decline of Psychosurgery and Other Radical Treatments for Mental Illness.* New York: Basic Books.

Valentine, C. W. (1930). The innate bases of fear. *J. of Genetic Res., 37,* 394–419.

Van Essen, D. C., Anderson, C. H., and Felleman, D. J. (1992). Information processing in the primate visual system: an integrated systems perspective. *Science, 255,* 419–423.

Varela, F. J., Thompson, E., and Rosch, E. (1991). *The Embodied Mind.* Cambridge, Mass.: MIT Press.

Vassilev, P., Kanazirska, M., and Tien, H. T. (1985). Intermembrane linkage mediated by tubulin. *Biochem. Biophys. Res. Comm., 126,* 559–565.

Vertosick, F. (1997). *When the Air Hits Your Brain.* New York: W. W. Norton & Co.

Wall, P. D. (1999). *Pain: The Science of Suffering.* London: Weidenfeld & Nicolson.

Wall, P. D., and Melzack, R. (Eds.) (1994). *Textbook of Pain*, 3rd ed. Edinburgh: Churchill Livingstone.

Warrington, E. K., and Duchen, L. W. (1992). A reappraisal of a case of persistent global amnesia following right temporal lobectomy—a clinicopathological study. *Neuropsychol., 6*, 437–450.

Warwick, K. (1998). *In the Mind of the Machine*. London: Arrow.

Weinberger, D. R., and Berman, K. F. (1998). Prefrontal function in schizophrenia: confounds and controversies. In *The Prefrontal Cortex*, A. C. Roberts, T. W. Robbins, and L. Weiskrantz (Eds.). New York: Oxford University Press, 165–180.

Weiskrantz, L. (1996). Blindsight revisited. *Current Opinion Neurobiol., 6*, 215–220.

———. (1997). *Consciousness Lost and Found*. New York: Oxford University Press.

Wells, M. (1968). *Lower Animals*. New York: McGraw-Hill.

White, M. (1997). *The Last Sorcerer*. London: Fourth Estate.

Whybrow, P. C. (1997). *A Mood Apart: A Thinker's Guide to Emotion and Its Disorder*. London: Picador.

Wildmann, J., Kruger, A., Schmole, M., Niemann, J., and Mathaei, H. (1986). Increase of circulating beta-endorphin-like immunoreactivity correlates with the change in feeling of pleasantness after running. *Life Sciences 38(11)*, 997–1003.

Willner, P. (1997). Validity, reliability and utility of the chronic mild stress model of depression. *Psychopharmacology, 134*, 319–329.

Winfree, A. (1987). *The Timing of Biological Clocks*. New York: Scientific American Library.

Winger, G., Hofmann, F. G., and Woods, J. H. (1992). A *Handbook on Drug Abuse and Alcohol: The Biomedical Aspects*. New York: Oxford University Press.

Wolpert, L. (1999). *Malignant Sadness. The Anatomy of Depression*. London: Faber.

Woolf, N. J. (1993). Cholinoceptive cells in rat cerebral cortex: Somatodendritic immunoreactivity for muscarinic receptor and cytoskeletal proteins. *J. Chem. Neuroanat., 6*, 375–390.

———. (1996). Global and serial neurons form a hierarchically arranged interface proposed to underlie memory and cognition. *Neuroscience, 74*, 625–651.

———. (1997). A possible role for cholinergic neurons of the basal forebrain and pontomesencephalon in consciousness. *Consciousness and Cognition, 6*, 574–596.

Woolf, N. J., and Butcher, L. L. (1991). Dysdifferentiation of structurally plastic neurons initiates the pathological cascade of Alzheimer's disease. In *Brain Cholinergic Systems*, M. Steriade and D. Biesold (Eds.). New York: Oxford University Press.

Woolf, N. J., and Wall, P. D. (1983). Endogenous opioid peptides and pain mechanisms: a complex relationship. *Nature, 286*, 155–157.

Woolf, N. J., Young, S. L., Johnson, G. V. W., and Faneslow, M. S. (1994). Pavlovian conditioning alters cortical microtubile associated protein 2. *Neuro Report, 5*, 1045–1048.

Xerri, C., Meztnich M. M., Peterson, B. E., and Jenkin, W. (1998). Plasticity of primary somatostasory cortex paralleling sensorimotor skill recovery from stroke in adult monkeys. *J. Neurophysiol., 79,* 2119–2168.

Yerkes, R. M., and Dodson, J. D. (1980). The relation of strength of stimulus to rapidity of habit formation. *J. Comp. Neurol. Psych., 18,* 459–482.

Young, G. B., Ropper, A. H., and Bolton, C. F. (1998). *Coma and Impaired Consciousness: A Clinical Perspective.* New York: McGraw-Hill.

Young, J. Z. (1978). *Programs of the Brain.* Oxford: Oxford University Press.

Zakay, D. (1992). The role of attention in children's time perception. *Exp. Child. Psychol., 54,* 355–371.

Zeki, S. (1993). *A Vision of the Brain.* Oxford: Blackwell Scientific.

INDEX

neuromodulation, 90, 214–215n.32

neuronal plasticity, 62–64, 164, 209n.19

neuronal wall, 8, 198–199n.16

neurons, 7, 34, 44
connections between, 61–66, 112
and consciousness, 164, 169–74, 179, 181–184, 187–193
effect of drugs on, 85–86

neurosis, 111–112

neurotransmitters. *See* acetylcholine; dopamine; norepinephrine; serotonin; transmitters

Newton, Sir Isaac, 230n.4

nicotine, 94, 216–217n.44

n-methyl-d-aspartate (NMDA) receptor, 223n.37

noradrenaline, 41, 175

norepinephrine, 91, 92, 123, 124, 140–141, 215n.37

novel stimulus, 113–114

objective reduction (OR), 189, 190

octopus, 167

Odyssey (Homer), 37, 206n.33

Olds, J., 16

opiates, 81–82, 85–86, 95, 213n.19

opium, 82, 85

pain
cyclic variations in, 133–134
and depression, 129, 134–135
and fear, 135–136
Gate Theory of, 222n.29
perception of, 224n.10
of phantom limbs, 131–132
physiology of, 129–31
relief from, 83, 84–85
survival value of, 136–137

pan-psychism, 34, 39, 204n.22

Papaver somniferum, 81

Papez, James, 196n.7

Parfit, Derek, 27, 28

pargyline, 123

Parkinson's disease, 205–206n.32

Pascal, Blaise, 33

passive avoidance, 17, 201–202n.32

Paulsen, Ole, 193

Penfield, Wilder, 145

Penrose, Roger, 189, 190, 191, 230n.5

peptides, 178–180, 184, 188

Pert, Candace, 179, 213n.15

phencyclidine, 133, 223n.37

phenelzine, 123

phenomenology, 36, 165

phenothiazines, 109

phobias, 110–113

Pinker, Steven, 8, 46–48, 200n.19, 218n.8

pituitary gland, 176–177

Pleasure Principle, 4

pleasure
drug-induced, 81–82
and fear, 113, 117
laughter as, 153–157
and loss of control, 102–103
model of, 34–35
nature of, 99–102, 150
and novelty, 113–117
rodent experiments, 16–17, 147–148
and stimulants, 93–95

poppy, 81, 213n.14

positron emission tomography (PET), 39

Prader-Willi Syndrome, 12, 201n.24

prefrontal cortex, 5, 29, 40, 109–110, 144–146, 203n.8

pro-hormones, 177

procedural memory, 66–67

Prozac (fluoxetine), 124, 125

psychiatry, 208n.7